Policy, Geophilosophy and Edu

Policy, Geophilosophy and Education

P. Taylor Webb
University of British Columbia, Vancouver, Canada

and

Kalervo N. Gulson
University of New South Wales, Sydney, Australia

SENSE PUBLISHERS
ROTTERDAM/BOSTON/TAIPEI

A C.I.P. record for this book is available from the Library of Congress.

ISBN: 978-94-6300-140-3 (paperback)
ISBN: 978-94-6300-141-0 (hardback)
ISBN: 978-94-6300-142-7 (e-book)

Published by: Sense Publishers,
P.O. Box 21858,
3001 AW Rotterdam,
The Netherlands
https://www.sensepublishers.com/

Printed on acid-free paper

All Rights Reserved © 2015 Sense Publishers

No part of this work may be reproduced, stored in a retrieval system, or transmitted in any form or by any means, electronic, mechanical, photocopying, microfilming, recording or otherwise, without written permission from the Publisher, with the exception of any material supplied specifically for the purpose of being entered and executed on a computer system, for exclusive use by the purchaser of the work.

TABLE OF CONTENTS

Acknowledgements	ix
Introduction: Notes on the Writing Experiment	xi

Part 1: Emergence

Chapter 1: Policy Scientificity 3.0: Theory and Policy Analysis in-and-for This World and Other-Worlds	3
Policy Scientificities in Education	5
Policy Scientificity 1.0	6
Policy Scientificity 2.0	7
Policy Scientificity 3.0	11
Policy Mutations	16
Chapter 2: Education Policy Geophilosophy: Theory and Policy Analysis for Emergent Worlds	19
Critical Parochialisms, or "Where Did My Ontology Go?"	22
The Spatialities of Education Policy (Analyses)	25
Unpredictable 'Agency': Emergence and Affect	26
What It Does (and Doesn't Do)…	31
Chapter 3: Policy Problematization	33
No Solution; No Problem: Policy Logics in Education	35
Policy	37
Problematization	38
Problematization: Contradictions, Recursions, and Events	39
Policy Problematizers	44
The Insufficiencies of Knowledge in Educational Research	47

Part 2: Intermezzo

Chapter 4: Policy Prolepsis: Phantasmic Encounters in Becoming-Policy	51
The Incompleteness of Policy	52
Policy Prolepsis	55
The Politics of Affective Space: Phantasmic Positionings	59

TABLE OF CONTENTS

The Politics of Absences and Presences: Policy Prolepsis in Time	60
Policy Prolepsis and Enacting Subjects	64

Chapter 5: Policy Intensions and the Folds of the Self   67

Critiquing and (Re)conceptualizing Policy Implementation	69
History of 'Policy Implementation'	70
Immanent Space and Emergent Geographies	72
The Immanent Space of Education Policy	74
Policy Intensions and the Geographies of the Self	75
Policy Cartographies and the Geographies of the Self	77

Chapter 6: The Neo-Liberal Policies of *Epimeleia Heautou* Caring for the Self in Education Markets: Mapping Biopolitical Catallaxies in Education Policy with Viviana Pitton   83

Neo-liberalism and Governmentality	85
Human Capital as Voluntary Formations of the Self	88
The Aporias of Neo-Liberal Equality in Education	92

Part 3: Connections

Chapter 7: Ambient Fear, Islamic Schools and the Affective Geographies of Race and Religion: "We Had to Hide That We're Muslim All the Time"   101

The Relational Geographies of Religion and Race	103
The Management of Religious, Educational (Suburban) Space	107
Islamic Schools and the Geographies of Ambient Fear	110
Histories of Fear and City Sedimentations	113
Marketizing Space and Commodifying Educational Difference	116

Chapter 8: Policy E(A)ffects: Spatial and Racial Encounters in the City   117

Oh, the Spaces You Will Go: Marketized Education and Culturally Focused Schools	118
Policy Effects: Representational and Material Manifestations of Education Policy	120
Space, Place and Encounters: A Conceptual Terrain for Rethinking Policy Effects	122
Education Policy and the Constituting of Geo-memories	126
The Racializations of Subjects/Objects: Material Encounters in the City	130

Chapter 9: 3.0: Lines: The Vectors of a Policy Geophilosophy	133
Line One: The Spatial and Affective	134
Line Two: Problematization for Emergent Ontologies	136
Line Three: Problematic Attachments and New Concepts	138
Moving with a Geophilosophy	140
References	143

ACKNOWLEDGEMENTS

This book greatly benefited from the assistance and input from many people. We are grateful to Peter de Liefde for his patience through the preparation process. We would like to thank several people for their time, encouragement, and keen editorial eyes, including: Stephen Ball, Eva Bendix Petersen, Matthew Clarke, Trevor Gale, Stephen Heimans, Bob Lingard, Amy Scott Metcalfe, Elizabeth St. Pierre, Greg Thompson, and Deborah Youdell. Thank you to Sam Sellar who provided detailed feedback on Chapters One and Two. We would also like to acknowledge the participants of the workshop on *Education Policy Analysis for a Complex World: Exploring the Possibilities of Post-structural Policy Analysis*. Chapter Six was supported by the *Social Sciences and Humanities Research Council* of Canada. We take full responsibility for the result.

Finally, and most importantly, we would like to thank our families and especially our partners: Amy Rudzinski and Owen; Kim Shaddick, Finn, Kobi and Aila.

We acknowledge with much gratitude the following publishing sources for the material used throughout the book. We appreciate their permission to modify and reprint those excerpts into this book.

Gulson, K. N., & Webb, P. T. (2013). We had to hide, we're Muslim: Ambient fear, Islamic schools and the geographies of race and religion. *Discourse: Studies in the Cultural Politics of Education, 34*(4), 628–641.

Webb, P. T. (2013). Policy problematization. *International Journal of Qualitative Studies in Education, 27*(3), 364–376.

Webb, P. T., & Gulson, K. (2012). Policy prolepsis in education: Encounters, becomings, and phantasms. *Discourse: Studies in the Cultural Politics of Education, 33*(1), 87–99.

Webb, P. T., & Gulson, K. (2013). Policy intensions and the folds of the self. *Educational Theory, 63*(1), 51–68.

Webb, P. T., & Gulson, K. N. (2015). Policy scientificity 3.0: Theory and policy analysis in-and-for this world and other-worlds. *Critical Studies in Education, 56*(1), 161–174.

Webb, P. T., Gulson, K. N., Pitton, V. O. (2014). The neo-liberal education policies of *epimeleia heautou*: Caring for the self in school markets. *Discourse: Studies in the Cultural Politics of Education, 35*(1), 1–14.

INTRODUCTION

Notes on the Writing Experiment

We wrote this book as an experiment. This book wanders through disciplinary and multi-disciplinary approaches to policy analysis, including: political science, policy sociology, policy archeology, and other critical and poststructural approaches. We should note that one of us begrudgingly entertains the term 'poststructural' for pragmatic reasons and one of us does not much care for the term – even though the latter has recently come to learn about the importance of the term in relation to it functioning as a shelter from physical and epistemological violence produced from 'science' – a violence that Lyotard (in Van Reijen & Veerman, 1988: 279) noted when he declared that "there is no reason, only reasons".

This difference however, is not indication of some fatal flaw. Difference is what brought this book together: a collective difference from the instrumentalism of techno-rational policy analysis; respective differences between geography and philosophy (and a shared sense of what they might do together); and, perpetual differences over what words to use, whether a hyphen should be used in the neologism 'neo-liberal', whether to have a glass of wine or a pint of beer, etc. All of this is just rambling on about the author-function, and noting how some words, concepts, and wines are selected for us already. It is fun to live vicariously every now and then, and much easier than trying to create other languages. We hope you will pardon us, however, if we do both in this book, often at the same time.

In thinking about how some of these chapters came together, the book started as a paper that we wrote when trying to think about how to research a policy change in Toronto, Canada. We had a suspicion that what we had been working with was not adequate for the job ahead. We used to work together at the University of British Columbia, Vancouver until Gulson left in 2010. Our research grant kept us connected, but we would read separate literatures that converged during our frequent, but long-distance conversations. Webb had sabbatical in 2011–2012 and read the works of Gilles Deleuze and the newly released lectures of Michel Foucault at the Collège de France. Gulson continued reading and thinking about spatial theories, especially that of non-representational theory (e.g., Anderson & Harrison, 2010). We have been writing 'empirical' case reports and conceptual papers separately, and together, for four years.

This book encapsulates some of our work but it is also a part of us opening up what we hope will be our next explorations into policy analysis. Writing has been provoking: we have reconsidered the ontological, representational and epistemological aspects of policy and the many different ways it is used and analysed. We also worked with the ideas of becoming and (philosophical/spatial) concept creation in relation to education policy. We were interested in continuing the idea of "policy theorists" (Simons, Olssen, & Peters, 2009a: 27) who,

> provide … answers to the epistemological challenges of post-structuralism and the current pluralist social world, and who also take up the difficult work of intellectually-based social criticism.

In this book we attempt a type of conceptual contribution – what we are calling *policy geophilosophy* – for a new way of undertaking policy studies that may possibly reinvigorate the field. We see this work as congruent with St. Pierre's (2011: 613) challenge and call for "a renewed commitment to a *reimagination of social science inquiry*" that is enabled by 'post' approaches, including poststructuralism. We argue that we need to develop new concepts for policy studies in order to contribute to the reimagining of inquiry and to hedge against undue ossification and co-option of critical policy studies.

Our project follows the strict mantra that it is much easier to develop new ideas once you let go of others' desires.[1] Deleuze and Guattari (1994: 8) contend,

> Although concepts are dates, signed and baptized, they have their own way of not dying while remaining subject to constraints of renewal, replacement, and mutation that give philosophy a history as well as a turbulent geography, each moment and place of which is preserved (but in time) and that passes (but outside time).

We are attempting to create a vocabulary and several concepts to generate different ways to understand education policy, on the premise that there is an impetus and momentum in contemporary policy studies to which we attempt to speak to, and, and times, with. This book includes published papers that emerged during our respective and collective journeys – what we have come to posit as a *policy geophilosophy*.

What will be clear from some of the chapters is that there are 'data' included in the sense that we speak of data as words external to theory, or words as interview transcripts. We are cognisant, following St. Pierre and Jackson (2014: 716) that this is a reading of,

> conventional humanist qualitative research, words in interview transcripts and in field notes are considered primary data, collected as they are in 'face to face' encounters in the *presence* of participants in their natural settings. Again, words spoken by participants are privileged regardless of their adequacy to respond to the study's substantive and theoretical demands.

As St. Pierre and Jackson (2014: 716) contend, this view privileges these words over those that might equally be adequate "to respond to the study's substantive and theoretical demands".

We do not presume what counts as data, and while people's words are included, we do not assume that these are the only 'data', nor other materials in the world, nor of course, *other worlds in materials*. If you do lean towards needing this type of validity and legitimacy we have done this type of work as part of other papers that have been published parallel to this book and the papers reworked within (see notably, Gulson & Webb, 2012; 2013a; 2013b). Our approach in this book has an affinity with what Brinkmann (2014: 722) posits as an abductive approach to analysis in which the "abductive tool-user, the bricoleur, the craftsperson, [is] the ideal qualitative researcher."

We wanted to know what happened when using abduction or an open-ended approach to approaching diverse signs and materials as 'data'. For example, some of our data includes snippets from literature (i.e., Tom Robbins, Olive Senior, Jack Kerouac, Dr. Seuss). We work from the premise that some of what we write are impressions, born from bewilderment (even when we should know better). While we might not quite want to be characterized as 'post-coding' researchers, we do think that what we are attempting to do is to undertake analysis that "occurs 'in the middle of things' (Deleuze & Guattari, 1980/1987, p. 293), without a beginning or end, without origin or destination. In this way, analysis occurs *everywhere and all the time*" (St. Pierre & Jackson, 2014: 717). We see the material as part of our lives as researchers and scholars and people, not something separate from our different roles. Continual analysis enables us, as scholars, "to be able to act in a specific situation" (Brinkmann, 2014: 722). For Brinkmann (2014: 722),

> [u]nlike induction and deduction – both of which address the relationship between data and theory – abduction is a form of reasoning that is concerned with the relationship between a situation and inquiry. It is neither data-driven nor theory driven, but break-down driven (Alvesson & Kärreman, 2011). It occurs in situations of breakdown, surprise, bewilderment, or wonder.

Some of the examples will seem to be singular, and in a sense, they are – e.g. a focus on one school. Like Berlant (2011: 12) we are interested in the idea of generalisability – that is, "how the singular becomes delaminated from its location in someone's story or some locale's irreducibly local history and circulated as evidence of something shared". As such, we are interested in how policy analysis is done and comes to be made stable – its scientificities – such that it is applied to all and sundry, regardless of temporal and geographical specificities. We are fascinated that we can "track the becoming general of singular things" (Berlant, 2011: 12). We welcome you to (re)read some of these previously published papers as chapters in this book – for we think they now sit as part of this conceptual program rather than as the initial exploratory forays designed as journal articles, with all of the limitations of that format.

EMERGENCE, INTERMEZZO, CONNECTIONS

The first section of the book – *emergence* – is comprised of three chapters. These chapters provide an introduction to the concept of *policy geophilosophy* in education.

INTRODUCTION

Chapter One discusses disciplinary and multi-disciplinary approaches to policy analysis as they have been developed or adopted in educational policy studies. The chapter lays out our understanding of the terrain we traverse, and explains why – and in what ways – a *policy geophilosophy* can assist us and others working within education policy (who isn't nowadays?) and, perhaps, working our ways out of it. The first chapter provides an overview of the various approaches or analytics to understanding such an object and its historical role(s) in education. We aim to map out the conceptual, methodological and ethical dimensions of policy analysis in education with a focus on the conditions of how policy analysis is done, and the ontological status of policy – what we have come to know as 'policy scientificities'.

Chapter Two, at the risk of appearing like a mystery novel, identifies the culprit of our text – *policy geophilosophy* – up front. Our *policy geophilosophy* examines *how education policy positions and constitutes objects and subjects through emergent and adaptive policy arrangements that simultaneously influence how policy is sensed, embodied, and enacted*. Here, we are interested in three things. The first is how policy as concept and action both endures (stabilizes) and mutates in and through space-times; second, the ways policy analysis refrains and constitutes the ontologies and epistemologies of policy and its objects; and third, how policy shapes and constitutes subjects.

With the culprit taken care of, Chapter Three discusses our approach to performing such analyses. Here, we articulate a *policy problematization* and discuss, for better or worse, the methods we use when approaching the object better known as education policy. The third chapter wrests directly within the supposed logics of education policy that portends 'solutions' to educational 'problems' and maps the disciplinary vagaries produced from such logics and objects. Our goal with problematizing policy is to think through the ontology of such an object rather than to only treat its remit as an epistemological enterprise beget with 'solutions'.

The second section of the book – *intermezzo* – contains three chapters (Chapters Four to Six). These chapters work in different ways, and for various purposes. Nevertheless, we believe that these chapters are talking to each other and to our concept of *policy geophilosophy*. The chapters introduce a few conceptual tools that have assisted us in rethinking education policy in the ways that we discussed in Section 1. We hope they may assist you too.

Chapter Four discusses what we have come to term a *policy prolepsis*. The import of such an idea is a return to material encounters with policy, an 'ontology', that works within and between different registers of representation, and in relation to ontologies that *themselves* are becoming. We argue in this chapter that policy material cannot be considered independent of the forces that produce it, and we stress the point that certain affective registers are used in the eventual political contests that attempt to settle ontological difference – including uncertainty. Here, then, our *policy prolepsis* identifies the many space-times in the enactments of policy becomings.

INTRODUCTION

Chapter Five discusses another concept that we use in our problematizations of education policy, namely *policy intensions*. Borrowing 'intension' from philosophy, a *policy intension* is a broad and ambiguous idea that attempts to capture the ways in which education policy is sensed, embodied, and eventually enacted. This chapter provides readers with our understanding of people, but we talk about this in relation to subjects/objects and the many different ways they move – and are moved – within education policy. We note how intensions are part of the processes of subjectification and use Gilles Deleuze's (1988) idea of *the fold* to think through the affective and shifting spaces of subjectivity produced in *policy prolepses* and enacted within *policy intensions*.

Chapter Six connects our discussion regarding subjects/objects and situates them explicitly within conceptions of neo-liberalism. Our goal in this chapter is not to rehash this edu-economic history, but to connect subjects/objects with the many different spaces of care that are practiced and enacted in relation to school choice. We conduct a problematization that attempts to recognize how neo-liberal education policy is being used to escape the inequities and educational inequalities produced in the (liberal) registers of race and ethnicity. This argument unearths historical and spatial conceptions of the subject, education, and economy and notes how these objects are changing – indeed becoming – in ways that are not immediately recognizable, in fact, in ways that are unsettled and uncertain.

The third and final section of the book – *connections* – contains three chapters (Chapters Seven to Nine).

Chapter Seven provides an 'empirical' or material example to the previous two chapters. We think through the development of government-funded private Islamic schools, and the local politics which emerged in relation to school choice policies. We use the idea of 'ambient fear' to illustrate our concepts of *policy prolepsis* and *policy intension*, and note how the affective registers of policy making are used, but in disproportionate ways depending on different representations of race and religion. We link the idea of 'ambient fear' to the idea of the city which, for us, remains an under-theorized space in educational policy studies.

Chapter Eight situates the city as a prominent object within the spaces of school choice and race. The chapter identifies the emergent relations of cities, and the emergent raciologies that are used to traverse neo-liberal education policy. This problematization relies on rethinking representational conceptions of space and noting what new set of relations are produced when non-representational conceptions of space are levied in relation to non-representational notions of race and ethnicity.

Chapter Nine is the final chapter of the book. These kinds of chapters are typically entitled 'conclusions'. We, however, have decided not to use this trope; instead, we have alternatively labelled the chapter 'lines'. The chapter discusses what we believe are some of the possibilities and opportunities that a *policy geophilosophy* provide. We also discuss what a *policy geophilosophy* does not, or cannot, do. Our hope is that

INTRODUCTION

this chapter provides others a way to engage in the difficult work of intellectually-based social criticism aimed at the routinised and domineering practices of education policy development and its analysis.

Off we go.

NOTE

[1] In other words, "Beware of the dreams of others, because if you are caught in their dream, you are done for.'" (Deleuze, 2007: 323)

PART 1

EMERGENCE

POLICY GEOPHILOSOPHY

How education policy positions and constitutes objects and subjects through emergent and adaptive arrangements that simultaneously influence how policy is sensed, embodied, and enacted.

This section examines and discusses:

- The disciplinary and multi-disciplinary approaches to policy analysis as they have been developed, adopted, and practiced in educational policy studies.
- How policy – as concept and action – both stabilizes and mutates in and through space-times.
- How policy analysis refrains and constitutes the ontologies and epistemologies of policy.
- *Policy problematization*, in contrast to other methods and epistemologies of policy analysis.

CHAPTER 1

POLICY SCIENTIFICITY 3.0

Theory and Policy Analysis in-and-for This World and Other-Worlds

What we are suffering from is not a void but inadequate means for thinking about everything that is happening. There is an overabundance of things to be known: fundamental, terrible, wonderful, insignificant, and crucial at the same time.
—Foucault, 1997: 325

In this chapter we provide a kind of topography of the disciplinary and multi-disciplinary approaches to policy analysis as they have been developed, adopted, and practiced in education. We aim to map out the conceptual, methodological, and ethical dimensions of policy analysis in education. While there is a sense of periodisation in these mappings, we are most interested in the contours of how policy analysis is done, and the conditions or ontological status of policy.

To do this we posit a typology and heuristic of three education 'policy scientificities' that correspond to, but should not be taken as being reduced to:

1. *policy scientificity 1.0* (i.e., the 'policy sciences'),
2. *policy scientificity 2.0* (critical policy studies, policy sociology); and
3. *policy scientificity 3.0* ('post' studies; e.g., post-human, post-structural).

If at any point during the mapping you step out for a coffee, we completely understand.

The following borrows heavily and is considerably reduced from Simons, Olssen, and Peters (2009a, 2009b: 1–95), Olssen, Codd, and O'Neil (2004), Rizvi and Lingard (2010), and Ball (1995). We cannot stress enough that you should read these first if you have come this far. These reviews or maps carefully articulate shifts in the ways policy analysis has been undertaken in education, and the conceptual, methodological and ethical dimensions produced through these shifts. We believe selective 'tune-outs' of some recent policy scholarship to be problematic in education, and we are convinced this 'selective muting' is why we perpetuate some of the same old problems in education, largely because we keep thinking with the same old solutions. This, 'muting' we contend, is applicable to social sciences more broadly. We elaborate on these ideas in Chapters Two and Three.

We use the term 'policy scientificities' in juxtaposition to the original 'policy sciences' articulated by Lerner and Lasswell (Lerner & Laswell, 1951). We flag the term 'scientificity' in relation to developments in the physical and natural

CHAPTER 1

sciences that investigate multiplicity, chaos, non-linear dynamics, and (non) representation with inter- and multi- disciplinary frameworks. The distinction that we wish to highlight between a policy 'scientificity' and a policy 'science' pivots on the conditions that policy analysis uses to produce and legitimate its intended objectives – this is, scientificity as the "constitution of science as science" (Lather, 2006a: 786) – particularly as changes are occurring in the natural and physical sciences. Foucault (1970: 400), however, gets right to our distinction when thinking about education policy when he stated,

> it is useless … to say that the 'human sciences' are false sciences; they are not sciences at all; the configuration that defines their positivity and gives them their roots in the modern episteme at the same time makes it impossible for them to be sciences …

Following Foucault (1974), policy scientificity is, therefore, how policy analysis "structures certain of its objects, systemizes parts of it, formalizes, underwrites strategies" (Lather, 2006a: 786), through its different outcomes and practices. But that is not all. Policy scientificity is also what is excluded when engaged with systematizing, formalizing, and underwriting objects for policy analysis. We discuss the idea of *policy absences* more fully in Chapter Two as part of our discussion on 'ontological politics'. Here, *policy scientificity* reanimates the notion of 'policy science' and points to the uncertainty of onto-epistemes in the natural and physical sciences, given the early evidence of adaptive, self-organizing, and emergent ontologies. This is not a condemnation of our colleagues who work in the 'natural' and 'physical' sciences, but an invitation to mutually celebrating not-knowing!

In what Nietzsche (1974: 301 cited by Lather, 2004a) discussed as the "unnatural sciences", policy scientificity locates, places, situates, or 'spatialises' researchers in analyses as "creative thinkers" (Olssen, 2008) and "policy problematizers" (see Chapter Three). These roles are in stark contrast to the preferred roles of researchers as 'problem solvers', 'solution providers', the eponymous 'knowledge transferrers' or people who 'mobilize knowledge' evident in so many disciplinary approaches to education policy. While we are not entirely sure what the last category even means, we have a sneaking suspicion that it is a thinly veiled characterization of the 'traveling knowledge salesmen' who is deeply connected to, and performed by, the un-reflexive and globalizing networks of policy mobility (McCann & Ward, 2013). We would add, too, that we are entirely aware of the privileges bestowed to such a figure by its gendered characteristics. Admittedly, then, our use of 'policy scientificity' is probably a poor strategy because of the dominance of so-called 'rational,' 'disciplinary,' 'instrumental,' and 'masculine' convictions circulating within global policy studies. Nevertheless, we hope that people still trained in techno-rational, positivistic, and disciplinary approaches to education policy will actually open and read this book, unlike the folks of Troy.

The metamorphosis of a 'policy science' into a 'policy scientificity' allows us, in a similar manner to seeing 'science' as an "arena of struggle in broadening the definition of science" (Lather, 2006a: 787), to focus on the representational and material aspects of policy analysis. We can, therefore, examine language, meaning, subjectivity, and the variety of ways that representation legitimates scientific and disciplinary criteria (and delegitimate or exclude competing criteria). The so-called human sciences, then, are a "'meta-epistemological' position [that addresses] finitude, relativity, and perspective" (Foucault, 1970: 355).

'Scientificity' allows us to shift focus "to the proper characterization of the object, not control of the subjectivity of the knower" (Lather, 2006a: 787). The object we wish to characterise, properly or not, is education policy and the concomitant objects brought forth within its purview. We believe the ontological question *what is education policy?* to be a very interesting one – even when colleagues have looked at us incredulously when we have raised it as such – particularly amidst the "blurred, intermediary and composite disciplines [that] multiply endlessly" (Foucault, 1970: 358). Our policy scientificities conceive of an invigoration of policy ontologies where "*ontologies* are brought into being, sustained, or allowed to whither away in common, day-to-day, sociomaterial practices" (Mol, 2002: 6).

And, finally, our apparent sequencing of policy studies (i.e., 1.0, 2.0, 3.0) is an attempt to capture some of the *cumulative* expectations piled onto policy analysis and education over the past sixty years. While our numbering of policy scientificities implies a kind of evolution or progression within policy studies, we certainly do not mean to suggest such a thing. Educational 'progress' is something best left to free market believers, development psychologists, and other transcendentalists. Rather, we are much more comfortable suggesting policy analysis has mutated in three discernible ways and now haunts education like a Cerberus.

And, yes, our numbering system is a nod to Lather (2009), who we think was onto something when she told us to "get lost" as a way to repudiate the instrumentalism embedded in contemporary policy science. Finally, our numbering also borrows from web development in the sense that now the internet is apparently adaptive with an impending "singularity"[1] about to occur any moment now (i.e., Web 3.0, see Kurzweil, 2005). We are not sure if 'singularity' is the most exciting or frightening thing we have heard in awhile, but we do think 'singularity' is a cognate way to describe the current state of education policy, particularly its global convergence and isomorphism (Sahlberg, 2011). And we are convinced that this is a truly scary idea for educators and scholars who work on the margins of multiplicity instead.

POLICY SCIENTIFICITIES IN EDUCATION

This overview and argument is not meant to be a straight line, despite the heuristic of *1.0, 2.0, 3.0*. Given our propensity to think with images, we imagine this disciplinary trajectory to be more like a möbius strip; twisted loops; the curves of schooling's eternal (capitalist) recurrence. We are seeking new concepts in thinking through and with these policy scientificities as the practice of '*thinking with theory*' (Jackson & Mazzei, 2012).

CHAPTER 1

POLICY SCIENTIFICITY 1.0

"Policy sciences" figured prominently within the social sciences as a multi-disciplinary approach that included politics, law, sociology, economics, and psychology. The term *policy sciences* was coined by Lerner and Lasswell in 1951 (Lerner & Laswell, 1951), and referred to the role public policy might play in providing solutions to the problems of the social welfare state, including the post war reconstruction and the spread of Western democratic values (i.e., employment, security, equality). The entire point of policy sciences, according to Parsons (1995), was to "manage the 'public' and its problems" which, conveniently, required specialist knowledge. Fay (1975: 14 cited in Ball, 1995: 258) described policy science as a,

> set of procedures which enables one to determine the technically best course of action to adopt in order to implement a decision or achieve a goal. Here the policy scientist doesn't merely clarify the possible outcomes of a certain course of action, he [sic] actually chooses the most efficient course of action in terms of available scientific information.

Rizvi and Lingard (2010: 1) summed up the policy sciences as ways to assist the state to "develop priorities and programs, and determine ways to ensure their efficiency and effectiveness."

Interestingly, and perhaps curiously, policy sciences assumed if analyses were based on a series of well-established and replicable methods, that policy analysis would provide ways of making and evaluating policy. The resulting knowledge for managing the public would, thus, somehow transcend the political apparatuses and machinations that govern the public in capitalist states. Lasswell (1970) amended his initial ideas to include a "policy process" to account for political machinations but insisted that 'policy scientists' remain 'problem-oriented', even within the vagaries of governance. Lasswell would eventually amend his model with what he called the "decision process" to account for the politics of science – which maintains the rationalized intentions of population control and remains a staple of policy analysis today.

For instance, we note that techno-rational ideas persistently surface in debates about 'policy cycles' and 'policy processes', and are supported and disseminated by numerous organisations like the American Educational Research Association and its affiliated journal *Educational Evaluation and Policy Analysis*, a journal for "those engaged in educational policy analysis, evaluation, and decision making". We use the term 'techno-rational' to refer to the kinds of positivistic assumptions guiding *policy scientificity 1.0* and the instrumentalist perspective of government in which 'solutions' can be 'implemented'. These positivistic and instrumental assumptions of how analysis should proceed and be applied also guide educational governance and decision making, including the kinds of 'predictive' claims such assumptions portend (see deLeon, 2005 for a critique of such claims). *Policy scientificity 1.0* continues into the 21st century in many ways, such as repeated calls for "scientifically based" studies in education (Eisenhart & Towne, 2003).

Yet, the 'science' of policy science was not, and is not, so clear-cut. The notions of contestation and incrementalism were part of *1.0*, such as Easton's (1953) notion that policy is the "authoritative allocation of values" and Lindblom's (1959) ideas of policy analysis as a "science of muddling through". *Policy scientificity 1.0*, nonetheless, remained and remains a settlement around instrumentalism and related rationalities of decision-making. Simons, et al. (2009a) pointed to the implications of such an instrumentalist orientation. They stated that the policy sciences,

> aim at the re-organisation of society through policy measures taken on the basis of scientific problem-solving rationality . Although there is a clear value-orientation, such as democratic values and the prevention of coercion, the epistemological and methodological assumptions of Lasswell and his contemporaries are clearly positivistic (that is, it is possible to reveal the nature of policy and decision making based on objective, empirical data or logical reasoning) and instrumental (to engineer policy based on positive knowledge of how it should be). (Simons et al., 2009a: 4)

Policy scientificity 1.0 became a very productive time for higher education and a strategic means to legitimate the academy itself (Simons et al., 2009a: 5–6). Fabianism, Keynsianism, and state policy, for example, were part of the welfare dispotif and at the same time deeply implicated in the management of the population.

1.0 continues merrily along today, in many ways, including in critical educational policy work using Geographic Information Systems (Taylor, 2007) and, as mentioned above, in repeated calls for "scientifically based" studies in education (Eisenhart & Towne, 2003). Much of this work continues to use ideas of 'school effectiveness' as a whipping boy to maintain the "capitalistic axiomatic" of schooling (Deleuze & Guattari, 1987: 214). This ethos continues into what we discuss as the next iteration in education policy studies – *policy scientificity 2.0*.

POLICY SCIENTIFICITY 2.0

Policy scientificity 2.0 emerged in the mid-to-late 1980s, and continues today. We would be remiss if we designated a single moment or event that signalled a switch from *1.0* → *2.0*. Even the idea that a 'switch' occurred is specious. We are not contending that the practices and assumptions of *1.0* have somehow been displaced with additional approaches to policy analysis. Instead, we suggest that *2.0* has had a kind of 'hardening effect' upon *1.0* as the latter defends itself from the critiques of the 'soft' and 'human' sciences.

We are contending that the policy sciences became an expanded field that incorporated new ideas involving the assertion of criticality, reflexivity and the precarious creation of multi-disciplinary approaches to policy studies. A set of interrelated factors contributed to rethinking the positivistic, technicist, and instrumentalist approaches of *1.0* by focusing on questions of how analysis could and should be done; including, but not limited to:

- the deliberate design of neo-liberal states,
- the uneasy relationships between government and academics – including the splitting of sociology of education into critical policy studies and school improvement studies in the UK (Ball, 2007),
- (multi) disciplinary feuds about 'science', and
- a rethinking of the relationships between criticality and methodology.

For our purposes, *policy scientificity 2.0* is the assertion of criticality and the precarious creation of multi-disciplinary approaches to policy studies, marked by three important turns, in addition to the shifts listed just above, including:

(a) new demarcations of heterogeneous locations of policy making, i.e., policy contexts, and for our purposes, 'policy spaces' where important political and power struggles occur in response to so-called 'implementation' attempts (e.g., the micropolitical, cities, districts, schools, classrooms);

(b) an explosion of theoretical and inter-disciplinary frames, especially from continental philosophy, from which to critique positivism (e.g., post-positivism, feminism, post-colonial, post-structural, etc. (e.g., Bensimon & Marshall, 1997); and

(c) a questioning about the nature of instrumental research and its relation to different educational milieus (and a questioning of whose utility it serves), including contestations between the discourses of 'improvement', 'reform', 'effectiveness' and 'critique' (and all the clever heroic moralizations contained within these discourses).

In general, *policy scientificity 2.0* emerged as a shift concerned with mapping the "contradictions, tensions, or general patterns and contingent or structural assemblages" of *policy scientificity 1.0* while noting an explicit "concern with education, power and with social regulation" (Simons et al., 2009a: 15). Policy sociology is emblematic of thinking about policy as a practice, rather than only a discursive instrument or technology, an overlooked and scourged scientificity within articulations of *1.0*. *Policy scientificity 2.0* then continues with the *1.0* trajectory of 'science', although in decidedly different ways, and refutes the claim that policy analysis is a neutral technical activity brought about to improve society.

Of course, the challenge to neutrality of knowledge reflected the great paradigmatic wars that were waged in educational research during this time (e.g., Gage, 1989) and that continued into the 21st century (e.g., Jacob & White, 2002). One of the key moves here was that psychology, or the 'psys' more generally, were displaced in education studies during *2.0*, but only to be replaced with an ascendency of sociology and anthropology ('ethnography') as a way to better understand and regulate ourselves (Rose, 1999a).

With a move to critical policy studies (Prunty, 1985) came the disciplinary entree of 'policy sociology' and its emphasis on power, politics and difference. This entree effectively layered additional meanings to policy with the activities that accompany both the development and uses of policy (i.e., the politics of education policy). *Policy scientificity 2.0* was concerned with "what do people do in the name of policy?" (Wedel, Shore, Feldman, & Lathrop, 2005: 35); that is with people as subjects and objects – as constituted in and by policy – rather than merely implementers, makers, and solution providers. Here, Jenny Ozga (1987) (to name just one) highlighted sociology as one of the multi-disciplinary approaches used previously in Lasswell's policy sciences. Ozga (1987: 14) noted that an education policy sociology was "rooted in the social science tradition, historically informed and [drew] on qualitative and illuminative techniques".

Policy sociology did "borrow a few techniques" from ethnography (Wolcott, 2008: 44), psychology (i.e., mixed methods, J. W. Creswell, 2013), and the Chicago School of Sociology (symbolic interactionism) in order to conduct such analyses, indicating, perhaps, an emergence of multi- and inter-disciplinary work in *2.0*. During this time Tom Popkewitz (1991) would introduce variants to the scientistic orientation that are worth noting, particularly his inter-disciplinary idea regarding a "political sociology" in education that historicizes the politics of policy concerned with education reform. Also included were critical implementation studies (Simons et al., 2009b) that reoriented studies of policy away from the state as primary actor and removed policy from the pedestal (Vidovich, 2007). This involved increasing use of theories of micro-politics and included the take up of Foucault (Ball, 1994) with an exploration of the contingent practices of policy research (Ozga, 2000).

Of course, (gender) 'trouble' emerged during this time that challenged 'coherent' categories of the policy subject (Butler, 1990). Such 'trouble' refracted some of the techno-rational assumptions contained in the educational categories concerning 'the subject' (e.g., 'girl', 'boy', 'at-risk', but also 'teacher', 'student', 'researcher'). This 'trouble' also highlighted some of the most pernicious policy ideas in education regarding the subject as 'human capital'. We examine the contemporary neo-liberal equivocations of education policy and 'human capital' ideas in Chapter Six, including the challenges to liberal conceptions of multiculturalism, representation, and recognition. The seductions of 'entrepreneurial subjects' and education policy produce any number of practices committed to forms of care and other educational self-investments.

For now, *policy scientificity 2.0* has become mired in debates about recognition, identity, representation, and difference as a way to produce ~~labor~~ educated people (Bauman, 2001; Fraser, 2000; Gilroy, 2000; Hall & du Gay, 1996; Honneth, 1995; Spivak, 1988; Taylor, 1994; West, 1993; Willig, 2012). Finally, *2.0* maintained disciplinary frames in relation to the policy sciences which expanded how one might conduct such work. We take this up in just a moment, in our discussion of *policy scientificity 3.0*.

CHAPTER 1

Coffee Break

Amidst the very real sufferings of, and in, education, we would note that *policy scientificity 2.0* is "an active point of escape where the revolutionary machine, the artistic machine, and the scientific machine, and the (schizo) analytic machine become parts and pieces of one another" (Deleuze & Guattari, 1983: 322). We apologize if these are not the words you would use, but to a large extent, *policy scientificity 2.0* resurrected enduring questions about the purposes of schooling, and placed such questions under a plethora of competing disciplinary sciences that deal explicitly with issues of power. The takeaway is that discussions concerning *1.0* → *2.0* are almost entirely epistemological which obscure analyses of the *different educational machines* that are produced from these conflicts and which perpetuate schooling as sites of biopolitical catallaxy (e.g., state and provincial governments). *2.0*, then, introduced a nagging splinter into policy analysis regarding the extent to which the very enterprise of education should be, and could be, 'repaired' through analysis and activism.

2.0 focused on the important shifts in understanding the changes to previous accepted links between education and society, and provided a re-articulation of the aims and possibilities of critique and transformation. Troyna (1994), for instance, insisted that critical social science ought not wholly be concerned with critique but with the act of political transformation. This does, however, come with a caveat. Simons, et al. (2009b) proposed that crisis of the welfare state and neo-liberal globalisation carry challenges to the normative function of critical policy studies.

> The connection being made between education and policy is traditionally a two-way connection; on the one hand studying the policy context of education but on the other hand studying how policies could be used to improve education and its role in society. The background for this critical orientation is clearly the modern welfare state that conceives of education as a major component of public policy. The general principles of welfare policy, often taken for granted by critical scholars, are 'the change of education through change of public policy' and 'the change of society through change of education'. What we want to stress is the importance of being aware of a sort of 'critical/advocacy parochialism' at the level of these principles. Facing the crisis of the welfare state and state government, these principles are no longer evident. Or to formulate this in a positive way, a major challenge will be to discuss what 'the public, and its education' is about in today's global context, and how education and policy are related and should be related. (Simons et al., 2009b: 37–8)

In this sense of *2.0*, education and education policy are not ameliorative activities, at least not in their current practices and usages. Some of *2.0* masked the instrumentalism contained in *1.0* and repackaged it as educational 'reform'

POLICY SCIENTIFICITY 3.0

or educational 'improvement' through a sense of 'criticality' that insisted on 'transformation' with its heroics and impositions.

With *2.0* still immersed in a form of (critical) instrumentalism, we note, along with Sarason (1990), that many attempts at educational reform and/or education improvement were zombie policies, lifeless and doomed to fail. Policy instrumentalism staggered forward in *2.0* amidst the apocalyptic wars concerned with 'science' (Jacob & White, 2002), 'culture' (Hall & du Gay, 1996), 'the subject' (Butler, 1990; Foucault, 1982b, 1994b), and the persistence of instrumentalist notions of 'critique' deeply embedded within the field of education (Ellsworth, 1989).

Please note, we are not disavowing *2.0*, for we are as implicated as the work we have noted, but we are positing that *2.0* faces similar problems to those which St Pierre (2011: 613) noted about qualitative research. In proposing a 'post' qualitative research, St Pierre contends that qualitative research "has been so disciplined, so normalized, so centred...that *it has become conventional*, reductionist, hegemonic, and sometimes oppressive and has lost its radical possibilities...". Education was considered a heretical act some time ago. It doesn't seem so anymore.

In the next section we suggest that *policy scientificity 3.0* might provide new radical possibilities for undisciplined policy studies.

POLICY SCIENTIFICITY 3.0

There has been proliferation of rich, single and multi-disciplinary approaches to policy analysis that have been developed over the past two decades – Scheurich (1994) created "policy archeology", Gale (2001) developed "policy historiography" and Shore and Wright (1997) proposed "policy anthropology".

We identify these disciplinary approaches as necessary contributions to what we are positing as *policy scientificity 3.0*.

In this final part of the chapter we outline four characterisations of *3.0*, and these are proposed as emergent ideas that are not clean breaks from *1.0* and *2.0*, but rather start to provide a mapping of a becoming-policy-analysis. We will not provide an exhaustive list of recent disciplinary developments in policy studies, nor review any of these recent policy sciences because your coffee might be getting cold, or dripping down the wall. However, like Patti Lather (2006b), we do believe that it can be instructive to think with proliferation. As such, if you do not see yourself in *3.0*, we believe that if you wait just long enough you will likely find yourself within a disciplining frame soon enough.

Or, you can develop your own. As recipients of various biopower subjugations – 'the knowledges' – it will not take long to find an articulation of your own disciplinary trajectory if you haven't already (although we can't insist enough that you don't let this popular task distract you from working with the ontological!). We may not believe in what others unabashedly declare as 'free markets', but we are firm believers that "the subject who desires can be made to desire its own

CHAPTER 1

repression" (Deleuze & Guattari, 1983: 105). What the following *policy scientificity 3.0* indicates are provocations, ruminations and abutments – unfinished thoughts and struggles about what constitutes the theories and methodologies for an emerging set of analyses; *policy scientificity 3.0* may include any or all of the following, or, in fact, be something completely different.

3.0.1: Parochial Pleasures of the Disciplines

Policy scientificity 3.0 is characterised by the competing epistemologies, or the lack of discipline of the disciplines – what some have characterised as the "science wars" (Lather, 2004b). The biopower techniques and the liberal epistemes that we have been discussing (i.e., the disciplines) are not a happy family; indeed they are in crisis (Hall, 1990). For instance, Stuart Hall (1990) proclaimed that he was happy to chair a sociology department now that sociology was dead. Likewise, Paul Rabinow (2003) read anthropology's obituary. Wendy Brown (2010) has informed us that political science and political theory are intending to eliminate each other. Philosophy, of course, has had a particular nasty feud with itself ever since Ludwig Wittgenstein (1953) continentally (i.e., linguistically) questioned himself. His analytical feud left him brown and blue (1965).

Moves to an inter-disciplinary approach to education policy studies are not, we suggest, a strategic move to avoid the disciplinary crisis. What does interest us in these types of approaches that can be typecast as *3.0* is that they *use* the disciplinary crisis and its multiplicities deliberately in its conception, particularly with respect to uncertainty and discord. In this regard, the inter-disciplinary approaches to policy studies that constitute *3.0* are attempts to avoid the disciplinary "parochialism" (Lingard, 2006) that haunts educational policy, and that reinforces "methodological educationalism" (Roberston & Dale, 2008) and/or "methodological individualism" (Bonta & Proveti, 2004).

In addition to disciplinary parochialism, critical parochialism is a key conceit in conceptualizing education policy. A third option of 'transdisciplinarity' has been offered as an alternative to forms of disciplinary and advocacy parochialism. However, any form of transcendence is not something that can be offered to readers in good faith: "a transcendent source of order 'rescues' a chaotic matter, is equivalent to the sort of 'vampirism' in which a higher-level constraint claims credit for reciprocally generated emergent order" (Bonta & Proveti, 2004: 35).

Policy scientificity 3.0, rather than being inter- or trans- disciplinary, is a transversal politics, where "transversal lines tend to transsectorally cross through several fields, they link together social struggles and artistic interventions and theory production" (Raunig, 2007). This politics would deliberately embrace multiplicity to develop new links between education policy and emergent ideas regarding the 'public' (e.g., Heimans, 2012). Here, we find that working with multiplicity and uncertainty to be really quite liberating in its penchant to 'not know', but rather 'to think'.

3.0.2: Methodology as Perpetual War

It appears that the social sciences in general have become worried, lethargic and a bit self-loathing (Law, 2004). To borrow from outside education for just a moment, *policy scientificity 3.0* is "war all the time" (Bukowski, 1984), "pure war" (Virilio & Lotringer, 1997/1993), but really a persistence concerning "war and truth" in the academy (Foucault, 2003). We are convinced, given our locations, and implications, in neo-liberal universities, that no return to an idyllic time of policy analysis or retreats into academic silos – i.e., 'programs', 'departments' – or methodological parochialism will stop this multi-disciplinary Cerberus. The question for us will be to what extent, if any, can policy scholars talk about, within and across difference (Gilroy, 2005; West, 1993).

The second characterization of *3.0*, thus, revolves around the methodological wars of *2.0* that we would note have only escalated in *3.0*, albeit in a kind of constant guerrilla arrangement that parallel modern military tactics of ambush, sabotage, subterfuge, jamming, and automation (e.g., drones). Proclamations of "evidence based" research, with its limitations on funding and contentions about what knowledge 'counts', have wound the clock back to continue the methodology wars in education (Jacob & White, 2002). And, as St. Pierre (2011) notes, an ossification and routinization of qualitative methodologies in education has re-inscribed the mechanic and instrumentalist versions they sought to disrupt. Here, some options that *3.0* might take up include *post-qualitative* methodologies (St Pierre, 2011) that are 'working the ruins' left from some qualitative predecessors (St Pierre & Pillow, 2000). In just a moment, we will briefly discuss a 'fieldwork in philosophy' as another option.

3.0.3: Difference, Representation, and Subject Catallaxy

The third characterisation of *3.0* addresses difference and representation, with particular attention paid to race and ethnicity as our areas of scholarship, although we note that we could have focused on other categories that are used to express subject positions; indeed, we note the veritable explosion of different subject categories, and in relation to ideas of difference and representation in education.

In many ways, the contemporary focus on performance has stretched the liberal political imagination away from forms of representation that constituted and occluded so many different groups of people in the first place. And this is the rub. For instance, West (1993) remarked that difference can be assimilated and elided in some kind of cosmopolitan fantasy ('we are the world'), and something that has been homogenized in relation to attempts at univocal, or at least coherent, political representation (i.e., 'identity politics').

Here, then, *3.0* analyses, identifies, and examines ideas of *difference* and *representation* in relation to the many registers "which govern the relationships of translation between them" (Hall, 1997: 21). In this sense, *3.0* borrows from Paul

Gilroy (2000: 34) to map the "radical forms of anxiety that flow from uncertainty about racialized identities" and to try and "recover the liberatory moment in the process of freeing ourselves from the bonds of raciology and compulsory raciality." Chapter Seven examines the "radical forms of anxiety" produced from racialized bodies, and Chapter Eight examines how these affects and raciologies are spatialised educationally throughout cities. Again, part of what we are interested in are the 'geos' in education policy and a significant space in the movement of education policy is the city.

If raciology is one form of translation between difference and representation, then this is no easy task. It is also a task that is under threat as many translation mechanisms are running out of steam or are being mutated (or maintained) within neo-liberal or post-liberal raciologies, for instance the aggregate of neo-liberal multiculturalism (Hale, 2005). *3.0* maps the many different translation registers as they erode and mutate within neo-liberal, post-liberal, and/or the contemporary catallaxy of raciology in education.

'Ethnoscapes', for example, are real in that they organise and mediate the political, cultural, and economic futures of many (Appadurai, 1996). Moreover, some ethnoscapes may require assistance when wishing to be 'represented' and 'recognised' in the "global cultural [educational] economy" (Appadurai, 1990). However, the *practices of recognition* are also the very objects that organise and palpitate various 'ethnic cleansings' within such economies (Appadurai, 2006). And while post-colonialism has at times been identified as a sub-set of post-structuralism, Ahluwalia (2005) asserts that this denies the colonial roots of post-structuralism, and therefore, it may be pertinent to examine the ways in which post-structuralism draws on the ideas of post-colonialism concerning "otherness, difference, irony, mimicry, parody, the lamenting of modernity and the deconstruction of the grand narratives of European culture arising out of the Enlightenment tradition …" (Ahluwalia, 2005: 2). *3.0* maps theories and practices of policy difference.

Alterity is a two-way street, and importantly, an engagement with different representations simultaneously generated of the Other. Here, Bifo (2008: 24) perceptively observed that "alterity sets the limit of the existent organism." *3.0* examines and reflects on the production of concepts that are sometimes identified as limited by their Euro-centric and occluding their connections to pernicious colonial geo-histories.

The work of Deleuze and the concepts such as nomadism, folds, and so forth, are ideas that are in a sense playful, but could be "seen to appropriate and intellectualise indigenous experience and ways of life" (Bignall & Patton, 2010: 2), which ostensibly function as an indifference to the conditions of colonised peoples. *3.0* is acutely aware that some of the concepts at play in *policy geophilosophy* could be seen to be abstract, and generated from a non-geography and non-history. We could, for example, note Deleuze's "preference for virtual creativity over analysis of actually existing political situations" (Bignall & Patton, 2010: 2). This might be seen to fall into what Edward Said saw as the irrelevance of criticism that was devoid of contact with the world. As Ahluwalia (2005: 141) noted: "[f]or Said, theory can be effective only when it is located firmly within the world".

The criticism then of Deleuze's work, and by default much of the work of post-structuralism as theory absent the world – as abstract – has been repudiated by Bignall and Patton (2010) (and many others) who suggest many of Deleuze's ideas are taken up by those supporting postcolonial politics, and that there are many resonances with various postcolonial concepts (see also, for example, Burns & Kaiser, 2012; May, 2005b; Nail, 2012). Thomas Lemke (2014) has made this case about Foucault as well (and Mark Olssen too (1999)).

3.0, however, maps the contemporary translation registers of neo-liberal raciologies, whereas the contemporary *catallaxy* of neo-liberal education policy frays the assumptions of economic activities that strive for unitary ends and singular purposes (e.g., racial and gendered equality in education based on 'coherent' categories of racialized and gendered subjects). Instead, neo-liberal catallaxy, as opposed to 'economy', rejects unitary ends and seeks to produce differentiation with multiple ends. Our *policy geophilosophy* maps the various forms of difference produced in the name of neo-liberal education policy, including what we see as very serious (and seductive) problematics associated with school choice policies as a way out of the liberal inequalities of schooling and earlier forms of compulsory raciality (Rofes & Stulberg, 2004). We discuss these issues in depth in Chapters Six, Seven, and Eight.

3.0 constitutes policy geophilosophy firmly within 'the world' that is concerned with the representations and materialities of policy. The effects, affects, disputations and re-articulations, and examples of policy processes and practices in the settler societies throughout the world that continue to (re)produce preferred colonial representations and materialities at such a rapid pace that the net effect is an erasure of many ethnoscapes (Appadurai, 1990). But, *3.0* simultaneously asks ontological questions about 'this very world' and the possibilities of other representations, non-representations, and those contained with developing new translation registers perhaps born from earlier forms of difference and representation but that are also not necessarily tied to those either. Again, the 'global cultural educational economy' is not something we believe we should be headed towards.

3.0.4: Complex and Uncertain Materials

The fourth characterisation of *3.0* is a general move to maintain or connect to a materialist orientation in education and educational policy studies. The 'materialist turn', a set of broad approaches that have attempted to bring together objects, knowledge, things, practices and subjects (Barad, 2007; Bennett, 2009), in "a radical ontological move that decentres the human and emphases the co-constitutive power of matter" (C. A. Taylor & Ivinson, 2013: 666).

This materialist turn has been debated in geography as part of non-representational theories (Thrift, 2008) that Murdoch (2006: 24) suggested are part of a materialist post-structuralism. That is, "forms of post-structuralism that are situated 'beyond the text' in the 'fleshy materialities' of the bio-social domain", including affect, and human and non-human agency. Non-representational theory, therefore, is understood "to be a necessary response to a contemporary political moment in which various non-representational modalities – including affect – are caught up in the emergence of new forms of sovereign and bio power" (Anderson, 2008: xx). This is to simply (actually, quite complexly) wrestle with scientificity in education policy studies. Stephen J. Ball provides good examples with his ideas about policy subjects, policy enactments and policy becomings.

Policy scientificity 3.0 does (or can) remain preoccupied by the subjugations that education policy produces. We try not to privilege the subject, only their innumerable enactments through, and of, policy – 'fleshy materialities'. We take up questions about 'agency' in Chapter Two, but for now, Bonta and Protevi (2004: 25) signal what this materialist view might look like if we took it up in education policy studies,

> … there is no exact quantitative solution. Nor can there be any qualitative, 'thick' narrative (for example, a Clifford Geertz-inspired ethnographic account) or even a qualitative-quantitative hybrid approach [mixed methods] that provides a full set of instructions. Rather, [problems] are 'resolved' only by the irreplaceable, un-reproducible, adaptive 'real-life operation' [that] indicates the irreducibility of distributed spatiotemporal networks of embodied artisans in 'resolving' complex problems by real-life operations rather than by the solution of exact equations or descriptions.

The emphasis on materialism is to use and think through the 'empirical' in policy studies while noting that these 'policy realities' and 'policy materialities' are constantly changing; indeed constantly emerging. This emergence is an important part of Actor Network Theory approaches to policy analysis, in which "[a]ny changes we might describe as policy – new ideas, innovations, changes in behaviour, transformations – emerge through the effects of relational interactions …" (Fenwick & Edwards, 2011). For example, philosophy itself has begun to 'experiment', and a fieldwork in philosophy (Bourdieu, 1990; Rabinow & Rose, 2003) allows us to: (a) develop concepts in situ; (b) collapse the endless debates about theoretical abstraction (or, conversely, to 'localize' theory) while still holding it as a very important area for development, and (c) note how we are ontologically implicated with and affected by objects of analysis (rather than just epistemologically positioned) – that matter matters (Barad, 2007; Bourdieu, 1990).

POLICY MUTATIONS

Finally, *policy scientificity 3.0* is not an 'evolution' of the prior and admittedly broad epochs of policy analysis in education. No. *3.0* is its third mutation. *Policy geophilosophy* still works within, around, and through the prior scientificities of *1.0, 2.0*. It is our modest attempt to contribute to Bakhtin's 'carnival' – the heteroglossia of policy studies and scientificities in education. These scientificities constitute policy scholars and their corresponding activities in different ways – as 'analysts' and 'solution providers', as 'activists', and as 'policy theorists' and 'problematisers'. While at various time-spaces we are constituted as all of these, it is clearly in the last type of work that we locate *policy geophilosophy*. We see it as having a decidedly marked difference from the kinds of instrumental and techno-rational policy research that claim 'solutions' to policy 'problems'. In fact, it is an attempt to map some of these sedimented logics.

Policy scientificity is also marked, for better or worse, as an inter-disciplinary approach that deliberately uses uncertainty and chaos rather than seeing them as things to avoid, sublimate, 'control', or neatly package away in a single discipline. We would never suggest a solution to your problems; we can barely keep abreast of our own. However, we are pretty sure that all educational problems are spatialized, temporalized and require new concepts in order for us to experiment with and muddle on.

Please move to the next chapter to see how a policy geophilosophy manifests.

NOTE

[1] The singularity is often referred to as a future point in time in which a constellation of events in artificial intelligence, human-biological changes, and/or human-machine interfaces will produce an emergent and superior form of 'intelligence'. The term refers to a moment, and for some, a thing, although it isn't clear if the singularity is a specific form of intelligence or an environment that contains multiple 'superintelligences'. Anyway, we consider policy to be a technology, and one that is adaptive and replacing some of our thinking.

CHAPTER 2

EDUCATION POLICY GEOPHILOSOPHY

Theory and Policy Analysis for Emergent Worlds

> If the protests of children were heard in kindergarten, if their questions were attended to, it would be enough to explode the entire educational system.
> —Deleuze and Foucault 1977: 209

Welcome back. For this chapter, we recommend something a bit stronger than coffee; perhaps a bitter or even something heavy on tannins. This chapter explains what we mean regarding an *education policy geophilosophy,* an approach we initially developed out of frustration because we could not believe what was being done to education in the name of policy. Of course, we were equally stupefied to witness what was done to policy through the sanctified fantasies of education. It is easy to ignore adults – we do it all the time – but, we wondered, is no one listening to five-year olds?

Education policy analysis has left us with a preoccupation with the 'knower' and displaced, or taken for granted, what it is to be known. Take for instance the definitiveness in the idea of a 'more accountable education system'. Or, 'academic achievement'. Or, to cite a couple of classics, 'educational equity' and 'educational success'. Conversely, we are interested, similarly to Lather (2009: 8),

> in a scientificity that is about imperfect information where incompleteness and indeterminacy are assets, more not less, central elements of a scientific posture of getting lost as a way of knowing. Here the absence of foundations is enabling, opening us to the other. Against the received objectifying, scientistic posture, this is a scientificity of engaged ethics grounded in a permanent facing of the undecidable, an ethical horizon of science more attuned to innovation than 'the epistemological quarrel over the conditions of scientificity.' (Dosse, 1999: 352)

As noted in the previous chapter, various scientificities have been mobilised in education policy to legitimate analysis and advocacy attempts over the past sixty years. These criteria for different forms of policy scientificity have shifted and have been debated. Mapping these three periods of policy scientificity allowed us to understand how education policy is a historical construction that is power-inscribed, and that both enables and constrains educational possibilities through various registers that simultaneously enunciate such possibilities and exclude other possibilities.

CHAPTER 2

In order for us to posit a *policy geophilosophy* in education, it was important to note the various disciplinary frameworks that have been developed, used and appropriated for different kinds of education policy studies. We are not disciplinary apologists, but we acknowledge that the liberal construction of education produced the biopower apparatuses (i.e., 'the knowledges') that we simultaneously critique and use. In this sense, we do not rewrite the historical "explosion of numerous and diverse techniques for achieving the subjugations of bodies and the control of populations" (Foucault, 1990: 140). No. Instead, like five-year olds, we are trying to get out from under them.

Policy geophilosophy has an affinity, though not equivalence, with "political informed use of complexity theory" (Bonta & Protevi, 2004: 3), which only means that "an education that is understood in complexity terms cannot be conceived in terms of preparation for the future. Rather it must be construed in terms of participation in the creation of possible futures" (Davis & Sumara, 2008: 43). These are wonderful ideas; particularly that we might be included in developing our futures – even at the age of five, and that the plural of 'futures' is not just some science fiction idea but a very real likelihood within the multiverse (Greene, 2011; Gribbin, 2010). *Policy geophilosophy* includes the ideas of *space* and *concept* in education policy studies so that they may be employed as strategies against the technicians of school behaviour, administrators of curricular subjectifications, and the education leaders of population control. Thus, our *policy geophilosophy* shares in some of the possibilities involved in kindergarteners' questions about exploding the education system.

We propose that a policy analysis needs a critical ethos committed to analysis as situated, spatial, contextual, and material. We find the term 'geophilosophy' a rich one that reflects our individual interests in geography and philosophy. If we look at our object of interest in this book, 'policy', and hence a 'policy geophilosophy', we are fascinated by three things: one, the way in which policy as concept and action both endures (stabilizes) and mutates in and through space-times; two, the ways in which policy analysis attempts to deal with, and constitutes, the ontologies and epistemologies of policy; and, three, how policy shapes, constitutes, and enacts subjects. Specifically, our policy geophilosophy is designed to examine *how education policy spatialises and constitutes objects and subjects through emergent and adaptive policy arrangements that simultaneously influence how policy is sensed, embodied, and enacted.*

We work with 'non-representational' theories, broadly part of poststructural geographies, that tend to deal with types of questions and problems in which we are interested. Anderson and Harrison (2010: 23–24) posed questions such as,

> how do sense and significance emerge from on-going practical action?; how, given the contingency of orders, is practical action organised in more-than-human configurations?; and how to attend to events – to the 'non' that may lead to the chance of something different or a modification of an existing ordering?

For our purposes, and we hope perhaps yours, a policy geophilosophy produces alternative and multi-disciplinary ways of understanding education policy, including a transversal politics (see Chapter One) which are so desperately needed. How much longer can we endure policy machines – i.e., *1.0, 2.0, 3.0* – that do not listen to kindergarteners? Please, do not misinterpret us. We are not entirely sure we like kindergarteners, but we think they may have a point. Would it really be so terrible to explode such a disciplining and overtly capitalist structure as the educational system? At the very least, maybe we might "cease to celebrate the creation of state schooling and see it instead as an 'inglorious moment' in the 'modern play of coercion over bodies'" (Ball, 2013: 118; quoting Michel Foucault, 1979: 191).

Because we suspect we have had our 'inglorious moments' in our collective and respective work, we are obliged to state that a policy geophilosophy can produce new formulations of education for emergent futures. Within such logics, we note a rapidly devolving disconnect between the parochial instrumentalism of education policy and the state. Our inter-disciplinary approach to policy studies, our *policy geophilosophy*, is not, however, an attempt to salvage that particular link, but is rather an attempt to develop additional links between education policy and the state that capture the many different ways education policy is being used, by whom, and for what purposes. Peters (2004: 218) stated that for Deleuze and Guattari, "philosophy cannot escape its relationship to the City and the State. In its modern and postmodern forms it cannot escape its form under industrial and knowledge capitalism". Sorry kids, you still have to go to school, for now.

And, right from the start, we have no qualms in jettisoning a techno-rational policy 'scientificity' and anything remotely connected to it. Well, the last part is not entirely true. We are interested in techniques and rationalities, and we still like to count things, but only because counting reminds us of the different flows that travel around and through sedimentations that have been brought to rest. We also count things because of the constant changes – indeed speeds – through which these movements produce space. Zeno brought this to our attention awhile back; Rene Magritte provides a constant source of inspiration and laughter here; and Gilles Deleuze reminded us of the beautiful potential of *becoming* more recently.

We are interested in the possibility of uncertainty and emergence in transversal-disciplinary frameworks that examine ideas of difference, non-representation, unpredictability and chance in education policy and policy studies. This is to work from and with the 'onto-epistemes' of *policy scientificity 1.0, 2.0,* and *3.0* discussed in Chapter One. The subsequent sections discuss the ideas of ontology and materiality, spatiality, agency, and emergence. These sections illustrate an indicative sense of a *policy geophilosophy* that we attempt in this book through concepts of *policy prolepses, policy intensions,* and *policy folds* (e.g., Chapters Four and Five). *Policy geophilosophy* is one way to understand complexity and uncertainty in education policy, and to connect with others who are developing a variety of multi-, inter-, and post-foundational analyses of educational policy (e.g., Heimans, 2012).

CHAPTER 2

CRITICAL PAROCHIALISMS, OR "WHERE DID MY ONTOLOGY GO?"

We propose *policy geophilosophy* as part of a critical ethos committed to analyze specific policy issues from situated, contextual, spatial and materialist points of view. A policy geophilosophy, as a form of 'criticality', offers "a critical attitude … and thus a way of relating to the present" (Simons, Olssen, & Peters, 2009c: x) that,

> create[s] a public, not in view of finding agreement (on facts or values), but by gathering people for whom something is at stake … that is, to help constitute 'matters of public concern' by transforming what policies or researchers regard as matters of fact into 'an issue to talk about'.

Our critical ethos may be a virtue (Butler, 2001), and is certainly aimed at developing an interdisciplinary "art of not being governed like that and at that cost" (Foucault, 2007: 29). Our concerns pertain to governance, and the changing nature(s) of education policy in relation to the varying modes of the state, especially the configuring of relations between the market, the state, 'civil society,' and its regulation (Ball & Junemann, 2012). Here, our sense of 'critique' is not aimed at transformation guided by ideas of transcendence (Torres & Van Heertum, 2009; cf. Foucault's genealogy of critique). We do not claim, as such, that what we (re)present is the only way to understand a *policy geophilosophy*, nor do we claim that *policy geophilosophy* is the only inter-disciplinary approach to education policy studies, or transversal politics. We do claim, however, and hope to demonstrate throughout this book, that a policy geophilosophy can assist scholars to examine the spatio-temporal aspects of education policy and to link to and create concepts that assist others understand education policy materialities differently (e.g., policy becomings; Ball et al., 2011).

Materiality and Ontological Politics

As we mentioned in Chapter One, the materialist 'turn' is an important one for us to recognise. While we draw on Deleuze in this book, Deleuze did not consider himself a materialist but he did see his work as 'vitalist' (Coole & Frost, 2010). We draw on the idea of 'lively' matter – especially regarding policy and objects such as schools in this book (see our discussion about 'agency' below). We are interested in the 'material turn' not because it is 'new' as such, but rather that, as Coole and Frost (2010: 6) suggested,

> [i]n terms of theory itself … we are summoning a new materialism in response to a sense that the radicalism of the dominant discourses which have flourished under the cultural turn is now more or less exhausted. We share the feeling current among many researchers that the dominant constructivist orientation to social analysis is inadequate for thinking about matter, materiality, and politics in ways that do justice to the contemporary context of biopolitics and global political economy.

The 'material turn' fits with our desire to delimit a set of 'ontological politics' that has been displaced in education policy analyses by an insistence on epistemology that strives for certainty, predictability, and instrumentalism. Law (2004) discussed "ontological politics" in ways that deliberately set out to destabilize onto-epistemes that strive for techno-rational singularity. According to Law, traditional ontology assumes (at least) five characteristics. It is: (a) independent of people; (b) 'out there' (spatial assumptions of the world); (c) anterior and precedes people (i.e., statements from God, truth, or science); (d) definite and singular (including constant and universal); and, (e) able to be represented.

When we speak of 'ontological politics' we posit and experiment with ontologies that challenge these five assumptions. For us, ontology is: (a) enmeshed with people (e.g., 'object-oriented-ontology' Morton, 2010); (b) not 'out there' but produced in various times/spaces (Morton, 2010); (c) not anterior (Hacking, 2004); (d) multiple (Mol, 2002), and (e) non-representational (Edwards, 2012). Our 'ontological politics,' then, posits a different world than the one used for reference in many (all?) education policies. But there is more to our politics than just assertions of difference.

Policy is produced through what Law (2004) describes as 'inscription devices'. The purpose of these devices is to trace or represent materiality (e.g., charts, graphs). However, within the production of policy much is deleted in order to produce preferred courses of action. For example, the use of charts in policy development almost always obscures the 'data' that is used. For our purposes, we are interested in what particular realities are constructed by particular inscription devices, and, more importantly, what particular realities have been erased, elided, and remain virtual as "conditions of possibility" (Foucault, 1970). Here, our 'ontological politics' is committed to showing and critiquing the "perspectival" (Law, 2004: 60) tendencies of education policy that seek singularity, independence, anteriority, definiteness, and representativeness. We think these tendencies are why so many people continue to clamour for singular 'evidence' in education. In effect, our politics seeks to thwart tactics involved in assumptions of education policy committed to singularities. Rather, our 'ontological politics' intends to illustrate the multiplicity, fractionality, and differences of education policy instead. We are convinced that the tracings of singular ontologies onto education policy are tantamount to erasures of multiplicities, and this, we believe, are serious political acts. Our 'ontological politics', then, focusses on the absences and presences within education policy, and we illustrate these ideas in Chapters Four and Five.

When we discuss notions of ontology, politics and policy we are interested in the possibility of thinking things differently.[1] This includes the political implications of ontologies and struggles over the object 'policy'. These struggles encapsulate and embody struggles over investments concerning what policy can 'do' when the question 'what is policy?' is answered. We are not positing a new material that we have 'discovered' in order to improve policy studies in education when we invoke the term of 'ontological politics'! We will leave that task up to astro/physicists! To contend/believe that policy is techno-rational, for example, is to adhere to the idea that there is no politics to policy, it is connected to ideology, but there is no politics regarding the object and associated and produced practices. The idea of multiple ontologies provides a way of disrupting political positions that are fixed and stable (i.e, essential and universal), though does perhaps fall down in providing a way of acting in reference to these multiple realities (S. Sellar, personal correspondence, 2014).

We poise an ontological question, *what is education policy and what roles does it enact in relation to the state (e.g., in relation to formal schooling)?* We are interested in the object 'policy', as part of a "reinvigorated account of objects and ... that objects present a starting point for analysis" (Ash & Simpson, 2014: 12). To return to St Pierre's (2011) idea of reimagining social sciences, and to pay credence to the critical policy studies and critical social science of *2.0*, educational policy studies has been preoccupied by an epistemological war tied to "necessary perspectivalism" (Lather, 2009) and quite cleverly displaced what Law (2004: 143) noted as the persistent war of "ontological politics". Singh, Heimans and Glasswell (2014: 3) posited that:

> what we 'do' as research is ontologically political. Research practices do not simply investigate or make sense of an external reality ... even when putatively, this might be the aim. The doing of research is an 'interference' [in] reality.

We are, similarly interested in an ontological politics of policy analysis. This is predicated on a politics that deals with the representational and material aspects of policy analysis "a politics that has to do with the way in which problems are framed, bodies are shaped, and lives are pushed and pulled into one shape or another" (Mol, 2002: viii).

We certainly do not believe, of course, that education policy and its recommendations are somehow independent from the research and the researchers that produce it. In this sense, policy scholars are called to task to state their research 'positions' and 'positionalities', even though we do not need to account for how these spaces have been created for us, by us, and through us (i.e., disciplinary knowledges). How did space become the preeminent and implicit focus in educational research (i.e., positionalities) with *little recourse to understanding how these spaces are produced*? Might policy scientificities affect educational systems more than the recommendations generated from within them? Part of what we are arguing in this book is that confessions about perspectival and disciplinary subjugations are necessary but insufficient with regard to clear statements about the ontologies of our educational subjects/objects. And, yes, we believe that many kindergarteners are asking ontological questions; and, yes, we believe too many adults have not had compelling or plausible answers to these questions.

THE SPATIALITIES OF EDUCATION POLICY (ANALYSES)

In the following chapters we assume that the education examples we examine are unstable, chaotic, or "far-from-equilibrium" (Bonta & Protevi, 2004: 18). We aim to produce different spatial readings to account for the emergence, for example, of a school or a city. While in the twentieth century there had been multiple spatial turns in various disciplines and fields, including linguistics, philosophy and geography (Peters & Kessl, 2009), the emphasis on space in the late twentieth century and early twenty first century, closely related to notions of space-time compression, simultaneity and multiplicity identified with phenomena such as globalization and transnational migration (Warf & Arias, 2009). This constitutes a heuristic point, predicated on the notion that: "Geography matters, not for the simplistic and overly used reason that everything happens in space, but because *where* things happen is critical to knowing *how* and *why* they happen" (Warf & Arias, 2009: 1).

We are fascinated by this 'spatial turn' for it calls into question, as Thrift (2006: 139) noted,

> categories like 'material', 'life' and 'intelligence' through an emphasis on the unremitting materiality of a world where there are no-pre-existing objects. Rather, all kinds of hybrids are being continually recast by processes of circulation within and between particular spaces. The world is made up of all kinds of things brought into relation with one another by this universe of spaces through a continuous and largely involuntary process of encounter and the often violent training that the encounter forces.

In the following chapters we work with ideas of space offered by Thrift (2006), predicated on:

1. the idea that "everything, but everything, is spatially distributed" (p. 140), an assertion that speaks to the necessary interrelations of one space with other spaces;
2. that distribution repudiates the possibility of boundaries, for "[a]ll spaces are porous to a greater or lesser degree" (p. 140);
3. that with everything being spatially distributed and with no boundaries, every space is thus in constant motion. This is not to say that movement is not challenged, and as we note in the following chapters policy is the enduring and always ultimately failed, attempt to stabilize space. Thrift (2006: 141) contended, "[t]here is no static and stabilized space, though there are plenty of attempts to make space static and stable. Process (or perhaps, more accurately, force-being) is all in that it is all that there is …".
4. that multiplicity needs to be applied to the type of space, that there is no one kind of space. That there are indeed abstract spaces, relative spaces, and relational spaces (Thrift, 2006).

CHAPTER 2

Spatial Conceptions in Education

Newtonian conceptions of space posit a discrete and autonomous container for action, that is, abstract space *contains* events and actions. Relative space is conceived as a plane with implications of distance and scale – in which space is defined relative to the objects and processes being considered in space and time; that is, there is not fixed relationship for locating things (Jones, 2009).

Relational notions of space, the ideas of which are our focus, are premised on notions of multiplicity and openness (Massey, 2005) and "an emphasis on the proliferation of diverse relations and strong sense that that the resulting orders are open, provisional, achievements" (Anderson & Harrison, 2010: 15). For instance, Massey (2005: 99) posited that space needs to be constituted as radically heterogeneous. She stated, "[p]osition, location, is the minimum order of differentiation of elements in the multiplicity that is co-formed with space". Anderson and Wylie (2009: 320 cited in Ash & Simpson, 2014: 11) similarly contended,

> heterogeneous materialities actuate or emerge from within the assembling of multiple, differential, relations and … the properties and/or capacities of materialities thereafter become effects of that assembling.

Space as constant emergence is intimately concerned with power rather than as a neutral container that exists *a priori* for activity which subsequently orders relations between humans and non-humans. As Massey (2005: 99) noted "… space is the dimension which poses the question of the social, and thus of the political (while 'actual' spaces are produced through the social and the political)," and, furthermore, space is "the sphere of coevalness, of radical contemporaneity."

Throughout the book we identify some of the spatial and conceptual equivocations that the neo-liberal education project uses to propagate itself. In Chapters Four and Five, we argue that education policy is a spatial process, and that implementation processes in particular produce crucial emergent geographies. We describe how emergent geographies are produced when policy *folds* actors through senses and enactments of policy. The idea that policy is sensed, embodied and enacted is developed into the concept of a *policy intension* which extends approaches to spatial, and in particular, micropolitical analyses in policy research.

UNPREDICTABLE 'AGENCY': EMERGENCE AND AFFECT

It may have been clear that there is some overlap with what we are discussing and notions of complexity theory. Following Olssen (2008) there are confluences between notions of distribution and relationality in the broadly poststructural approaches we are taking, and the ideas of interactions in complexity theory. Notably, as Olssen (2008: 108) posited,

> Interactions take place in open systems through 'self-organisation' by adapting dynamically to changes in both the environment and the system.

Self-organisation is an emergent property of the system as a whole. An emergent property is a property that is constituted due to the combination of elements in the system as a whole. As such it is a property possessed by the system but not by its components.

Interactions and emergence are part of the lack of borders and simultaneous multiplicity that constitute our (relational) readings of space. Spatialities emerge, we suggest in education policy, as forms of ordering and stabilization (see Gulson, 2011). Thrift (2008: 121) posited that,

> space-times ... generate many of the unactualized possibles without which they cannot be sensed and described. The distribution of space-times is complex and the response to this complexity is not theoretical but practical: different things need to be tried out, opened up, which can leave their trace even when they fail.

Complexity theory also carries with it ideas of 'self-organization', which admittedly, is tricky for our avowedly social purposes that rely a great deal on ideas of power and politics. Protevi (2009: vii) proposes the notion of 'bodies politic' as an attempt to demonstrate "the ways in which politics, psychology, and physiology intersect in socially embedded and somatically embodied affective cognition". We wish to highlight how these ideas of 'self-organization' and 'bodies politic' assist us to map conceptions of education policy that are instrumental, mechanistic, techno-rational, and that claim to deterministically cause (or produce) a desired state of affairs. For our purposes, we will capture this conception with the term of emergence rather than 'self-organization', where emergence refers to the "(diachronic) construction of functional structures in complex systems that achieve a (synchronic) focus of systematic behaviour as they constrain the behaviour of individual components" (Protevi, 2006: 19). Temporality, and not just history, is crucial to our formulation of emergence and we discuss this idea in Chapter Four in the form of a *policy prolepsis*.

Further, we assume that emergent structures are patterned (but not normalizing), where we have "a qualitative knowledge of the emergent properties of a system" (Bonta & Protevi, 2004: 19). Emergent structures can arise through either patterned conditions or properties that are unexpected but explainable from non-linear rules, and emergence occurs through un-patterned processes that "are not deducible even in principle 'from the most complete and exhaustive knowledge of their emergence bases'" (Biesta, 2010: 6, citing Kim, 1999: 3). Either. Both. Biesta (2010: 6) is helpful here in outlining the notion of emergence as a norm rather than exception,

> What is particularly important is the ability to understand the open, recursive, organic, non-linear and emergent dimensions of physical and social processes as positive and necessary aspects of complex systems, rather than as deviations from the norm or as epiphenomena that need to be explained away. This is also the case in the field of education where complexity has provided a language for articulating the fact that educational processes and practices

tend to be characterised by nonlinearity and unpredictability .... Moreover, the idea of emergence not only makes it possible to highlight that knowledge, understanding and reality are themselves emerging through educational processes rather than that they are simply represented in and through education (see Biesta & Osberg, 2007; Osberg & Biesta, 2008). Complexity also makes it possible to highlight the fact that individuals emerge in and through educational processes in unique and unpredictable ways.

We think educational organizations, institutions, and what are characterized as systems (e.g., school districts, national systems) are good examples of these ideas. Stephen J. Ball (2007, 2012; Ball & Junemann, 2012) provides excellent examples of the kinds of complex adaptive systems that we are talking about in education policy. Ball's mapping of various private and public partnerships constitutes a form of *policy emergence*. We further think cities might be good examples. And people. 'Systems' are constituted through mutation and emergence related to events that do not, in and of themselves, 'predict' outcomes – indeed, produce emergent spaces, uncertain concepts, and difference. For instance, Ball (2009) noted how heterarchies and network theory functioned with these characteristics, including the slippery neo-liberal catallaxy which produces and simultaneously capitalizes on the differences it requires and produces.

A politically informed sense of complexity theory affords us the luxury to discuss 'agency' – but really *activity* – in relation to much broader, open, and adaptive environments; that is, to understand 'agency' in education within *policy ecologies* (Weaver-Hightower, 2008), *policy ensembles* (Ball, 2006), *policy assemblages* (McCann & Ward, 2012) and *policy dispositifs* (Bailey, 2013) that are uncertain, chaotic, and emergent. As Coole and Frost (2010: 9) contended, new materialities require that,

> the whole edifice of modern ontology regarding notions of change, causality, agency, time, and space needs rethinking. ... [N]ew materialists are rediscovering a materiality that materializes, evincing immanent modes of self-transformation that compel us to think of causation in far more complex terms; to recognize that phenomena are caught in a multitude of interlocking systems and forces and to consider anew the location and nature of capacities for agency.

Policy 'actors', for example, are simultaneously policy subjects (Ball et al., 2011) within and various dispositifs of networked governance (Metcalfe, 2010) or "societies of control" (Deleuze, 1992). We note an affinity between what we are attempting with our geophilosophy and what Thrift (2008) has noted as the complicated links between complexity and materiality. A politically informed sense of complexity theory examines traditional forms of 'agency' as,

> an escape route from the conceptual gridlock of 'structure' as either a merely homeostatic self-regulation or a postmodernist 'signifier imperialism' and

'agency' as a mysterious exception somehow granted to individual human subjects in defiance of natural laws and lithely free of social structure. (Bonta & Protevi, 2004: 6)

That is one way to say it. Michel Foucault said it differently: "People know what they do; frequently they know why they do what they do; but what they don't know is what what they do does" (Dreyfus & Rabinow, 1982: 187). Foucault suggested that activity is generated but that it enters complex systems that are also generating action. Foucault troubles *intention* that is conceived as 'lithely free of social structure and natural laws'.

For instance, might all the 'agency' going on in the world influence subsequent action? And, might agency simply be the production of more and more rules to follow and break? Bonta and Protevi (2004: 5) crystallized this idea when they stated that "'agency' thinking seems mired in a quasi-existentialist affirmation of 'resistance'", which we would note is perpetuated by all the insistence on 'having' agency, which is precisely the polyvalent technologies provided by governments nowadays. A major goal of what we are trying to achieve in this book, through working through and with a *policy geophilosophy* in education, is to rearticulate and reorganize the spaces that influence actions rather than to insist on 'agency' to 'resist' these spaces (see also Butler, 2004; Youdell, 2010).

At the risk of making things even more complicated, neo-liberalism – the *sin qua non* of education policy – encourages subjects to increase 'their' agentic spaces (e.g., entrepreneurial, self-responsible, self-determining) within rapidly reterritorialized educational places. Neo-liberal 'agency' is always mediated through race and gender, and to the extent to which capital facilitates somatic mobilities to places that better mediate sexist and racist ecologies. Of course, questions about identity, difference, and representation are questions that kindergarteners also ask (McGlynn, Bekerman, Zembylas, & Gallagher, 2009). Here, our *policy geophilosophy* identifies the equivocations of the biopolitical subject that the neo-liberal education project uses to propagate itself through its assertions and inducements for different subjects to claim 'their agency' on economic grounds. We devote Chapter Six, Seven and Eight to an analysis of some these ideas.

Policy Affects and Effects: Action in the World

Educational representation appears to be a slippery slope of 'agency-thinking' when the need for reconstructing epistemologies that have colonized our memories and aspirations obfuscate the maintenance of the intersubjective project that organizes the preconditions for political activity in the first place. If indeed it is the case that recognition and representation have become the neo-liberal epistemologies for action, we examine the potential of *policy geophilosophy* for non-representational action – perhaps even an *Anonymous politics* (Coleman, 2013) and/or a *politics of imperceptibility* (Grosz, 2002). Perhaps the best we can do is examine to what extent 'action' can be conceived within education policy, and to what extent indeterminacy and incompleteness can contribute to a political informed sense of movement. We understand what the intentions are for neo-liberal free markets and we are not impressed.

In another sense, however, 'agency' is deeply rooted in sense-making and environmental cues or triggers. A great deal of movement is produced when

> at critical thresholds some physical and biological systems can be said to 'sense' the difference in their environment that trigger self-organizing processes. In this way, signs ... are not only conceptualized as occurring beyond the registers to the human and even the organic [e.g., linguistic], but also are understood as triggers of material processes. (Bonta & Protevi, 2004: 4)

This notion of triggers is a key part of *policy geophilosophy*, and no amount of italics can signal how subject/object movement is influenced to various degrees when sense-making and affect are actuated by environmental cues and triggers. Here, we can see that the scientificities of *3.0*, in which *policy geophilosophy* sits, are part of debates about the separation of affect and intention and cognition, and about 'location' of intentionality in relation to the subject (e.g., Altieri, 2012; Leys, 2011; Connolly, 2012). On the one hand, Leys (2011, 2012) has argued that one consequences of an adherence to anti-intentionalist theories of affect is to jettison the conceptual necessity underpinning 'critical thinking'. On the other hand, responses to this critique (Altieri, 2012; Connolly, 2012) contend that Leys narrows understandings of emotions, affects and intentionality to a notion of concept definition (Altieri, 2012), while also using the term 'anti-intentionalist' to conflate multiple literatures on intentionality (Connolly, 2012).

In this book we are tending towards the multiple notions of intentionality. We are interested, as such, in two things: one, how policy organises affective life; and, two, the relational spatialities of affective policy life. As Thrift (2008: 175) posits,

> *affect is understood as a form of thinking*, often indirect and nonreflective true, but thinking all the same. And, similarly, all manner of the spaces which they generate must be thought of in the same way, as means of thinking and as thought in action.

The focus on affect as part of policy analysis is done not to emphasise that policy generates and is a reaction to feelings or emotions, but rather that, as Thrift (2008: 173) maintains there are increasingly "diverse ways in which the use and abuse of various affective practices is gradually changing what we regard as the sphere of 'the political'". We also see this, like Thrift (2006: 143), as concerning relationships between sensing, affect and space, where space is "constructed out a spatial swirl of affects that are often difficult to tie down but are nevertheless crucial".

WHAT IT DOES (AND DOESN'T DO)...

Here, it bears repeating, what a *policy geophilosophy* attempts to do. As we move through our conception of a *policy geophilosophy*, we focus deliberately on, to reiterate the above, *the many ways policy subjects/objects are positioned spatially and philosophically by emergent and adaptive policy formations which influence how subjects/objects sense, embody, and enact policy*. Like the sensing cats and dogs do moments before large earthquakes. Like the sensing of a drop in air pressure that in turn produce migraine headaches. Like the intuitions of five-year olds regarding their impending subjugations as good little capitalist labor. Butterfly effects, each and everyone of them.[2]

We imagine that we will be charged with a kind of neo-phenomenology with regard to *policy geophilosophy*. Fine, as long as the subject is understood to be producing and produced (as in reciprocating). Deleuze & Guattari (1994: 149–150) are helpful here,

> Phenomenology wanted to renew our concepts by giving us perceptions and affections that would make us give birth to the world, not as babies or hominids but as beings, by right, whose proto-opinions would be the foundations of this world. But we do not fight against perceptual and affective cliches if we do not fight against the machine that produces them. By invoking primordial lived-experience, by turning immanence into an immanence to a subject, phenomenology could not prevent the subject from forming no more than opinions that would already draw the cliche from new perceptions and promised affections.

In other words, note all the instrumentalisms smuggled into 'your' feelings and experiences. The environmental triggers that cue policy sensings will be analyzed in this book in terms of expressions, not in terms of foundations of science, human essentializations, or phenomenology. We are interested in the question of 'how is affective life an object-target for specific and multiple forms of power?' (Anderson, 2014: 4).

The *policy geophilosophy* we envisage has an affinity with cues from 'complex adaptive systems' which investigate how social systems adapt to changing environments to increase survivability – which may be just another fancy way to examine how educational neo-liberalism supports itself. Again, we do not claim that we are outside of the dispositif, but that shouldn't mean that we cannot comment on it either. And if kindergarteners can do that, so can we.

Moreover, we clearly admit that *policy geophilosophy* is limited with regard to modelling and predicting the spatialities and complexities of social systems and education policy in particular. While we rarely have access to definitive information in education policy, even in the best of studies, so much of education policy is levied in relation to future imaginations that deliberately omit the attractors and bifurcations that emerge when closing particular modalities. Again, we use uncertainty in our analyses, not try to control for it.

NOTES

1. There are, of course, critiques of the connection of ontology to politics. See, for example, a somewhat humorous contribution to the debate on political ontology here, throughout the comments section, http://sites.williams.edu/cthorne/articles/to-the-political-ontologists/. Thanks to Sam Sellar for the link.
2. Butterfly effect as the sensitive dependence on initial conditions, of which, minute variations in sensing generate sizeable differences (e.g., scale) in outcomes.

CHAPTER 3

POLICY PROBLEMATIZATION

There is no solution because there is no problem.
—Marcel Duchamp[1]

This chapter examines and critiques the instrumental ontologies of education policy analysis related to 'solving problems'. We use Michel Foucault's (1982b, 1985, 1988b, 1994a) concept of problematization to query the roles associated with researchers who believe they are solving problems, and posits alternative roles that policy researchers might assume when working in education. The chapter, then, takes up our idea of a *policy scientificity* as a way to think through, re-articulate, and challenge the many ways education policy has been legitimated as a social and political instrument.

Our goal is to examine a key assumption of policy related to 'solving problems' through such technologies. We also query the ironies of creating problems when under the impression of working on solutions. We discuss the potential problematization has to alter conceptions of policy research; and, through this discussion, we provide a set of alternative pragmatics with which to conduct research for, on, and through education policy.

This chapter works against the backdrop of the persistent methodology wars in education that have lasted roughly into their fifth decade (Howe, 2009); what we characterised as the 'perpetual war' in *policy scientificity 3.0*. In this chapter we locate a pervasive logic that maintains educational problems can be solved in, with, for, or through policy. The only question is which kind of 'science' is required. Policy, itself, is rarely questioned. This logic plays out against a stubborn backdrop of proliferating methodologies and a dizzying array of algorithms that have territorialized educational problems and solutions in largely binary ways; for instance, in the irony of methodologies that are 'double-blind' (Feuer, Towne, & Shavelson, 2002), or in tautologies directed at 'thematizing' human beings in narratives that express 'experiences' and 'voices' (St. Pierre, 2008).

We considered an explicit return to the paradigm wars as a way to frame this chapter, but a return to the paradigm wars suggests that we left these battles, or that the wars were – or can be – 'won' in some way. Rather, we believe these conflicts are a persistent part of educational research, with many conducting their respective work in 'the ruins' for decades (St. Pierre & Pillow, 2000). Within this lived archeology, we believe it is best to think methodologically – if this is what we do – in terms of "pure war" (Virilio & Lotringer, 1997/1983) and in relation to "war machines"

(Deleuze & Guattari, 1986b) which constantly remind us of the ethics of conducting educational research in the first place.

We could scrap educational methodologies entirely and place them under erasure, for instance, '~~methodologies~~'. Of course, if we did, we would have little to say, and we believe there are still important remnants of these wars remaining in education policy research. Following St. Pierre (2008), the syntactical of '~~methodologies~~', then, signals our continuity with questions concerning the utility of educational research (Popkewitz, 1984). More importantly, the syntax demarcates a series of questions that interrogates assumptions about the world which are intimately connected to ~~methodologies~~ when it is further assumed that the world can be represented and manipulated (and usually in ways that serve to legitimate particular ontologies while erasing other ontologies). For us, ~~methodologies~~ signals an important and overlooked 'ontological politic' that has been erased or forestalled for a set of preferred 'knowledge practices' that simply accept and reify specific ontologies while maintaining preferred ideas of the subject, subjectivity, and epistemology (Law, 2004; Mol, 2002; St. Pierre, 2011).

It is within these 'knowledge practices' that a variety of "smug humanitarianisms" (Marcus, 2010: 270) are used to avoid what Paul Rabinow (2003: 30) noted as "the arbitrariness, contingency, and powerful effects" of placing "oneself amidst the relationships of … contending logoi." In other words, methodologies might drop the pretence of solutions and various moralisations (e.g., 'transformations') and instead "open up fields of discussion, in which there are many possible solutions, each which captures something, but not everything, put before us by the problem" (May, 2005a: 83). We are aware that any committed ontological politics will need to engage with preferred knowledge practices and preferred humanitarianisms in order to identify alternative worlds.

For instance, and in refrain of a policy historiography (Gale, 2001), what is it that we can learn from so many contrived attempts to solve educational problems over the past century – the so-called manufactured crises (Berliner & Biddle, 1996)? Or, in refrain of a policy archeology (Scheurich, 1994), what can we take away from such busy, constant, and persistent activity to solve educational problems when so many have failed, and will likely fail in the future (Sarason, 1990)? Is education policy research simply a compilation of discursive ruins, perhaps better understood with a *policy forensics*? Or, have the endless recommendations for policy and practice, sedimented by more and more problems – and more and more solutions – produced a *policy geology* that contains the strata of conflicting educational moralizations? Or, is education policy studies a spatialisation of conflicting desires and heterotopias, better understood through *policy geographies*?

Our purpose for this chapter lies in critiquing the persistence of *policy scientificity 1.0* and some of *2.0* that rely on rationalistic policy methodologies that claim to solve problems. In so far as this goes, we explain why and how we ought to problematize education policy rather than accept the normative practices of governments, institutions, analysts, and researchers that weigh policy down with developing, designing, implementing, and evaluating solutions (loosely, the 'policy cycle').

We discussed these logics in the first chapter, and specifically as part of the rationales that supported *policy scientificity 1.0* and some of the 'parochial criticalities' of *policy scientificity 2.0*. We now further ask: To what extent does policy benefit from espousing 'problems' and 'solutions'? Who benefits? Who does not? Should researchers participate in providing solutions, or the more contemporary 'knowledge transfer' and 'knowledge mobilization'? Should researchers assist others in 'solving problems' by tapping into 'participatory' and 'community' sentiments? What alternative roles might policy researchers assume within a framework of problematization? As we move through this chapter, we will argue that so much is lost when researchers do not map the contours of thought that generate the very ontologies that affect ourselves. This is a major goal of our *policy geophilosophy*.

NO SOLUTION; NO PROBLEM: POLICY LOGICS IN EDUCATION

Our approach to this chapter is to begin with three interpretations of Marcel Duchamp's epigraph above, "there is no solution because there is no problem." Our discussion of Duchamp's aphorism is a way to locate various assumptions about educational research and its relationships to policy. Following our discussion of Duchamp's statement, we discuss education policy as an enacted phenomenon that illustrates the purposes of a policy problematization. The third section discusses the concept of problematization more fully around ideas of contradictions, recursions and events, and we conclude with considerations for researchers engaged in a policy problematization.

To begin, the first interpretation of Duchamp's enigmatic phrase is to understand it as a popular logic that draws attention to ways of understanding its converse; namely, that research is concerned with developing solutions to educational problems, and that this knowledge can be mobilized, transferred, sold, exchanged, indeed, traveled through policy (Ozga & Jones 2006). While we reiterate our uncertainty concerning these edu-capitalist highways, we are, to repeat from Chapter One, fairly certain that 'commodified knowledge' produces the 'traveling knowledge salesmen' who is deeply connected to, and performed by, the un-reflexive and globalizing networks of policy mobility (McCann & Ward, 2013).

In this first sense of the aphorism, then, the practice of the converse can be found increasingly outside the academy, evidenced in any number of satellite, ghost, shadow, and above all, partisan networks and 'think-tanks' that develop policy to solve (their?) problems (McGann & Sabatini, 2011). Here, the policy 'scientist' of *1.0* (Fay, 1975) and the 'qualitative researcher' of *2.0* (St. Pierre, 2011) located in the university may be an endangered species, perhaps already a policy-analyst fossil. Increasingly the relevance of the academy reverts to the claiming of theoretical innovation – and we may well be implicated in this – as 'useful' analyses of 'society' and 'social problems' are undertaken by corporations and think-tanks (Savage & Burrows, 2007).

The second interpretation of Duchamp's enigma is to identify the challenge to researchers to engage in problem development, problem design, and problem formulation. This is the contemporary curricula in many graduate policy studies, particularly when policy is seen as inextricably linked to the ubiquitous containers of 'leadership' and 'educational administration'. In this second sense of the aphorism, a proliferation of methodologies has exploded, in what our dearly departed friend and exceptional methodologist described as a "morass of methodologies;" whereas researchers are only limited to conducting research to problems that can be developed.

Please note the politics of problem formulation within the second enunciation of the aphorism that essentially 'wags the tail of the dog' or creates problems for desired and ostensibly, already designed solutions – 'manufactured crises' and 'inside jobs' but also 'human rights' and 'social justice' – the double entendres of educational moralizations within methodologies (Rabinow, 2003). A second interpretation of Duchamp's puzzle reveals rationalism's plasticity and serves as a reminder that policy research is irrevocably political, a condition that Lyotard (1988: 279) succinctly described when he declared that "there is no reason, only reasons" (in Van Reijen & Veerman, 1988).

A third interpretation of Duchamp's statement is to take it simply at face value – that is, literally: there are no solutions because there are no problems. Neither. None. Policy problematization is not nihilism, but it does accept and examine the very real possibilities involved with educational *indeterminacies* and *contingencies*. The third interpretation of the aphorism leaves us with only rigorous forms of problematization and thinking that position policy as a set of intentions and enactments in relation to contingencies, indeterminacies – what Derrida (1994: 75) discussed as "aporia[s] of undecidability."

Deleuze (2004: 63) noted as "[n]either the problem nor the question is a subjective determination marking a moment of insufficiency in knowledge. Problematic structure is part of objects themselves …". In this final sense of Duchamp's aphorism, problematization explicitly acknowledges – and depends on – the political conditions of policy while revealing its rational and moralizing posturings. Here, mapping the morass of methodological proliferation alongside uncertainty can be instructive in the development of alternatives to not only policy analysis, but social sciences more broadly (Lather, 2006b).

The remainder of the chapter discusses this third interpretation more fully and concludes with considerations for policy researchers engaged in problematization. And, we would be remiss if we didn't mention Carol Bacchi's (2012b) wonderful take on the same.[2]

POLICY

Policy is both text and action, words and deeds, it is what is enacted as well as what is intended.
—Stephen J. Ball, 1994: 10

Before discussing problematization, we would like to review the object of our analysis a bit more thoroughly. At this point, we have discussed education policy as a technology that is used within, and contributes to, different games of reason, for instance, the policy scientificities of *1.0*, *2.0*, and *3.0*. Now, we would like to locate these games within different, competing, and intersecting locales – spaces that are uncertain, contingent, chaotic, complex, indeterminate, but always producing. In so doing, our brief discussion of education policy is an attempt to not take this object for granted; indeed, we want to discuss this object differently.

Ball's (1994) definition of policy (above) is an important springboard for the ways we think about policy problematization. In particular, Ball's notion of enactment signals the ways policy interacts with thinking and practice, or the "collective efforts of interpretation and translation (creative enactment) and the policies are enacted in material conditions, with varying resources, in relation to particular 'problems' that are constructed nationally and locally" (Ball et al., 2011: 11). Policy enactments re-introduce policy 'actors' and 'subjects' as integral (and under theorized) composites and objects within policy research (Ball et al., 2011). Elsewhere, one of us has discussed these composites as part of a policy assemblage (Webb, 2009). Fenwick and Edwards (2010) discussed this similarly in education as an actor-network methodology that makes visible the 'messy objects' of policy, as part of sociomaterial assemblages. In any case, a tremendous amount of activity is created in the production of policy, but more importantly, a tremendous amount of activity is produced when policy is actualized, sensed, embodied, and practiced. It is in reference to this subsequent function of policy – the so-called 'implementation' – that we suggest problematization operates.

Traditionally, academics have 'problematized' policy at the level of text and with a variety of methodological tools involved with analysis that problematize policy rhetoric, puffery, spin, and other discursive and linguistic features of policy. In many ways, policy research in education has problematized the intentions developed in written texts as a form of critique (e.g., racist, sexist, homophobic, neo-liberal, partisan, etc.). Importantly, the mediatization of policy suggests a 'policy aesthetics' that incorporates visual methodologies into discursive analyses of policy (Lingard & Rawolle, 2004). Educational solutions, if this is what they are, are now packaged into very appealing documents and circulated through various electronic networks and within and through intermediary organisations, such as policy think-tanks, that create, disseminate, and recommend conditions of implementation (Lubienski, Scott, & DeBray, 2011).

Enactments, however, recognize that policies "are translated into practice" and "in this way policies are almost always localized and customized" (Ball et al., 2011: 11). Enactments are not attempts to disassociate policy research from its political production or from its textual representations and rhetorical devices – what we will discuss in Chapter Four as a constellation of policy affects circulated through *policy prolepses* and *policy phantasms*. However, policy enactments also "cannot be read-off from texts and neither can they be reduced to anything that might be called an 'implementation gap'. Policy is always contested and changing (unstable) – always 'becoming'" (Ball et al., 2011: 10–11).

The notion that policy is becoming is an important formulation of policy enactments, and, as we will discuss in the next chapter, this implies that far from policy being a reflection of, and intervention into, order, policy is an always already failed attempt to manage chaos. Policy enactments and policy becomings, then, "cannot be understood as either active resistance or passive acceptance, but the continuous transformation of a token by many different people" (Ball et al., 2011: 11).

PROBLEMATIZATION

According to Rabinow and Rose (2003), Michel Foucault introduced the idea of a 'problematization' in his book *Discipline and Punish* (1977). A bit later, Foucault (1985) explained that the term signalled the central concept guiding his methodologies of archeology and genealogy. For instance, in the introduction to the *Use of Pleasure*, Foucault (1985: 11) reflected on the methodology, declaring it to be "a matter of analyzing, not behaviours or ideas, nor societies and their 'ideologies,' but the problematizations through which being offers itself to be, necessarily, thought – and the practices on the basis of which these problematizations are formed".

Foucault described problematizations as explanations of how available objects of thought and practice come to be. According to Foucault (1988b: 257), a problematization,

> Does not mean the representation of a preexistent object nor the creation through discourse of an object that did not exist. It is the ensemble of discursive and nondiscursive practices that make something enter into the play of true and false and constitute it as an object of thought (whether in the form of moral reflection, scientific knowledge, political analysis, etc.).

Problematization denies that thought and practice are 'preexistent' or have been determined in some other *a priori* fashion, for instance, and what we contend constitutes the policy scientificities of *1.0* and *2.0*. In this sense, policy enactments are decidedly unpredictable if not chaotic. As such, problematization seeks explanations about the ways thinking is practiced and produced. In education, we might situate pedagogy or teaching as a significant practice that is produced, but one that is not preexistent even if policy continues to understand pedagogy as a largely technical, rational and unproblematic endeavour (e.g., 'best practices'). Rabinow and Rose (2003: 13) suggested that "to analyze problematizations is not to reveal a hidden and suppressed contradiction: it is to address that which has already become problematic".

Foucault's insistence on thought and practice to understand problematization coincides with analyses of policy that include intentions and enactments. Representation and materiality matters when understanding educational policy; otherwise, as we noted earlier, it may be best to treat policy as (only) text and study it with literary/textual theory (e.g., rhetorical analysis). Nevertheless, local enactments of policy are not univocal, and thought and practice are produced within historical (sedimented) ambiguities, contingencies, indeterminacies, and contradictions. Returning to the example of pedagogy, McLaughlin (1987: 172) observed that teachers' policy interpretations "…often seemed quite idiosyncratic, frustratingly unpredictable, if not downright resistant…". Foucault (1994a: 118) argued similarly,

> when thought intervenes, it doesn't assume a unique form that is the direct result or the necessary expression of these difficulties; it is an original or specific response – often taking many forms, sometimes even contradictory in its different aspects – to these difficulties, which are defined for it by a situation or a context, and which hold true as a possible question.

Policy problematizations, then, take into account a particular milieu that desires a specific outcome(s). In other words, problematizations arise when contexts "make it uncertain, to have made it lose its familiarity, or to have provoked a certain number of difficulties around it. These elements result from social, economic, or political processes. But here their only role is that of instigation" (Foucault, 1994a: 117–8), rather than 'solution'.

PROBLEMATIZATION: CONTRADICTIONS, RECURSIONS, AND EVENTS

> Only expression gives us the method.
> —Deleuze, 1986a: 16

The idea that policy is unpredictable, chaotic, and contradictory strikes at the assumed rationality that directs its development, so-called implementation, and its desired causality, a rationality evident in the propositions of policy scientificities *1.0* and some of policy scientificity *2.0*. Foucault (1994a: 118) addressed the simultaneity of contradicting thought and practice when he observed,

> [t]o one single set of difficulties, several responses can be made. And most of the time different responses actually are proposed. But what must be understood is what makes them simultaneously possible … in their diversity and sometimes in spite of their contradictions. It is problematization that responds to these

difficulties, but by doing something quite other than expressing them or manifesting them: in connection with them, it develops the conditions in which possible responses can be given; it defines the elements that will constitute what the different solutions attempt to respond to.

Policy problematizations attempt to identify conditions and registers in which problems and solutions have been enacted and expressed. More importantly, policy problematizations identify conditions and registers that have disqualified parallel (i.e., rival, contradictory) thoughts, practices, and enactments – what Lather (2006b) described as the "unviable" or what Butler (1993) explained spatially as the "constitutive outside" (quoted by Lather, 2006b: 41). We discuss our ontological politics as a series of *policy presences* and *policy absences* when conducting problematizations.

John Law (2004), when discussing Annemarie Mol (2002), noted how the ontological is precisely produced in practice and how alternative ontologies are displaced by practices in particular ways. Deleuze (2004: 178–9) would make a similar observation,

> [b]y 'problematic' we mean the ensemble of the problem and its conditions. If the differentials disappear in the result, this is to the extent that the problem-instance differs in kind from the solution-instance; it is in the movement by which the solutions necessarily come to conceal the problem ....

Unique to problematization is the identification of conditions that produce problems (and solutions) and that can be used to produce and cancel other possible thoughts and practices (i.e., conditions that contain multiplicities). In this sense, a policy problematization is primarily concerned with developing opportunities – creative possibilities – rather than understanding a situation as problematic that requires a single solution, often conceptualized as a 'silver bullet' in education policy (e.g., Eisner, 1992; Fowler, 2003). In this sense, problematization does not seek solutions, but rather, it seeks to identify difference and multiplicity at levels of thought, practice, and enactment (and, we would note, conditions that censure alternative practices).

Deleuze would often discuss ideas of ontological possibilities (presences and absences) with the idea of the *virtual*. Borrowing from Deleuze, Todd May (2005a: 95) noted that problematizations "offer us a virtual realm of pure difference, a problematic field in which solutions do not overcome problems but simply actualize them under specific conditions." Here, we note, those under the impression of generating solutions are likely just creating problems. Policy problematizations, however, are attempts to make the "unviable" viable, or to at least identify the "constitutive outside" (note the spatial description in Butler's formulation) and/or the "virtual". In this sense, a policy problematization is a recursive methodology that seeks difference and complexity in thinking and practice rather than a recursion that seeks repetition of the same (see for instance, Deleuze, 2004; Peters, 2008). We discuss the recursive features of a policy problematization that seek difference and complexity next.

Problematization: Historical Recursions, Heterotopias, and Events

Conditions that produce 'problems and solutions' are a game unto itself; or put more directly, problematizations are recursive. Foucault (1994a: 118–9) noted this feature of problematization when he stated,

> [problematization] is a question of a movement of critical analysis in which one tries to see how the different solutions to a problem have been constructed; but also how these different solutions result from a specific form of problematization. And it then appears that any new solution which might be added to the others would arise from current problematization, modifying only several of the postulates or principles on which one bases the responses that one gives.

We hinted at the recursions of problematization when we mentioned a *policy geology*. Rabinow (2003) believed that the recursive features of problematization were a unique contribution to methodologies. Rabinow (2003: 19) noted, "what is distinctive [about problematization] is Foucault's identification of the problematic situation, the situation of the process of a specific type of problem making, as simultaneously the object, the site, and ultimately the substance of thinking."

Foucault's "adding of solutions" broadens the scope of policy research beyond the traditional 'literature review', for example, and into a deliberate study of policy's sedimented conditions: conditions that (a) signal many different possibilities, including the many possibilities of enacting policy, and (b) fold researchers within different geologic and geographic traditions of research (Petersen & Davies, 2010). That is, if the ubiquitous literature review provides a summary of, or thinking about, particular problems, they also contribute to the problem itself (if not produce the problem directly) which produce the researcher in particular ways. These policy and self-recursions, then, are objects of analysis within a policy problematization, rather than just routines practiced within preferred methodological approaches that attempt to step outside of the problem.

Eventalization

Another way we have understood the recursions of problematization are in relation to *eventalization* that contrasts notions of causality often entrenched in *policy scientificity 1.0*. When defining eventalization, Foucault (1987: 104–5) stated,

> [f]irst of all, [eventalization means] a breach of self-evidence. It means making visible a singularity at places where there is a temptation to invoke a historical constant, an immediate anthropological trait, or an obviousness which

CHAPTER 3

> imposes itself uniformly on all. To show that things 'weren't as necessary as all that' .... A breach of self-evidence, of those self-evidences on which our knowledges, acquiescence and practices rest .... Secondly, eventalization means rediscovering the connections, encounters, supports, blockages, plays of forces, strategies and so on which at a given moment establish what subsequently counts as being self-evident, universal and necessary. In this sense one is indeed effecting a sort of multiplication or pluralization of causes .... Causal multiplication consists in analysing an event according to the multiple processes that constitute it .... 'Eventalization' thus works by constructing around the singular event analysed as process a 'polygon' or rather a 'polyhedron' of intelligibility, the number of faces is not given in advance and can never properly be taken as finite. One has to proceed by progressive, necessarily incomplete saturation. And one has to bear in mind that the further one decomposes the processes under analysis, the more one is enabled, and indeed obliged to construct their external relations of intelligibility.

Foucault's 'adding of solutions' and 'effecting a pluralization of causes' are related to his ideas about the 'conditions of possibility' where we might take the idea of policy events as contingent, but a contingency enacted within a set of engendered solutions and performed within conditions embedded in the problem. In other words, for our purposes events are not only rooted in the past, but in education policy studies, events are imagined policy futures and these futures are tied to 'polyhedrons of intelligibility'.

Similarly, Deleuze (2004: 188–9) would think through problematization with events, noting that,

> [p]roblems are of the order of events – not only because cases of solution emerge like real events, but because the conditions of a problem themselves imply events such as sections, ablations, adjunctions. In this sense, it is correct to represent a double series of events on the level of the engendered solutions, and ideal events embedded in the conditions of the problem ....

Here, the recursions of problematization must account for the ablations and adjunctions that occur within any enactment of policy. Otherwise, causal 'events' are simply "to read solutions back into problems, to approach problems in terms of solutions ... [it] is to confuse the actual with the virtual" (May, 2005a: 85).

John Law (2004) noted the conditions of possibility as registers for 'ontological multiplicity', and we would add that the elimination of possibilities in education policy consist of a tactics involved in a politics committed to notions of ontological singularity. High-stakes testing and policies like *Race to the Top* in the United States, for instance, literally create worlds that support particular (capitalist) relations (i.e., testing corporations, but many others as well) while simultaneously eliminating other worlds (e.g., fully funded schools). In this example, the ontologies (pl) of 'school' and 'schooling' are not questioned, only which version will be supported and which won't be supported. A world without schools, for instance, is not entertained.

Temporal Recursions

A historical analysis is a necessary recursion within a policy problematization, but in relation to two further points. One, that policy problematization is concerned with aspects of time more broadly than just the past and intimately linked to ideas of space (Massey, 1992; 2005). Most policy invariably places intentions into a stream of anticipated states of affairs – utopias, educational imaginations, future fantasies. However, a good example of educational dystopia is how neo-liberal policy has invested policy desires into anticipated economic outputs (e.g., gross national product growth), policy outcomes (e.g., educational markets) and sometimes policy throughputs (e.g., vouchers). In other words, policy problematizations ought to consider thoughts and practices in relation to contextualized temporal sequences – past and future – and within a spatial politic of heterotopias. We continue our discussion of the temporal aspects of policy in the next chapter.

We invoked the idea of heterotopias earlier through the related ideas of the 'unviable,' the 'constitutive outside,' 'differentials,' and the 'virtual'. Foucault (1986: 24) noted that heterotopias consist of "a sort of systematic description ... that would ... take as its object the study, analysis, description, and 'reading' (as some like to say nowadays) of these different spaces, of these other places". Heterotopias function as an analytic space that signal the creative possibilities within a policy problematization. Rabinow (2003: 19) noted the heterotopic recursions when he stated,

> [w]hat Foucault is attempting to conceptualize [with problematization] is a situation that is neither simply the product of a process of social and historical construction nor the target of a deconstruction. Rather, he is indicating a historical space of conditioned contingency that emerges in relation to (and then forms a feedback situation with) a more general situation, one that is real enough in standard terms but not fixed or static.

The recursions of a policy problematization signal a second consideration that amount to creative activity designed to identify contingencies, or alternative games of truth, that might produce 'new' possibilities for thinking, engagement, and enactment (Osberg, Biesta, & Cilliers, 2008). Ball (1995: 266) noted the creative possibilities of problematization when he challenged education policy researchers to "de-familiarize present practices and categories, to make them seem less self-evident and necessary, and to open up spaces for the invention of new forms of experience". Here, the recursive possibilities of a policy problematization portends a creative aspect that applies to the researcher as much as it applies to the objects of thought under investigation.

CHAPTER 3

POLICY PROBLEMATIZERS

The first consideration for researchers engaged in a policy problematization is to examine the recursive relationships between thought and problematization. Researchers could provide nuanced accounts of their current positioning within objects of thoughts. Rabinow (2003: 20) explained as much,

> [t]he defining trait of problematization [turns] on the type of relationship forged between observer and problematized situation. The specificity of that relationship entails taking up the situation simultaneously as problematic and as something about which one is required to think.

The recursive aspects to problematization require accounts of how researchers currently situate themselves within various identity politics and 'standpoint theories' (Lather, 2006b) and additionally, in relation to how this self-positioning functions with regard to thought and thinking. Deleuze (2004: 169) noted – with scare quotes – that the very invocation of a problematic inculcates the subject into a heterotopic realm of representing objectivity, or, if not too far from that meaning, representing ontology: "'[p]roblematic' does not mean only a particularly important species of subjective acts [i.e., research], but a dimension of objectivity as such which is occupied by these acts." In addition to research design and political stance (i.e., researchers' biases), problematization requires researchers to examine themselves as thinker in relation to objects of thought. This is to realize that ontology is also implicated in research, and not only epistemology. Rabinow and Rose (2003: 13) explained,

> [t]he specific diacritic of thought is not only to be found in [an] act of diagnosis. It also rests on the attempt to change the way in which a situation is apprehended: from seeing it as 'a given' which generates problems that must be resolved, to seeing it as 'a question' whose formation and obviousness must itself be subject to analysis. To enquire into this transformation of difficulties into problems which demand solutions is not to arbitrate between existing responses, but to 'free up' possibilities. The act of thinking is an act of modal transformation from the constative to the subjunctive, from the necessary to the contingent.

Policy problematization requires the researcher to recognize how their thinking processes apprehend situations (i.e., events) and objects, and more importantly, how their thinking might re-apprehend events and objects into contingencies. A declaration of political sensibilities is not the same thing as a recognition of preferred thought and thinking patterns in relation to objects that produce this thinking.

A modal transformation from the constative to the subjunctive – subjects and objects – is, in many ways, a de-familiarization of the self as much as it is a de-familiarization of an event. For instance, St. Pierre (1997) exemplified an approach of de-familiarization through her discussion of older, white Southern women from the United States. St. Pierre (1997) problematized acts of representing research participants, and through writing, thought differently about research and about thinking. St. Pierre concluded that the de-familiarization of thought is an important site of ethical work for researchers.

Likewise, Todd May (2006: 103–8) argued that problematization requires an inquiry into the self as much as, or directly in relation to, the objects of inquiry. May (2006: 106) noted, "problematizations open up certain paths [of thinking] and discourage others: they involve actions upon actions that contribute to creating certain ways of being". Unfortunately, the idea that education policy researchers think differently about themselves and their work is likely to be interpreted as a platitude. Nevertheless, Foucault (1994a: 118) argued that this was crucial to formulating a problematization. He said, "this development of a given into a question, this transformation of a group of obstacles and difficulties into problems to which the diverse solutions will attempt to produce a response, this is what constitutes the point of problematization and the specific work of thought".

In order to sharpen this particular point, Eva Petersen (2007) argued that traditional practices that ask students in research apprenticeships to situate themselves positionally are reinscribed as micropolitical techniques in the formation of particular subjects. The apprenticeship model suggests that positionality statements in educational research are necessary but insufficient practices in the development of policy problematizations. Positionality statements that situate researchers into various standpoint politics – a kind of ideological sublimation within the body – must, we contend, also indicate the ways in which standpoint theories involve or implicate thinking about the ontological and its objects.

Without recourse to a broad understanding of methodological difference, apprenticeship practices in research preparation amount to practices that simultaneously reify particular research positions, reify existing practices of thinking and 'knowing', and ultimately function as processes of epistemic and ontological 'othering.' Here, the beleaguered and perpetual wars we noted in *policy scientificity 2.0* and continuing in *3.0* (i.e., methodology) that avoid discussions of thought and thinking have not dissipated, but instead, have been sublimated within the academy. Now, the perpetual methodology wars in educational research amount to a 'silent war' within the academy that perpetuate the tradition of normalizing epistemic and ontological violence (e.g., 'quantitative and qualitative') while authoring epistemic and ontological Others (Foucault 2003: 16). This silent war conveniently functions to situate itself within an assumed air of 'providing different solutions to different problems' while precluding discussions about other ways of thinking about and enacting policy (e.g., post-foundational methodologies; St. Pierre, 2011).

CHAPTER 3

Assembling the Real, Assembling the Self

Another consideration in the practice of a policy problematization was alluded to earlier but bears repeating. Problematization is not an attempt to establish an ontology, preexistent 'nature', or *a priori* existence of specific thoughts and ('best') practices of policy, including the presumptions of implementation. Rather, problematization analyzes how thoughts and practices are materially and contradictorily produced and actuated within a period of time and with reference to a specific milieu. Rabinow (2003: 15) is helpful here,

> ... the one thing we should not be doing is attempting to find a new, hidden, deeper, unifying rationality or ontology. ... Rather, using the concept of problematization ... we can direct our efforts toward inventing means of observing and analyzing how the various logoi are currently being assembled into contingent forms.

This consideration re-situates policy researchers away from roles as 'problem solvers' and toward methodologists who try to understand the conditions that produce problems and solutions. Again, Rabinow (2003: 18, quoting Foucault) noted that "the primary task of the analyst is not to proceed directly toward intervention and repair of the situation's discordancy but rather to understand and to put forth a diagnosis of 'what makes these responses simultaneously possible'". Likewise, Rabinow and Rose (2003: 13) argued that "the task of the analyst is not to adjudicate between [difficulties]", but rather, that the researcher treats indeterminacies, contingencies, and difference as assets rather than as disconfirming evidence that feeds into already established logics of 'science' and established logics of 'justice'. To repeat what we noted in Chapter Two, as Lather (2009: 348, quoting Dosse, 1999: 352) explained,

> incompleteness and indeterminacy are assets, more not less, central elements of a scientific posture of getting lost as a way of knowing. Here the absence of foundations is enabling, opening us to the other. Against the received objectifying, scientistic posture, this is a scientificity of engaged ethics grounded in a permanent facing of the undecidable, an ethical horizon of science more attuned to innovation than 'the epistemological quarrel over the conditions of scientificity.

This consideration is not just an attempt to remain consistent. Rather, this final consideration is designed to thwart the scripts of 'recommendations' that have already been established and buttressed through various institutional policies – the always already 'realities' of governance (power), budget (money), and calendar (time), and, of course, juridical precedents of (in)equality, justice, and property. The third consideration for policy researchers is to claim a more modest approach to unknowing, and, perhaps, to deliberately not-know (but consciously think). We conclude this chapter by discussing a claim to not-knowing as a consideration for researchers engaged in a policy problematization.

THE INSUFFICIENCIES OF KNOWLEDGE IN EDUCATIONAL RESEARCH

Fail to know what everyone else knows and you have a chance to create something interesting.
—Todd May, 2005a: 149

The purpose of this chapter was to explain how policy is enacted and what factors enable and constrain, at times contradictory, enactments. More importantly, a policy problematization placed these enactments in relation to an assumed role of policy to 'solve' 'problems'. Policy problematizations, then, are designed to understand the simultaneity of contradictory thoughts and practices in education – indeed, designed to understand the different possibilities of thought and practice rather than to seek solutions to always already defined problems and ontologies.

Protevi (2004: 1) suggested that problematization should be contrasted with procedures of axiomatization – the "proposing of laws which can be judged by the adequacy of the solutions they provide". Using this contrast as an example, we might say that *policy scientificity 1.0* and *2.0* have become increasingly dominated by logics of axiomatization (e.g., 'evidence-based') rather than problematization (e.g., St. Pierre, 2011). The assumption within a paradigm of research axiomatization is that thought and practice can be governed by particular laws in relation to particular problems. Instead, a policy problematization can identify the conditions which generate objects of thoughts and identify the available logics of problem-solving that provide the registers for different enactments. Policy problematizations, furthermore, are designed for creative possibilities, and the development of new educational concepts.

These creative possibilities are certainly directed at 'ontic-epistemic imaginaries' and/or what Karen Barad (2003) discussed as the intra-actions involved in "onto-epistem-ology", but also, and invariably, question methodological and ontological responsibilities (Law, 2004). Lather's (2009) notion of 'getting lost' and May's (2005b) approach to unknowing locate the responsibilities of problematization within a more modest (honest?) approach of policy enactments, rather than adopting condescending airs regarding 'knowledge production' and 'solution provider' – the contemporary transformation of a 'more useful' academic. Notions of 'getting lost' and unknowing assist problematization avoid current structures of science and knowing that eliminate, preclude, or ostracize creative possibilities, including creative possibilities of responsibility involved in becoming. More importantly, these notions are the kinds of political tactics needed to thwart ideas of ontological singularity that, in turn, pathologizes policy enactments that 'don't fit' engendered solutions embedded within assumed (and preferred) conditions of policy.

CHAPTER 3

Lather (2009: 354) clarified her exhortation to researchers to 'get lost' when she stated, "what I am urging is that qualitative research resist the siren call to socially useful research that positions it within repositivization and, instead, work toward embracing constitutive unknowingness, generative undecidability, and what it means to document becoming". Policy problematization, then, seeks contingencies and indeterminacies that might provide a way out of established systems, worlds, ontologies, and logics, and that may provide moments of becoming different. Giroux (2000: 179) would make a very similar point when he stated,

> … it makes more sense in the present historical moment to educate students to theorize differently about the meaning of work in a postmodern world. Indeterminacy rather than order should become the guiding principle of a pedagogy in which multiple views, possibilities, and difference are opened up as part of an effort to read the future contingently.

A suggestion for Magistral and doctoral theses engaged in a policy problematization would be to develop 'aporias for policy and practice' and 'theoretical practices' rather than the ubiquitous 'recommendations' for policy and practice that assume and accept so many preexistent ontologies (which, of course, are terribly problematic). We submit that a policy problematization can assist students, researchers, and the public to think differently about education, and through this rethinking, perhaps create something interesting.

In the next chapter, we illustrate how policy problematization can map the ways policy enactments are effectuated by policy sensings of multiple policy encounters. We develop the inter-disciplinary concept of a *policy prolepsis* that helps us conceptualize policy enactments as forms of policy subjectifications that occur within: a) educational actors' senses and affects of policy and their estimations of possible outcomes, and b) the emergent spaces and times (histories and futures) produced in the multiple ontologies within policy becomings.

NOTES

[1] As cited by Cacinovic, N., Golding, S., & Maharaj, S. (2001). Maastrict: Institution and research. In A. W. Balkema and H. Slager (Eds.) *Concepts on the move*, vol. 17. Amsterdam: Lier en Boog (p. 99).
[2] Bacchi's (2012) excellent (and complimentary) take on 'policy problematization' emphasizes how policy legitimates particular policy initiatives, which reinforce a set of political and ontological dispotifs (e.g., her emphasis on governmentality). Problematizaton, thus, has a powerful possibility to thwart such processes. Similarly, ours emphasizes the relationships between policy enactments (and, thus, subjectivity) and ontology. There are a number of intersections and similarities between the two texts.

PART 2

INTERMEZZO

POLICY GEOPHILOSOPHY

How education policy positions and constitutes objects and subjects through emergent and adaptive arrangements that simultaneously influence how policy is sensed, embodied, and enacted.

This section examines and discusses:

- *Policy prolepses*; the material encounters with policy that work within and between different registers of representation, and in relation to ontologies that themselves are becoming.
- *Policy intensions*; the ways in which education policy is sensed, embodied, and eventually enacted within.
- *Spaces of care* that are practiced and enacted in marketization efforts, and particularly school choice initiatives. We examine and discuss how neo-liberal education policy is used to escape the inequities and educational inequalities produced in the (liberal) registers of race and ethnicity.

CHAPTER 4

POLICY PROLEPSIS

Phantasmic Encounters in Becoming-Policy

Prolepsis (n.) – The representation of a thing as existing before it actually does or did so.

In Chapter One, we noted that *policy scientificity 1.0* assumed education policy represented the implementation of solutions to educational problems, and that educational research should and could contribute to policy effectiveness (Simons, Olssen, & Peters, 2009a, 2009b). Within this construction of policy, the ontological status of 'policy' was not questioned because the practices and logics concerning 'solution ↔ problem' were not challenged either – in fact, the academy used such logics to legitimate itself. Policy problematizations, as discussed in Chapter Three conversely, are rare in educational policy studies because of the apocryphal emphasis on epistemology, knowledge, and 'the disciplines' that privilege Euro-American conceptions of ontology (Law, 2004).

While in the 1990s and 2000s, *policy scientificity 2.0* challenged notions of 'policy science' supporting *1.0*, *policy scientificity 2.0* replaced one epistemology with another that ushered forth a perpetual war that contributes to what we call *policy scientificity 3.0*. Further, we have argued that an instrumental and techno-rational characterization of education policy retains a stranglehold on education policy makers and educational researchers. Again, the *ontology of policy* remains unchanged within an instrumental understanding of such technologies, it is only the epistemologies that are in question.

Techno-rationality in the development and implementation of policy is paralleled in educational policy research which is increasingly required to be for policy and the expected 'solutions' to indeterminate 'problems,' and eventually, to be aimed at evaluating the efficiency and effectiveness of reforms (Rizvi & Lingard, 2010). *Policy geophilosophy* is concerned with a different rationality, one that maps the contours of various critical and methodological parochialisms. Debates about policy have become claims and counterclaims about methodology and related issues of rigour and what counts as legitimate evidence (Wiseman, 2010).

Techno-rational approaches to policy development and research imply that variations in policy meaning, implementations, and outcomes are attributable to subject's incorrect interpretations, or imply a certain set of literacy skills in reading or decoding policy have atrophied (Cohen, 1990). More importantly, different policy scientificities ascribe different understandings of the subject (e.g., 'teacher'). We pick up this idea explicitly in Chapter Five. For now, *policy scientificity 1.0*, and to some extent *2.0*, suggest that (predetermined) subjects have misinterpreted a 'fixed meaning' of policy, thus assuming these meanings are objective, accessible, and complete.

THE INCOMPLETENESS OF POLICY

In this chapter we critique the realm of policy implementation, including the when, where, and how policy gets *done*. When we talk about policy interpreters we refer to subjects, or crudely, end-users of policy, in what Bowe, Ball, and Gold (1992) identified as the context of practice, or the realm of "policy enactments" (Braun, Ball, Maguire, & Hoskins, 2011). We argue, in refrain of Ball (1994) and Braun et al. (2011), that various levels of policy, including the complexities, ambiguities and ambivalences associated with making, delivering, receiving, resisting and/or transforming policy, require analyses of policy that acknowledge and work with problematizations that we discussed in the previous chapter, rather than attempts to reduce or 'control' complexities. This is to work with and within, what Youdell (2011), following Deleuze and Guattari, has termed the *education assemblage*.

Furthermore, and against the above backdrop, our departure point for this chapter is to work from a critical policy studies orientation. This orientation allows us to rethink and reorient a key claim made consistently in critical policy studies over the last twenty years: that policy is not a seamless process from development to implementation.

With Ball (1994: 10), we agree that policy is characterized by incompleteness, ad hocery and "the 'wild profusion' of local practice." Policy is always and only a contingent and provisional fixing. Part of these claims of the provisional lie in the idea of interpretation, that educational policy is involved with semiotics (D. Ball, 1990), including teachers as semioticians of curriculum policy (Rizvi & Lingard, 2010).

In refuting ideas of techno-rationality in analyses of neo-liberal policy implementation, we do not relinquish politics. In fact, our argument in this chapter is that by working from an interdisciplinary "art of not being governed like that and at that cost" (Foucault, 2007: 29), we *increase space* for a multitude of political action. Like Youdell (2011: 10), we believe that various forms of post-structural analyses of education,

> … and the practices they espouse have received varying degrees of recognition and takeup in the mainstream of education theory and practice, and while for the most part they have been remained marginal, they have been legitimate, recognizable and speakable.

What interests us in this chapter is that in the midst of recurring turbulence surrounding education policy – constant crises of falling standards, perpetual calls for innovation, and the maintenance of human capital endeavours, and so forth – the concept *policy* remains untouched. It is the legitimacy of evidence, for example, that is contested, not what policy is (cf., Ball, 1994), nor whether policy can actually do the work for which it is claimed, and what effects are produced – and continually produced – in the name of this object.

Our understanding of education policy is informed from Ball's (1994: 10) idea that "policy is both text and action, words and deeds, it is what is enacted as well as what is intended." Throughout this chapter, we refer to policy documents, including: press releases, government decisions, legislation, formal authorizations, mandates, laws, speeches, white papers, reports, and curricula. We also refer to policy intentions that attempt to construct, prevent, and/or 'solve' a 'problem' (Miller & Rose, 2008); send a (symbolic) message; resolve political tensions; and maintain the status quo (e.g., regulate, standardize, cement). Policy enactments, then, are produced from a myriad of objects and intentions.

In this chapter, we explore the ideas of policy ad hocery, indeterminacies, and so forth, using Deleuze's (1990) ideas of affect, encounters, and becomings. We are concerned about not only the epistemology of policy studies but also the ontology of policy and practice; an ontological politics, or a politics of becoming-policy. This chapter introduces the concept of a *policy prolepsis* in education, and we argue that *policy prolepsis* is *a category of becoming-policy that actualizes educational practices within the spaces of desired, yet not fully developed, policy initiatives and policy implementations*. For instance, educational budgets are often developing policies that, nevertheless, actualize practices during the budget's development, or during its ratification, and/or, more likely, during its adjustments and eventual replacement. Thus, a budget can be used to illustrate how policies are represented in various moments of development (perhaps in practice, perhaps in a memo) even though budgets are continuously ongoing and rarely read by policy end-users.

Becoming-Policy and New Spaces for Educational Politics

Policy prolepses represent a range of emergent policy ontologies and subsequent enactments that are produced through the interface of educational subjects' senses of policy and their estimations of possible policy outcomes. We use Deleuze's (1990) idea regarding the logic of sense to argue that becoming-policy occurs in a pre-conscious space, and that this space is able to be manipulated. Educational policy, then, is a diverse ontological activity representing a swarm of policy outcomes through the management of semiotic desires and subjects' inferences about these persuasive signs.

CHAPTER 4

To accomplish these goals, we utilize Deleuze and Guattari's (1987) idea of *becoming* to form our conception of a *policy prolepsis* in terms of sense, through attention to affect, percept, and so on. As a site of scholarship, this paper links the idea of becoming to Deleuze's (1990) ideas about a *logic of sense*. Becoming, then, is a materiality of policy and subjectivity produced through the senses of those expected to implement it and the multiple expressions of various objects in different milieus. Prolepses signal the many ways becoming-policy is rhetorically figured, affectively constituted, and materially expressed. Deleuze and Guattari (1987: 293–294) explained that,

> a line of becoming is not defined by points that it connects, or by points that compose it; on the contrary, it passes between points, it comes up through the middle ... a line of becoming has neither beginning nor end, departure nor arrival, origin nor destination .... Becoming is the movement by which the line frees itself from the point, and renders points indiscernible: the rhizome, the opposite of arborescence; break away from arborescence.

Our notion of policy prolepsis intends to move thinking about policy as discourse or as text (Ball, 1994), to indicate a materiality of policy bodies, or bodies doing policy, and various technologies of the self that are intimately constituted and enacted in policy texts and discourses. This is to begin to see policy as part of education's rhizomatic terrain, and to consider,

> ... how [education] ... renders particular educational subjects and how it provokes and corrals affectivities suggests a complex map of education that brings together forces, orders, discourses, technologies, practices and bodies; from the legislative functions of the state to the affective eruptions of the playground. (Youdell, 2011: 55)

Policy prolepsis is a cartography that maps the constructions of policy subjects, and in particular, subjects and the requisite styles of practice and styles of care (e.g., 'professional').

For example, we hope teachers and other educational practitioners (targeted subjects of neo-liberal education policy) can utilize the idea of a policy prolepsis to ascertain the particular ways education policy induces and prompts particular enactments and desires. More specifically, a *policy prolepsis* can assist educational subjects/objects develop ideas and practices for a care of the self that consciously uses the resistances, variegations, and uncertainties that arise when confronting the unrelenting semiotics of policy. Thus, one, though of course not the only, possibility, is that policy prolepses may become a powerful heuristic for educators to transform the oft-used action research methodologies into a fieldwork of the self[1], rather than, and only as, a particular methodology to regulate themselves and their practice against curriculum policy directives. We believe that the idea of *policy prolepsis* can assist others in their own analyses of educational policy and practice, and provide a way to discuss a much wider *politics of becoming-policy*.

The chapter, then, illustrates the idea of a *policy prolepsis* by demonstrating how *policy apparitions* use fear in becoming-policy. We return later to the idea of fear in Chapter Seven as this particular affect is, perhaps, the quintessential prolepsis in neo-liberal constructions of education. *Policy apparitions*, then, are just one species of policy prolepses that utilize the affect of fear to manipulate educational actors' interpretations. These interpretations and inferences are produced politically and are used strategically for desired, yet ostensibly unformed, policy outcomes.

POLICY PROLEPSIS

Every orientation presupposes a disorientation.
—Hans Magnus Enzensberger, 1966[2]

We discuss policy prolepses in relation to semiotics – processes involved with signification, circulation, and communication of signs. We situate the concept of policy prolepses within rhetorical designata (semantic) and within cognitive interiorities (pragmatics). Our discussion develops two entangled politics within education policy studies, separated only for analytical purposes: a politics of sense and a politics of time. We argue that policy prolepses rhetorically figure policy interpretations through sense making, and subsequently position subjects (e.g., 'teachers') and their practice in particular ways that are not apparent or recognized.

Semetsky (2006: 27, citing Peirce, 1955) provides a definition of semiotics:[3]

> A sign can be anything that stands to somebody, a sign-user, for something else, its object, in some respect and in such a way so as to generate another sign, called its interpretant, to designate a sign, in agreement with the word representation describing both the dynamic process and the terminus of such a process, by which one thing stand for another.

We use the triadic model – interpretant, sign-user, representamen – to explain the concept *policy prolepsis*. However, rather than use the term 'representamen' to refer to the process and objects of a semiotics, we have selected the term prolepsis instead. The term 'representamen' suggests something that exists, whereas, the term 'prolepsis' denotes the representation of something that does not exist (and/or, in the process, perhaps perpetual, of becoming). The term prolepsis originates from rhetorical studies and our use of the term signals a *politics of becoming-policy* with rhetorically figured – and rhetorically figuring – signs.

Policy prolepses are a category of becoming-policy, produced rhetorically and used politically, that shape policy interpretations and shape educational practices within the spaces of desired, yet incomplete, indeterminate, and ad hoc, policy initiatives and implementations. Policy prolepses demarcate a wide range of emergent policy ontologies and fragmented enactments produced through educational actors' senses of policy and their subsequent interpretations of policy, including calculations of policy outcomes.

CHAPTER 4

Policy Prolepsis, Affective Tones and Triggers

Deleuze (1990) argued that semiotic sign-encounters occur pre-consciously and thought and thinking follow a sensory-sign encounter. Within such a configuration, policy interpretations are second-level thoughts influenced from sensed-signs, perhaps better described as rationalizations of sign-perceptions. Deleuze (2004: 139) described the process of affective sensing, or sign encounters, and its preceding role in thinking,

> [s]omething in the world forces us to think. This something is an object not of recognition, but a fundamental 'encounter' .... It may be grasped in a range of affective tones: wonder, love, hatred, suffering, [fear]. In whichever tone, its primary characteristic is that it can only be sensed. In this sense it is opposed to recognition.

The Deleuzian and Guattarian (1987) idea of affective sensing has been taken up by a number of scholars in education. For instance, Masny and Cole (2009: 5) described creativity and alienation as powerful affective tones that organize thought and thinking. In another example, Semetsky (2006) suggested that the idea of intuition is another way to understand how signs are sensed in addition, or in combination, with wonder, love, hatred, suffering, fear, etc.

In Chapter Two, we mentioned that policy enactments are deeply rooted in sense-making and environmental cues or triggers. We noted that a great deal of action is produced when,

> at critical thresholds some physical and biological systems can be said to 'sense' the difference in their environment that trigger self-organizing processes. In this way, signs ... are not only conceptualized as occurring beyond the registers to the human and even the organic [e.g., linguistic], but also are understood as triggers of material processes. (Bonta & Protevi, 2004: 4)

The notion of triggers is a key part of *policy geophilosophy* and provides us with ways to talk about policy objects and how objects and bodies express signs. Here, we want to reuse our previous definition (that is, Bonta & Protevi's definition) to indicate how different *policy signs* trigger sense making of policy subjects and the subsequent enactments of policy, and as triggers to non-human material processes and subsequent expressions thereof. By 'non-human' we mean the myriad of other bodies that interact and spatially position educational subjects: cities, schools, classrooms, educational objects, other policies, textual and mediatised features of policies, and so forth.

Initially, we might speak of ontological expressions as "material agency" borrowing from Andrew Pickering and his astute observations about the *Mangle of Practices* (1995). Here, then, 'non-human' bodies like cities, schools and textual features of policy are not mere representations of educational intentions but machines that organize the liminal spaces between 'human' and 'non-human'. This is to note the performative aspects of non-human bodies. The notion of 'agency' however is one that we find a bit troubling as we discussed in Chapter One, whether ascribed to 'humans' or 'material'. Nevertheless, Pickering's (1995) ideas about semiotic "tunings" and "signals" are entirely consistent with our ideas about non-human expressions and policy sign triggers. The divergences between our ideas of 'agency' do not diminish our agreement with Pickering (2008: 8) when he suggests that policy enactments destabilize policy intentions to the,

> extent that the world becomes sufficiently full of explicitly and self-consciously decentred practices and their products that an ontology of becoming becomes the natural ontological attitude, exposing dualist detachment for what it is: just one tactic of being in the world that we have at our disposal.

For instance, the dualist detachment of 'solution ↔ problem' is the *sine qua non* of representational policy making, implementation, and evaluation – one that we argued against in Chapter Three. Such a dualist detachment is consistent, but practiced differently, across *policy scientificities 1.0* and *2.0*. In this sense, both *1.0* and *2.0* obfuscate the performative ontologies of policy. This is to treat matter seriously, and in the ways Karen Barad (2003: 828) noted,

> [a] crucial part of the performative account ... is a rethinking of the notions of discursive practices and material phenomena and the relationship between them. On an agential realist account, discursive practices are not human-based activities but rather specific material (re)configurings of the world through which local determinations of boundaries, properties, and meanings are differentially enacted. And matter is not a fixed essence; rather, matter is substance in its intra-active becoming – not a thing but a doing, a congealing of agency.

At this stage, we are likely are a bit more "citationally" predisposed than what Barad (2003: 828) is getting at in her ideas of performing – and becoming – matter. Nevertheless, as we move through our ideas of a policy geophilosophy we want to note the predominance of signs circulated throughout different educational human, non-human, and more-than-human bodies (Whatmore, 2006) in the guise of the unexamined ontologies of *policy scientificities 1.0* and *2.0*. In Chapter Five, we take up the idea of subjectification, and the idea of the *fold* explicitly, as one way to extend a 'citationally' focussed understanding of policy into an intra-active one.

The idea of affective sensing and triggers applies to expressions of these bodies as well, and we want to focus on the many ways policy subjects/objects are positioned spatially and philosophically by emergent and adaptive policy formations which trigger how subjects/objects sense, embody, and enact policy. Figure 1 represents policy prolepses in affective tones, where signs are affectively encountered prior to understanding or recognition, and that influence subsequent thought.

CHAPTER 4

Policy prolepses operate through affective tones, or affective sensings, that function without certainty, and indeed, without recognition. In its opposition to recognition, policy prolepses are sign-encounters mediated through a logic of sense (Deleuze, 1990). The distinction between encounter and recognition – what we are calling 'phantasmic space' – destabilizes notions that policy has an established identity or fixed meaning. For example, how teachers make sense of, or understand, policy (e.g., Achinstein & Ogawa, 2006; Patterson & Marshall, 2001), and the ways teachers 'misinterpret' policy (D. Ball, 1990; Cohen, 1990). McLaughlin (1987: 172) observed that teachers' policy interpretations "…often seemed quite idiosyncratic, frustratingly unpredictable, if not downright resistant …".

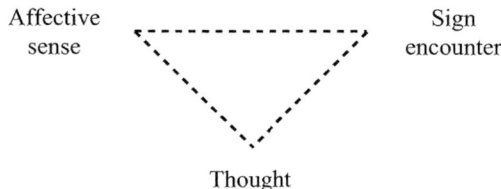

Figure 1. Phantasmic space: Policy prolepsis in affective tones

Given educators' positions within phantasmic space, Schwille et al. (1983: 377) noted that teachers,

> … are better understood as political brokers than as [policy] implementers. They enjoy considerable discretion, being influenced by their own notions of what schooling ought to be as well as persuaded by external pressures.

As we have noted elsewhere in our respective work, policy-signs of race and racism are powerful influences for thinking about schooling (Gulson, 2006; 2011) and powerful influences on teachers' policy enactments (Webb, 2001). We devote substantial attention to how race and space operates as event and encounter in Chapters Six, Seven, and Eight.

Furthermore, and with some affinity for work that demonstrates how policy practices are underpinned by complex and often contradictory premises (Ball, 2003), a distinction between encounter and recognition destabilizes ideas that policy interpretation is a conscious and rational process of 'reading' fixed policy meanings – if read at all – and developing 'correct' or 'incorrect' interpretations. In fact, policy interpretations are developed or 'read' through "random collisions of affects" (Masny & Cole, 2009: 5). For instance, policy subjects might sense a policy's intentions from its marketing gimmicks, or interpret it from a distance, for instance, develop an understanding from someone else's interpretation or sense of a policy.

Here, *policy prolepsis* articulates a kind of 'intra-activity' that Barad (2003) speaks about, at least in relation to the imbrications of signs and subjectifications.

Policy and its meanings are indeterminate, contingent, paradoxical, contradictory, and disorienting (often deliberately) – "every orientation presupposes a disorientation" (Enzensberger, 1966, p. x, cited by Calvino, 1986: 23). Notions of policy 'interpretations,' then, are transformed into a politics of controlling affective registers of meaning, if not attempts to control affects themselves. Policy prolepses, then, can be understood as the ways policy signs are rhetorically figured to influence those sensings and the ways educators make sense of policy, shape their practice, and eventually, create themselves in relation to perceived signs.

THE POLITICS OF AFFECTIVE SPACE: PHANTASMIC POSITIONINGS

Policy prolepses are coded affectively (e.g., wonder, love, hatred, suffering, fear, humor) and rhetorically position subsequent policy interpretations and, eventually, position subjects themselves. Deleuze (1990) used the notion of phantasm to explain sign encounters and to explain how subjects are positioned in phantasmic space. Deleuze (1990: 276) noted that phantasms are,

> constituted by simulacra which are particularly subtle and agile. capable of supplying the animus with visions. all of the images which correspond to desire. Not that desire is creative here; rather, it renders the mind attentive and makes it choose the most suitable phantasm from among all the subtle phantasms in which we are immersed.

Deleuze borrowed his ideas of phantasm and seduction from Laplanche and Pontalis (1964/1968). They noted how subjects are positioned by phantasms when they stated, "phantasm is not the object of desire, it is a scene. In the phantasm … the subject does not target the object or what stands for it; rather he figures there himself, caught up in the sequence of images" (p. 1868).

Kenneth Burke (1966) argued similarly, albeit more linguistically and explicitly dramaturgically, that affects function as *terministic screens*. Burke noted that affects were rhetorically figured and direct "attention into some channels rather than others" (p. 45), and constructions of "'reality' may be but the spinning out of possibilities implicit in our particular choice of terms" (p. 46). Likewise, Peirce (1955) anticipated a range of possible ontologies when he queried, "consider what effects, that might conceivably have practical bearings, we conceive the object of our conception to have. Then our conception of these effects is the whole of our conception of the object" (cited by Semetsky, 2006: 27). Finally, Blackburn (1990) argued that affects are constantly 'filling in space,' producing a myriad of different ontologies, or becomings, when trying to categorize and understand signs. Blackburn (1990: 62) noted, "[dispositions] might only bring us to the instancing of a power … at some region of space explained by the instancing of some other power at some related region of space." Blackburn's (1990) *filling in space* provides our prolepsis with one way to discuss how subjects make sense of, or enact, the indeterminacies and contradictions of policy – subjects fill in these spaces affectively.

Educational researchers have identified ways affects shape policy interpretations. For example, Honan (2004) developed a 'rhizo-textual analysis' of policy texts, which explored the construction of the subject position teacher through teachers' sensings of policy. Honan explained how teachers understood policy through the affects of *independence, self-doubt, denial,* and *inadequacy*, and she illustrated how these sensings consequently shaped enactments of policy and practice (pedagogy).

Similarly, Roy (2003) developed the idea of 'aura,' based on his interviews with teachers as a way to explain how teachers are rhetorically positioned through policy. Roy (2003: 112–113) explained that an aura is "an indirect acknowledgement of the presence of the absent" which "leaves room for the [subject's] becoming in the encounter, of the possibilities of realizing unsuspected relationalities that striated space excludes in its reinforcing of rigid boundaries." In his work, Roy (2003) noted how stress shaped teachers' senses of policy and their subsequent policy interpretations and, ultimately, their pedagogy.

In the next chapter, we use the powerful endogamous/exogamous imagery of Delueze's (1988) *fold* to illustrate ways in which one's relation to oneself could be seen to take place in different settings. We show how the self is folded in on endogamous parts of policy, and how policy is folded onto exogamous elements of the body, or what we might term the intra-actions of *policy prolepses*.

THE POLITICS OF ABSENCES AND PRESENCES: POLICY PROLEPSIS IN TIME

A *policy prolepsis* generates various registers of interpretation. However, the significance of policy prolepsis is that policy interpretations are never removed from their initial sensings of rhetorically figured signs and spaces – signs and spaces that figure thought, interpretations, practice, and subjects. Deleuze (1983: 108) noted the time between a sensory-sign encounter and the subsequent thought produced when he stated, "we are awaiting the forces capable of making thought something active, absolutely active, the power capable of making it an affirmation."

Policy prolepses occur in time and identify the intermediary spaces between policy-sensings and subsequent policy interpretations – the wait-times, the intermezzo, or, "the waiting of that which is going to come about as a result, and also of that which is already in the process of coming about and never stops coming about" (Deleuze, 1990: 242). For our purposes, we want to link metaphor with materiality, and posit that time represents both an absent space of policy prolepses and spaces where/when policy interpretations are developed – the thinking about sensed-signs. We represent policy prolepses in time in Figure 2 where we have placed our previous figure (Figure 1) within crude axes of temporal space.

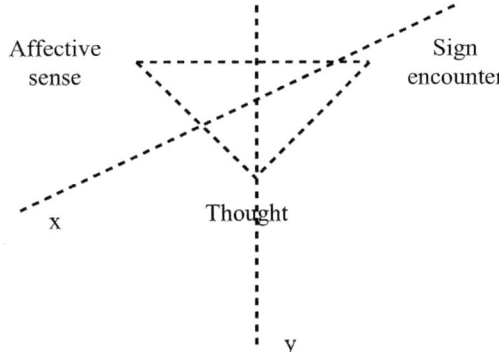

Figure 2. Temporal phantasms: Absent spaces in policy prolepsis

Just as policy signs are figured rhetorically, absent spaces of *policy prolepses* are mutable and controllable. For instance, the mediatization of education policy produces unprecedented number of sign-encounters for educators (Rawolle, 2005). The mediatization of education policy also accelerates the circulation of policy-signs while seemingly simultaneously compressing space (e.g., geographical, Cf., Harvey, 1989), and policy-signs traverse, or 'cross fields' (Lingard & Rawolle, 2004). Time can also be manipulated through the (all too) frequent distribution of multiple policies to educators (Honig, 2006). Multiple policies reduce the time to meaningfully engage with them individually. As a result, multiple policies that are not accompanied with support structures to *increase time* position educational subjects to only 'read' policy as sign-encounters. In effect, multiple policies on educators' desks ironically ventriloquize the message 'do not read' or 'only encounter' as a result of reducing time.

While manipulating time with education policy is nothing new, what is interesting within such strategic games is how the time involved in education policy making is structured already, and those with knowledge of these structures are able to use time to their advantage. For instance, Thompson and Cook (2014: 706) borrow Deleuze's (1994) idea of 'habit' to argue that "the habit of education policy-making ... is the collective contraction of past events into a lived present that is future oriented", wherein, education policy-making "contracts past events or problems into a solution-focused lived present as a means to build a better future."

Contraction of past events accentuates how time is understood in order to reproduce the past, present, and future through the logics of 'solution ↔ problem'. Unfortunately, the 'habits' of education policy-making do not afford analyses that seek temporal recursions and heterotopias of the 'unviable', the 'constitutive outside', and the 'virtual' that we discussed in the previous chapter. Thompson and Cook

(2014: 706) argue that "because the temporalities to which policy-making activities give rise have not changed, the thinking is trapped in old temporal circuits." The upshot to how time is structured in education policy-making is that it repeats and 'colonizes' educational subjectivities through memory while obfuscating and erasing possible futures not "coordinated and created by the present and past" (Thompson & Cook, 2014: 707).

In other words, the manipulation of time through policy results in a series of tactics aimed at an ontological politics committed to singularity rather than multiplicity; "an ontological politics … [designed] to reorder organizational and professional relations" (Law, 2004: 76). In effect, as Mol (2002: 97) presciently noted,

> … the warning against expertise [i.e., techno-rationalism] and the plea for an alternative science, get lost when 'reason' and 'force' (or other social mechanisms such as consensus and negotiation [and their resultants, like 'policy'] are listed alongside each other as equally plausible mechanisms for the closure of controversies.

In the end, the manipulation of time (reducing, accelerating, repeating habits, and memory) creates a myriad of affects, notwithstanding feelings of stress and inadequacy, which are prevalent affective orientations for policy prolepses (Honan, 2004; Roy, 2003).

The time of policy prolepses are spaces where/when sensings produce policy interpretations. Semetsky (2006: 33–4) discussed these middle spaces and their relationships to thought. She stated:

> It is the very presence, that is, the included middle of the transversal link … which does not rely on absolutes, but aims 'to bring into being that which does not yet exist' [Deleuze, 1994a: 147] … that which is as yet imperceptible by means of laying down a visible map of some invisible territory or, in other words, creating a mediatory space between discursive and non-discursive formations. The very 'interstice … between seeing and speaking' [Deleuze, 1988a: 87] is the place where thinking occurs.

As Murdoch (2006: 92) noted, and this provides another way into what we are discussing,

> … [m]ultiplicities conceive spatial forms through their generative capacities, and these depend on the emergent properties (or 'affects') that come into being as relations are formed between entities of various kinds.

The phrase 'absent space,' then, is used to signal the intermediary and political spaces involved in policy prolepses which are, of course, constantly present, or as Doel (2000: 125) definitively asserted, "space is immanent." Thus, we recognize the apparent contradiction in our conception of absent space; however, we hope readers afford us the semantic pleasure of using 'absence' even if we mean invisibly present, unviable, hidden, virtual, not readily apparent, ontologically forthcoming, or, of course, ontologically forestalled. Our 'absent space', then, is entirely related with our discussion in the previous chapter of the 'unviable' and/or the 'constitutive outside'. Likewise, the term 'negative space' is an idea that is used in art and architecture and generally refers to the space around and in-between images and signs. Negative space is apparent when the space around a sign forms a counter space that produces additional signs, effectively defining the boundaries of a thing. Moreover, negative space, like our absent space, is synthetic with artists, architects, city planners, and policy authors, to name but a few, skilled in manipulating this space.

Policy Apparitions: Examples of Policy Prolepsis and Fear

In this last section, we briefly illustrate the idea of policy prolepsis by demonstrating how fear constituted absent spaces of educational policy in our respective works (Gulson, 2011; Webb, 2009). Chapter Seven will provide more examples, but for now, these brief illustrations provide an indication of what we are talking about.

While others have approached fear and policy with great precision (e.g., Berliner & Biddle, 1996; Ginsberg & Cooper, 2008), our examples intend to demonstrate how policy itself is a semiotic monster that uses sensing of threat-fear to assemble intended and unintended educational acts and subjectivities. Bullen, Fahey and Kenway (2006), for instance, discussed how risk economies are spectral images – ghosts – designed to mobilize action through fear and understood with Derridaean 'hauntology'. We use the idea of a policy apparition to signal the senses of ephemerality, uncertainty, doubt, and fear that inscribe cases of policy implementation. What follows, then, are two brief examples of becoming-policy of school restructuring and accountability to provide illustrations of policy prolepsis through the primary sense of fear. The first example is concerned with how apparitions produce subjectivities, and the second example is concerned with identifying the assemblages of fear and uncertainty in policy apparitions.

In the first example, accountability polices instilled fear in teachers and described how teachers generated fabrications as spectral responses to the surveillance of pedagogy. Fear was produced in teachers through a fear of punishment and a fear of losing one's job. For instance, one participant noted,

> [test] scores are published. They're on radio; they're in the news, on the television. They are in the newspapers – I'm hypersensitive to it, being it's my job [at stake], but they're everywhere. They're on the Internet. They compare the schools to different schools. (Webb, 2009: 106)

The fear instilled by accountability policy was transmitted onto teachers by circulating test scores (i.e., signs) through the media (i.e., time). More importantly, teachers created and used fabrications to refract the surveillance of pedagogy. Consequently, teachers acknowledged their concomitant schizophrenia as a result of performing fabrications, to different audiences, a political response to accountability-policy-fear. Teachers noted how, and in which ways, their selves were changing as an assemblage of accountability fear, fabricated performances, and the swirling micropolitical pressure at the school. Thus, teachers were fearful and felt threatened, and responded to interpretations of policy that attempted reduce fear.

Our second example pertains to a policy text proposing inner city public school restructuring in Sydney, Australia, initially released as a draft proposal for public feedback. We want to draw attention to the designation of this policy as a 'draft,' and suggest this allowed for both absence (as in 'this is not really the policy') and apparition, that is these proposals may or may not be taken up. With the uncertainty of a draft policy, fear circulated through the city and the schools which operated in a local K-12 education market. We also want to note the ambiguity and uncertainty meant that what was encountered and manifested was fear of the non-White 'other' in the inner city, notably fear of Aboriginal students and parents. Aboriginal students were a central part of schooling in the inner city while simultaneously feared if they continued to be so. Some inner city schools were majority Aboriginal which carried with it the generation of non-Aboriginal fear of poor academic performance, violence and other forms of unsanctioned behaviour. One aspect of the draft policy proposal was to amalgamate these majority Aboriginal schools with a majority white student school.

Apparitions of race and policy were thus always already becoming, that is as form, despite being in draft. The point we want to make from this brief example is that this draft operated as a policy apparition in which fear, Aboriginality and education markets were inexorably linked (Gulson, 2006; 2011).

POLICY PROLEPSIS AND ENACTING SUBJECTS

In this chapter we created and played with the idea of *policy prolepsis* as the process of forming multiple ontologies and erasing other ontologies, that is the 'real,' in relation to sense-encounters of policy. We wanted to reinforce ideas that policy inherently contains multiple, contradictory, incoherent, and fluid meanings and are always becoming through assembling senses. We also wanted to posit this chapter as part of a rhizomatic politics (Youdell, 2011), for we believe that a *policy prolepsis* can be a powerful heuristic as part of a *policy geophilosophy* for policy researchers and educators to better understand how policy positions problems, solutions, and more importantly, subjectivity.

Policy prolepsis can be used to identify constructions of professional identities and map styles of practice. Teachers, practitioners, and policy researchers can use policy prolepses to identify the ways education policy induces and prompts particular behaviours and desires. More importantly, policy prolepses can assist 'end users' of policy to develop their relationships with themselves and develop ideas and practices for caring for the self. We believe these practices of the self, or becoming-teacher, may be different than those expected from policy. Specifically, becoming-policy can be identified by distinguishing it from a notion of policy as fixed in meaning (techno-rational policy analyses, official documents, of single meaning). This suggests that far from policy being a reflection of, and intervention into, order, policy is an always already failed attempt to manage chaos. Policy thus can be construed as always and only a matter of orientation that presupposes a disorientation.

A *policy prolepsis* may be our 'best guess' about the meaning of a policy, but the prolepsis is derived from wisps of textual, spoken, sensed, intuitive, and graphical instances of policy – policy rhetoric – and where policy meanings are hidden, indeterminate, ad hoc, contradictory and designed to provoke action in particular ways. The absent spaces of *policy prolepses* produces 'phantasmic space' which is relational, recursive, material, intersticed, and temporal. Thus, *policy prolepses* are always becoming with "neither beginning nor end, departure nor arrival, origin nor destination" (Deleuze & Guattari, 1987: 293). We attempted to illustrate this idea using the notion of 'policy apparitions', and we would like to remark in finishing that 'policy apparitions' are but just one conceivable way to illustrate *policy prolepsis*. Depending on a myriad of affective tones, policy prolepses might resemble, for example, *policy seductions* (desire), *policy learnings* (wonder), *policy repulsions* (hatred), *policy hypnosis* (intuition), and *policy nostalgia* (sufferings).

NOTES

[1] And very much related to Pinar's (2004) ideas of currere and complicated conversations.
[2] Cited in Calvino, 1986: 23.
[3] We have decided to not cite the original in order to highlight the important research that Inna Semetsky has done in the field of education and Deleuze studies.

CHAPTER 5

POLICY INTENSIONS AND THE FOLDS OF THE SELF

Everything is political, but every politics is simultaneously a macropolitics and a micropolitics.
—Deleuze and Guattari, 1987: 213

This chapter theorizes and critiques the processes and practices associated with 'policy implementation'. We do so in order to illustrate (a) the impoverished conceptions of space, and (b) the impoverished conceptions of the self and subjectivity. Our claims of impoverishment are levied in relation to the instrumental convictions of 'solution providers' found throughout the policy scientificities of *1.0*, and too many of *2.0*, utilizing the techno-rational strategy of 'implementing solutions'. Impoverished conceptions of the self illustrate how education policy continues to be wielded in ways that maintain a 'human capital' conception of people (and, more broadly, a conception that allows some to speak about others and their (capitalist) futures).

To accomplish these goals, we, again, posit policy as an inchoate, chaotic, and contested set of enacted practices and processes (Ball, 1994). We replace the rationalism of 'policy implementation' with the idea of *policy intensions* (with an 's') which illustrates how policy folds "onto bodies and produces particular subject positions" (Ball, Maguire, & Braun, 2012: 3). We are interested in the spatial aspects of the folds between policy and bodies, because, as we will argue, it is axiomatic to contend that space matters when examining education policy practices and processes.

There has been substantial research on links between local areas and schools, including (a) neighbourhood studies of inequality and school provision, (b) student and teacher practices in schools and cities that mediate policy initiatives relating to school choice, and (c) studies on the implementation and associated practices of policies such as 'inclusion', behaviour and discipline policies (Armstrong, 2003; Lipman, 2011; Lubienski, Culosino, & Weitzel, 2009). Surprisingly, given that policy takes and makes place, there has been relatively little education policy research using a spatial theory approach – as distinct from a description of spatial facets – to examine the micro-geographic practices of policy and the relations with subjects and objects associated with it[1] (see Gulson & Symes, 2007).

As noted in Chapter Two, space matters not merely for the simplistic reason that everything happens somewhere, but that "*where* things happen is critical to knowing *how* and *why* they happen" (Warf & Arias, 2009: 1). In this chapter, we add *to whom* they happen – but really, to *how whom* happens (or, for those really into the multiplicity, to *how whom becomings* happen). It is the spatial aspects of

CHAPTER 5

policy processes, policy enactments, and policy bodies that we think can be better understood by conceptualizing a *policy intension*.

The examination of space within education policy is to have a relationship with theory in the following way: "the role of space in the construction of theory is itself important, not only in the ways that theory might apply to a spatially distributed world, but in the spatialities that allow thought to develop particular effectivities and intensities" (Crang & Thrift, 2000: 3). Specifically, we use ideas of *relational space*, drawn from non-representational theories (Anderson & Harrison, 2010; see Chapter Two), with particular attention to the work of Gilles Deleuze, who conceives of a particularly rich non-representational geophilosophy that we use to disrupt the prevalent time-spaces of policy implementation. Notably, Deleuze's geophilosophy is concerned with situated, indeterminate, contingent concepts, and a positing of enlivened space – space as vital, material, immanent – that provides new spaces for living and new ways of becoming (Doel & Clarke, 2011). We propose that the ideas of an enlivened space brings a rich vein of thought to the emerging work on the links between policy, subjectivity and ontology.

Ours, then, is a spatial (re)conceptualizing of policy, and a deliberate critique of the so-called 'implementation gap' – what Foucault (1988c: 154) considered "a matter of making facile gestures difficult." Our focus on space-times of education policy shifts analytic emphasis away from political contestations of problem formulation and policy design during the initial stages of policy-making. We characterized these stages as the habitual wrangling over educational purpose and educational theory within the eternal recurrences of *policy scientificities 1.0* and *2.0*. Our focus on space-times also shifts analytic emphasis away from the so-called final stages of policy assessment and evaluation – the perpetual wars and endless debates over evidence, methodology, and 'science' of *policy scientificity 3.0*.

Instead, we argue that spatial analyses of education policy – using a relational -material framework – can powerfully identify the *effects* and *affects* of policy on subjects/objects. In this sense, this chapter could be considered our contributions to a geophilosophy ethics that emerge when folding policy bodies. For instance, those familiar with policy implementation research will note that we shift the traditional focus on institutions – the so-called 'black box' of reform – and instead, we examine the obscured subjectivity of policy subjects and actors during processes designed to 'reform' or 'improve' them. We draw attention to the ways policy speaks about and writes subjects. This is related to an ethics involved in education policy when policy entombs or forestalls possible subjectivizations.

Policy is always (already) contested, and a process whereby contradictions, indeterminacies, and contingencies are folded into policy and, subsequently, folded into subjects. Even in the eventual political compromises that produce education policy, policies maintain a number of political contestations folded within, and which end up folding subjects during implementation. We identify the ways policy contradictions are distributed and sensed by policy subjects, and thus, our analysis focuses on the 'intermezzo,' 'interbeing,' or the 'in between' of education policy

(Deleuze & Guattari, 1987). In other words, we conceive of *policy intermezzos* rather than 'implementations' as ways to create new analytic possibilities, for we contend *policy scientificity 1.0* and *2.0* have already structured 'implementation' (a) in simple Newtonian spaces (i.e., not in non-representational spaces), (b) with simple, much too simple, logics of 'solution ↔ problem', and (c) conceptions of time that reproduce and repeat the past.

This chapter will be primarily of interest to policy scholars, but we also believe that educators – the so-called 'end-users' of policy – can utilize the idea of a *policy intension* (which we develop shortly) to ascertain the ways education policy induces desired behaviours. More importantly, a *policy intension* can assist educators develop practices to care for the self (and others). Thus, one possibility of *policy intensions* is that they may become powerful tools for educators to utilize the macropolitical desires of policy in ways that assist in the accomplishment of their work rather than as, and only as, prescriptions developed to regulate their practice and themselves alongside neo-liberal directives.

CRITIQUING AND (RE)CONCEPTUALIZING POLICY IMPLEMENTATION

A critique is not a matter of saying that things are not right as they are. It is a matter of pointing out on what kinds of assumptions, what kinds of familiar, unchallenged, unconsidered modes of thoughts, the practices that we accept rest. …. Criticism is a matter of flushing out that thought and trying to change it: to show that things are not as self-evident as we believed, to see that what is accepted as self-evident will no longer be accepted as such. Practising criticism is a matter of making facile gestures difficult.

—Michel Foucault, 1988c: 154

In this chapter, we continue to build upon Ball's (1994: 10) ideas of policy enactments and stress the importance that education policy is characterized by incompleteness, partiality, fractional objects and "the 'wild profusion' of local practice." We laid the groundwork for much of this in Chapter Four with our development of a *policy prolepsis*. Here, we shift our focus away from the citational signs of policy and examine the emergent spaces produced from these signs and how they interact with policy subjects/objects. We develop the idea of *intensions* which are the micro-perceptions that sense, embody, and eventually, enact policy and its many triggers. Thus, *policy intensions* signal that education policy is an intra-activity that is performed through senses of the subject and which enact any number of *policy prolepses*.

The popular and preferred term 'implementation' belongs to a previous (for us, rejected) linear/temporal conception in which policy is idealized in sequential steps from drafting/writing to application/implementation, and eventually, evaluation (aka, 'the policy cycle'). We characterised and constituted the cycle as part of the instrumental and techno-rational scientificities of *1.0* and some of *2.0*. The linear/

temporal understanding of policy, discussed in the previous chapter obfuscates many of the geographies of policy while simultaneously positioning policy authors as the rational 'solution-providers' to the fractional worlds of practice (Mol, 2002).

The partiality of policy counters characterizations of policy as rational 'solutions' to educational 'problems' often described as the techno-rational approach to policy and its implementation developed since the mid-1950s (Datnow & Park, 2009). Techno-rational approaches to policy implementation utilize management theory to invest authority into "new school executives" (Maxcy, 1991: 172) and, thus, away from those implementing corporate managerial desires. These kinds of bureaucratic machines, then, make it very difficult to perform the kinds of policy problematizations that we discussed in Chapter Three. This is in large part due to the overwhelming amount of resources invested into education machines reliant upon Euro-centric understandings of ontology (Law, 2004). It is cheaper to routinise and/or try to ameliorate education rather than explore the possibilities contained in kindergarteners' questions about exploding the education system.

HISTORY OF 'POLICY IMPLEMENTATION'

Richard Elmore (1979–1980: 601–616) described the techno-rational approach as movement, whereas it is a process of policy implementation that occurs "top-down" and is concerned with "forward mapping" which produces a hierarchical spatial politic as policy makers attempt to control and direct policy desires for some future state of conditions. Policy subjects in techno-rational conceptions of policy are expected to comply with hierarchical desires by virtue of new spatializations of power and governance (Gulson, 2011; Webb, 2008).

During the policy scientificities of the 1980s (*2.0*), educational researchers mapped the considerable influence that policy subjects wielded over the processes and outcomes of so-called 'policy solutions'. Researchers observed that implementers responded to policy "in what often seemed quite idiosyncratic, frustratingly unpredictable, if not downright resistant ways" (McLaughlin, 1987: 171). Amanda Datnow and Vicki Park (2009: 349, our emphasis) described the considerable influence 'implementers' wielded when "… even fully planned, highly coordinated, and well-supported policies ultimately depended on how individuals within the local context interpreted and *enacted* policies; in other words, local factors dominated policy outcomes." Given policy subjects' influence on policy, Elmore argued that implementation can be understood from a 'bottom-up' perspective and through 'backward mapping' of policy intentions and desires. The influence of policy subjects/objects on policy inverted the direction of movement of techno-rational policy conceptions. Datnow and Park (2009: 350) described this inversion as "reflect[ing] larger debates surrounding the macro-micro theoretical divide."

Historically, this moment of policy analysis was captured by some through a (inter) disciplinary focus of 'policy sociology' in education – and *policy scientificity 2.0* specifically – that we noted was part of a larger critique of *policy scientificity 1.0*. We continue this important cross-paradigmatic approach to policy research. However, our approach to inter- and multi-disciplinary analyses of policy is better described as developing approaches and transversal politics to our *policy geophilosophy*. Again, ours is focussed on moving beyond a description of the spatiality of education policy and toward an attempt to use transversal disciplinary approaches to theorize spatialities in education policy.

Implementation and the Subject

Contemporary research into policy reintroduced policy subjects as central interpretative objects involved in increasingly complex processes; notably that policy subjects: a) *sense* policy and act accordingly without recognition (prolepsis – Chapter Four); b) *make sense* of policy through different reasoned interpretations and estimations (Spillane, Gomez, & Mesler, 2009); c) co-construct or *intra-act* with policy during implementation (Datnow, Lasky, Stringfield, & Teddlie, 2006); and, d) *enact* and *perform* policy (Braun, Ball, Maguire, & Hoskins, 2011).

These contemporary views of policy research account for the spatial politics of policy more or less as "a relational sense of context" that "… assume[s] that people's actions cannot be understood apart from the setting in which the actions are situated; reciprocally, the setting cannot be understood without understanding the actions of the people within" (Datnow & Park, 2009: 350). Our focus on *policy intensions* accounts for how policy is sensed and enacted. Importantly, however, policy intensions are not a subtle way to reintroduce the policy end-user as a rational actor in policy research. Policy intensions help explain how, why, where, and who responds to policy and signal how policy subjects/objects are written by policy.

Discrepant Policy Subjects/Objects and the Intra-Activity of the Policy Self

The literature on policy implementation has used discrepant descriptions of subjects and subjectivity (e.g., obedient, resistant, sense-making, co-constructing). Further, these discrepant descriptions obscure an understanding of policy as a spatial phenomenon, and, reify and routinize implementation as a process concerned primarily with efficacy, evaluation, and linearity – so-called 'solutions'. The attribution of subjectivity is central to understanding how policy is a spatial phenomena that is enacted and performed. As such, discrepant descriptions of policy subjects produce a muddied ethics when policy is enacted.

A *policy intension* is clearly associated with policy intentions, but signal the ways policy actors sense, encounter, embody, enact, and respond to policy triggers, often without recognition of policy desires. That is, *policy intensions* signal how policy is affectively encountered and *prior* to understanding or recognition of policy intentions. Intensions, moreover, signal the ways *policy prolepses* are subsequently enacted and embodied. It is these intensions that influence subsequent thought and action, which are also *in-tension* and *intense*.

For example, while policy intentions can be, literally, folded into documents – signalled by the various dog-eared policies of assessment and accountability, class composition (sorting), behaviour (classification), etc. – our purpose is to illustrate how policy *intensions* fold policy subjects. In this sense, policy asks subjects to face themselves differently; that is, policy insists that subjects consider themselves in relation to a myriad of 'better/best' practices: 'improved,' 'effective,' 'accountable,' 'knowledgeable,' and so forth. However, feelings of inadequacy compete with feelings of being effective once policy is 'implemented'. Policy writes subjects by folding them along different affects: educators as in/effective and in/adequate. And, policy implementation folds subjects along different ideas of being independent (or 'autonomous') and becoming dependent on curriculum policy: educators as in/dependent. We might consider the syntax of '/' as the fold where affective lines compete for expression along intersecting vectors that both combine and shear subjects' feelings (Webb, 2013). Education policy is frequently engaged with folding subjects along many affective lines, if not twisting them into knots.

Policy intensions assist understanding how policy desires move through different policy spaces, including the geographies of the self which have all-too-often been relegated as non-placed during policy implementations. Space is not simply a metaphor or amorphous realm that policy subjects inhabit, but something that folds onto and within subjects.

IMMANENT SPACE AND EMERGENT GEOGRAPHIES

Deleuzian space is not above and beyond nor is it inside or outside but rather self-referential in its time as an event. This is the space that the creation of a concept delivers us unto.

—Dewsbury & Thrift, 2005: 105–6

Deleuze and Guattari (1987: 213) noted that "everything is political, but every politics is simultaneously a macropolitics and a micropolitics", insisting that the so-called macro-micro theoretical divide is an illusion that can be collapsed by more thorough exegesis on the concept of space. In this chapter we work with the the ideas of relational space as outlined in Chapter Two which emphasized multiplicity and openness. This conception of space, often framed as part of a material post-structuralism (Murdoch, 2006) has an affinity with one interpretation of Deleuzian space – space is emergent and exigent to social relations. This aspect is evident in education policy literatures (discussed above) that use ideas of "relational contexts" to explain how subjects are folded in policy. Non-representational theory has taken this idea of relationality and focused on relational-materiality. This requires us to "think through the specificity and performative efficacy of different relations and different relational configurations" (Anderson & Harrison, 2010: 16).

Intensions as Territorialization Events: The Four Folds of Policy

We utilize the idea of space as predicate to suggest that the notion of event as predicate is significant when considering policy. That is, we can conceive of policy as predicate – *to space* and *to take* place. However, we consider policy as a particular kind of *event* where "an event is the potential immanent within a particular confluence of forces" and "events carry no determinate outcome, but only new possibilities, representing a moment at which new forces might be brought to bear" (Stagoll, 2010: 90–91). Implementation, for instance, assumes we can know where, when, and how policy is to be implemented by whom (e.g., as organizational designation). This 'fixing' of policy presumes that implementation is effecting change as designed – as in "taking place" or occurring. Implementation, then, is treated as a predictable event.

For our purposes, the assumed fixity of implementation is contrasted with policy implementation as a *territorialization event* which deliberately treats space as a predicate – to space, to take place, and soon, to fold. In this sense, the policy predicate of "taking place" is understood as not 'occurring,' but rather, *territorializing*, as in the state of being taken, acquiring through force, or obtained. Here, we follow the idea of predicating policy, as in "to space," and consequently, we follow a question posed by Deleuze (1995: 160): "what becomes of the subject, if predicates are events?"

The outcomes of even well-planned and conscientious territorialization events are not predictable, and, in fact, chaotic and uncertain. As a territorialization event, policy engineers four unpredictable policy topologies:

1. The self and its relations to the materialities of worlds; its enfoldings in different locations and material circumstances;
2. Force or politics as expressed through various technologies and competing rights to govern *and* the ways in which subjects think about these relationships, i.e., self-governance;
3. Knowledge as expressed through policy content (e.g., budget, curriculum, sequencing, assessment, etc.), but more importantly, policy scientificities in relation to various truths to self, and;
4. The "fold of the outside itself" (Deleuze, 1988: 104) which refers to how the self imagines and understands existence, death, and im/mortality – the temporal limits of itself (futurings).

These four folds of policy – perhaps imagined as a braided rope – represent a rough map of emergent, unpredictable, and chaotic spaces that loosely correspond with four folds of subjectivity identified by Deleuze (1988: 104–105). The four folds constitute a "set of particular positions" (Deleuze, 1988: 115) that combine to constitute bodies in space – namely "of bodies and space; of force; of truth in relation to self; and of the line outside [i.e., existence]" (Malins, 2004: 485). Policy intensions, then, signal how educators become-policy.

CHAPTER 5

THE IMMANENT SPACE OF EDUCATION POLICY

Doel and Clarke (2011: 125) argued that it would be better to consider space as a verb rather than a noun. They stated,

> [t]o space – that's all. Spacing is an action, an event, and a way of being. …. Space is immanent. It has only itself …. Spacing is what happens and takes place: it is the differential element within everything that happens; the repetitious relay or protracted stringiness by which the fold of actuality opens in and of itself onto the unfold of virtuality.

The four folds of policy are produced once implementation is understood as a territorialization event. While there is some affinity to policy fields and concomitant notions of spatiality within field analyses (Lingard & Rawolle, 2004), policy territorialization events indicate how policy attempts to space end-users' bodies in overtly political ways (rather than, for instance, as a set of cultural practices). Likewise, implementation attempts *to take place* of particular knowledges; *to take place* of particular technologies of governance; and, as noted above, *to fold* indeterminate desires into policy subjects.

Once policy is considered a territorialization event, we can play with this idea to consider the possibility that policy implementations are little more than a hopeful approximation to create change in a desired way. Policy as a *territorialization event* represents a shift to conceiving place as "both NowHere and NoWhere" (Doel, 2000: 125). The immanence of space does not delimit social space, and refuses any certainty and security of orientation because "everything takes-part and in taking-part, takes-place: everything happens, everything acts" (Anderson & Harrison, 2010: 14). Doreen Massey (2005: 139) suggested that it is not tenable to presume that place is a fixed location in accordance to time – rather place can be thought of as a multiple becoming. She noted, "The 'here' is no more (and no less) than our encounter, and what is made of it. It is, irretrievably, here and now. It won't be the same 'here' when it is no longer now."

Rather than understanding policy as struggles between educational hierarchies, we follow Deleuze and Guattari who suggested an understanding of the symbiotic and emergent relations that develop between micro- and macro- milieus. This is to see that policy, and the effects of predicating implementation, can be conceived in a similar way to place, as "the coming together of the previously unrelated, a constellation of processes rather than a thing" (Massey, 2005: 141). Hence, the four territorial folds of policy discussed above are better understood by mapping them together as möbius topologies assembled through the subject. Next, the imagery of the fold will be used to illustrate how the self is folded in on endogamous parts of policy and how policy is folded onto exogamous elements of the body.

POLICY INTENSIONS AND THE GEOGRAPHIES OF THE SELF

The concept of a *policy intension* signals the ways policy actors sense, encounter, embody, enact, perform, and respond to policy desires. Intensions indicate how policy is affectively encountered *prior* to understanding, recognition, or interpretation. It is these intensions that influence subsequent thought and action, so-called policy interpretations, which are also *in-tension* and *intense*. Our policy intensions are micro-sensings of policy which subsequently fold policy subjects. For instance, the apparently endless policy desires about policy subjects rest on the expectation that policy subjects are *pli-able*; that they can be folded. Semetsky (2006: 19), quoting Deleuze (1993: 95) explained,

> the unconscious perceptions are implicated as minute, or microperceptions: as such – and *le pli*, the root of the *im-pli-cated*, means in French *the fold* – they are part of the cartographic microanalysis of establishing 'an unconscious psychic mechanisms that engenders the perceived in consciousness'.

When considering the imagery of the *fold*, the "outside is not a fixed limit ... folds and foldings that together make up an inside: they are not something other than the outside, but precisely the inside of the outside" (Deleuze, 1988: 96–97). The *fold* challenges conceptions of subjectivity that stand independently apart from – and rationally in control of – shaping/producing space. The idea of the fold, then, is a "critique of typical accounts of subjectivity, that presume a simple interiority and exteriority" (O'Sullivan, 2010: 107). The idea of the fold was developed as a way to study thought, thinking, and subjectivity; or more precisely, to study the relationships one has to oneself, and others.

Folds are where "subjectivity becomes an ongoing negotiation of things perceived, both consciously and unconsciously, within and outside of the body" (Conley, 2005: 171) and where "thought is placed in action and action is placed in the world" (Anderson & Harrison, 2010: 11). Subjectivity *is* the inside of the outside; two sides of a single surface – entangled. Folding signals how policy and subjects are intimately connected and produce each other; but more importantly, the fold indicates where and how subjectivity is becoming.

For instance, Kaustuv Roy's (2003) study on teachers who developed a new "innovative" or alternative school illustrates how the idea of the fold assists an understanding of the spaces of the self. In Roy's study, teachers developed the school to better meet the needs of youth who supported themselves and their families. These youth often moved, and lived in unsafe neighbourhoods where drug problems, teen pregnancy, and dropout rates were high. Among the many challenges that teachers experienced during their time developing the school, the idea of the self changing during school reform was particularly evident and difficult. As Roy (2003: 173) noted, the,

CHAPTER 5

> ... grand schemes of reform and change are rapidly taken over by territorializing forces, but an imperceptible rupture remains the hidden, unnoticed fault line that can allow what Britzman and Dippo (2000) have called "awful thoughts" or dissident movements to surface. ... What this signifies is that the grand-scale reforms and large structural initiatives [policy], although the may look impressive, are less important from the point of view of real change than the minor movements of disorientation and dissidence at the micropolitical level.

In a different example, one of us observed how accountability policy folded teachers into paranoid and schizophrenic subjects (Webb, 2009). As the result of intense scrutiny from state and district accountability policies, teachers created pedagogical fabrications intentionally and individually. Teachers discussed their feeling of schizophrenia and paranoia as a result of performing pedagogical fabrications to different audiences. A teacher explained how they became fabricated,

> I keep portfolios of the kids' work and I assess quite frequently and so the principal assumes that I'm a good teacher. She's popped into my classroom [unannounced] and asked me 'how are you going to teach this-and-this' and 'how are you going to assess it.' Kind of this bullshit thing we do. And you know, I'm prepared now. I show her the portfolios. Mind you, I don't have to show what's in the portfolio – just the idea that I have a portfolio [indicates to her that] I'm on the ball. (Webb, 2009: 113)

Teachers noted how, and in which ways, they folded themselves within prevailing discourses of performance accountability. The enactments of fabricating pedagogy were produced by teachers' policy intensions of the swirling accountability registers at the school (e.g., standardized scores, local codes of behaviour, parental expectations) and trying to meet those intense, and in-tension, demands on a daily basis.

In another example, one of us explained how the policy intensions of fear of the racial other was used to position parental policy subjects within a environment of school choice in multicultural, inner city areas (Gulson, 2011). A paradoxical positioning was most evident in the practices of choice of white, middle class parents. These parents were making residential choices based partly on a desire to live in an 'edgy,' multicultural area of the city, in order for their children to be exposed to cultural diversity which meant somatic difference and commodifications of ethnicity such as restaurants, while simultaneously sending their children to a school that was predominantly white. These intensions were part of contradictory discourses of multiculturalism and choice, enmeshed in complex assemblages of schools and dangerous, immutable, bodies of colour.

As part of the contradiction, policy circulated intensions of fear through the city and the schools which operated within the local K-12 education market. Here, a teacher noted that "I've dealt with specific cases of racism where parents have said 'I do not want my child to sit next to that brown child'" (Gulson, 2011: 61).

Holding these contradictory desires to be with and apart from difference, illustrated that in inner city education markets, education policy folds racial difference as "a heterogeneous process of racial differentiation" (Anderson & Harrison, 2010: 19).

Thus, when policy is 'implemented', it is not a Cartesian-self that is moving through Newtonian-space considering different folds to inhabit in a rational and conscious deliberation of policy expectations. Rather, the policy subject is flooded with a "swarm" of subjective folds within an immanence of territorialized spaces (Deleuze & Guattari, 1987: 7). Subjectivity is produced through the interface of subjects' senses of policy and their estimations of possible policy outcomes. The pliable foldings of education policy and the self are,

> an interiorization of the outside. It is not a doubling of the One, but a redoubling of the Other. It is not a reproduction of the Same, but a repetition of the Different. It is not the emanation of an 'I', but something that places in immanence an always other or a Non-self. It is never the other who is a double in the doubling process, it is a self that lives me as the double of the other: I do not encounter myself on the outside, I find the other in me. (Deleuze, 1988: 98)

Education policy, therefore, is neither an articulation nor a representation of a solution. Rather implementation can be considered a momentary point along a *line* of desires or a *vanishing point* of unfulfilled intentions, *policy vectors*. Marcus Doel (2000: 128) explains,

> [l]ike the vanishing point in a perspectival painting, such a point points into that which it vanishes. And since a point, no less than a space, is folded many ways, this directional aspect takes on an infinite complexity and intensity.

Flooded with swarms of policy contradictions, policy intensions fold subjects and their practice in ways that are not apparent or recognized. For instance, in what we would see as an example of policy prolepsis, numerous studies have discussed how fear is wielded adeptly in education policy to achieve particular outcomes (e.g., Ginsberg & Cooper, 2008). Moreover, education policy has capitalised on 'manufacturing crises' in order to persuade policy actors in particular ways (Berliner & Biddle, 1996).

POLICY CARTOGRAPHIES AND THE GEOGRAPHIES OF THE SELF

> What's your road, man? – holyboy road, madman road, rainbow road, guppy road, any road. It's an anywhere road for anybody anyhow. Where body how?
> —Jack Kerouac, 1957, *On the Road*

We have argued that the taken-for-granted processes of policy fold the *affects* of policy users through speculative claims about what policy can do – that is, through policy's purported *effects*. We noted that intermediary spaces, or emergent geographies, are produced in policy, and in the subjectivity of actors once policy is implemented. We discussed these emergent geographies as important middle spaces for policy research, better understood by mapping the four folds of policy. We used the idea of the *fold* to illustrate how policy implementation is a spatial-temporal politic, rather than, or only, a rational-temporal process of policy initiative, development, and implementation.

This politic, then, is used to disorient subjects and re-orient their relationships with themselves in various ways once policy is sensed, embodied, and enacted.[2] The idea that policy is sensed, embodied, and enacted was developed into the concept of a *policy intension*. We believe that a *policy intension* extends approaches to micropolitical analyses of education policy in order to demonstrate the ways implementation folds affects and writes bodies with policy.

We are interested in whether policy may or may not be helpful to those that are using and being used by it, and in the ways policy implementation is part of that which it wants to create (ideal subjects, change, etc.). For this task we use the idea of a map, or in the words of Jack Kerouac "where body how?" This is to consider:

> The map is open and connectable in all of its dimensions; it is detachable, reversible, susceptible to constant modification. It can be torn, reversed, adapted to any kind of mounting, reworked by an individual, group, or social formation. It can be drawn on a wall, conceived as a work of art, constructed as a political action or as a meditation. (Deleuze & Guattari, 1987: 12)

This concept of a map is significant because it has to do with performance, it is the notion of the map employed differently from assumptions of representation – it is imbued with poetics and imagination; with openness, diversity, and creativity (West-Pavlov, 2009). Similarly, there is "a variety of modalities of folds: from the fold of our material selves, our bodies, to the folding of time, or simply memory. Indeed, subjectivity might be understood as precisely a topology of these different kinds of folds" (O'Sullivan, 2010: 107). Research into policy can be similarly entered from diverse points and located as part of diverse practices. In the final section of the paper we discuss how the four territorial folds of policy provide a constellation of folds that can be examined through cartographical methods.

Mapping the Folds of Policy Implementation

When discussing subjectivity, Inna Semetsky (2006: 21) explained that,

> subjectivity exists as a territory and constitutes itself via the cartographic method: it engenders itself through multiple connections by mapping both "psychic and the social" (Bosteels, 1998: 150) that is, the dimensions constituting the fold of both inside and outside: the inside of the outside.

Likewise, Tom Conley (2005: 172) explained the cartographical potential of subjectivity when he stated,

POLICY INTENSIONS AND THE FOLDS OF THE SELF

a person's relation with his or her body becomes both an 'archive' and a 'diagram', a collection of subjectivations and a mental map charted on the basis of the past and drawn from events and elements in the ambient world.

Borrowing from Steve Pile and Nigel Thrift's (1995) *Mapping the subject* that insists on "wayfinding"[3] rather than on re-presenting 'fixity', our purposes are to reorient policy implementation research and to consider more fully "a different logic of social practice, an intensive and affective logic of the included middle" (Bosteels, 1998: 151). Our purpose to develop modes of analysis and inquiry is to better understand the ethics involved in folding end-users, and how policy prolepses and intensions effectuate such foldings. Our cartographical methods do not fix our understandings of policy nor bodies, but rather, produce multiple foldings that better inform how policy intensions form the topologies of education policy, whereas the relationship between mapping and space is crucial. Buchanan and Lambert (2005: 5) emphasize this point when they stated,

> [t]his mapping of the different kinds of space that mix in each assemblage (social, political, but also geological, biological, economic, aesthetic or musical and so on) becomes the major task set out by the project they define as pragmatics or micro-politics.

Mapping different kinds of space reiterates that there is a four-fold politics to researching policy. Implementation events are always becoming with "neither beginning nor end, departure nor arrival, origin nor destination" (Deleuze & Guattari, 1987: 293). As such, researchers could begin discussing micropolitical action as a re-politicizing of education from the 'middle,' 'intermezzo,' or 'interbeing' rather than at policy's provisional beginnings (i.e., design) or policy's ostensive end (i.e., evaluation). From this, a spatial politic is born from which to address schooling *micropolitically*. Thus, policy is an event that is concerned with multiplicities that emerge from within four topological folds of policy.

Conceiving policy as a 'chart' *implicates already* with that which it interacts and relates. That is, policy implementation is not an application of a solution; rather, policy can be conceived as an interval. Policy cartographies map the embodiment of indeterminate outcomes and map the intervals of effects and affects that perform and enact policy geographies. Cartographical methods that examine implementation deliberately place policy intensions into various networks and registers that are too often "non-placed" and obscured in research (Buchanan, 2005).

This is not to suggest that policy end-users do not resist policy. Indeed, resistance is a sign of the complex processes subjects are engaged in when negotiating subjectivity: "there will always be a relation to oneself which resists codes and powers; the relation to onself [sic] is even one of the origins of these points of resistance ..." (Deleuze, 1988: 103). Deleuze (1995: 176) continued,

> [i]t definitely makes sense to look at the various ways individuals and groups constitute themselves as subjects through processes of subjectivation: what

CHAPTER 5

counts in such processes is the extent to which, as they take shape, they elude both established forms of knowledge and the dominant forms of power. Even if they in turn engender new forms of power or become assimilated into new forms of knowledge. For a while, though, they have a real rebellious spontaneity. This is nothing to do with going back to "the subject," that is, to something invested with duties, power, and knowledge.

Policy folds become creative responses to implementation rather than conceptualized as 'illegitimate' or 'repressive' forms of resistance to 'hierarchical' forms of authority. Nevertheless, the self is not 'outside' the places and spaces of its becoming – that is, not "lithely free of social structure" (Bonta & Protevi, 2004: 6). Rather, the self is intra-acting with the emergent spaces of its becoming and integrally im*pli*cated through its sensings and responses to these emergent spaces. The 'relation to oneself' is a set of power relations and the self "will be reintegrated into these systems from which it was originally derived. The individual is coded or recoded within a 'moral' knowledge, and above all [s/]he becomes the stake in a power struggle and is diagrammatized" (Deleuze, 1988: 103). Tom Robbins (2004: 86–87) gets to the creative aspects of the self's diagrammatization,

> [t]he magician was at work on his magical things. Sprawled upon a pallet of skins, he attended to his maps.... Unlike poor Rand McNally, Ziller was not obliged to limit his cartograms to representations of the earth's familiar surface; no, his maps could and did indulge in languorous luxuriation, in psycho-cosmic ornament that may or may not be helpful to motorists seeking the most convenient route from there to here. If, with appropriate geographical symbols, they indicated the presence of mountain ranges, forests and bodies of water, they seemed also to indicate psychological nuances, regional flavours, genito-urinary reactions and extrasensory phenomena – those 'other dimensions' of voyage so well known to the aware traveller.

Topologies of resistance identifies how subjects develop and use 'new' liminal geographies (i.e., folds) delineated from revised boundaries of previously occupied territory. Hence, the "notion of ownership might itself be reconfigured as a question of folding: to have is always to fold. We *fold* that which is outside, inside" (O'Sullivan, 2006: 124). 'Ownership' is particularly important in light of neo-liberal attempts of deterritorialization that remove forms of practice from policy subjects and inserts others. Implementation deterritorializes previous forms of subjectivity and replaces them with new folds.

Neo-liberal policy invests, or takes a stake, in the ownership of subjectivity. This is a re-appropriation of materiality – here as micro- or fleshy- materialities – and a redefinition of property, of materiality. Implementation is the predicate act of *taking place* of subjectivity and therefore *to own*. Mapping policy folds indicate how subjects are socially and spatially constituted and reconstituted. More importantly, mapping policy subjects identifies the territory and materialities that structure the topologies of subjectivity – "with what folds can I surround myself or how can I produce myself as subject?" (Deleuze, 1988: 114).

In closing, Deleuze entertained how the fold might be used for creative possibilities of self-making, borrowed from Michel Foucault's (1982: 237) observation that "from the idea that the self is not given to us, I think that there is only one practical consequence: we have to create ourselves as a work of art." Indeed, Deleuze (1995: 114) would similarly state that "subjectification is an artistic activity." Likewise, Tom Conley (2005: 172) noted that "the struggle for subjectivity is a battle to win the right to have access to difference, variation, and metamorphosis."

In this spirit, we believe that cartographies of the four territorial folds of policy can be a powerful heuristic for critical policy researchers and for those expected to 'implement decisions' to better understand how policy positions problems, solutions, and subjectivity. Cartographies of implementation events assist policy subjects to develop their relationships with themselves and develop practices for caring for the self. We believe these practices of the self may be different than those expected from policy. It is this spirit of self-creation that we join Jack Kerouac on the proverbial policy road and evoke the methodological imperative: "Where body how?"

NOTES

[1] We note there is extensive work on childhood and socio-spatiality (e.g., Kraftl, 2010).
[2] With affinities to Naomi Klein's (2007) *Shock Doctrine*.
[3] Pile and Thrift (p. 1) use Mathy (1993) ideas of wayfinding: "Visiting in turn all, or most, of the positions one takes to constitute the field...[covering] descriptively as much of the terrain as possible, exploring it on foot rather than looking down at it from an airplane"

CHAPTER 6

THE NEO-LIBERAL POLICIES OF *EPIMELEIA HEAUTOU* CARING FOR THE SELF IN EDUCATION MARKETS

Mapping Biopolitical Catallaxies in Education Policy with Viviana Pitton

This chapter examines neo-liberal education policy as part of developing our *policy geophilosophy*. Specifically, the chapter re-theorizes neo-liberal policy in order to illustrate different conceptions of the subject/object within arguments that advocate for the deregulation and marketization of education. As an aside, we do wonder if there are there other kinds of policies in contemporary education apart from neo-liberal ones? Anyway, we imagine this chapter has come too late for some, and is completely irrelevant for others due to the ubiquity of, and varied responses to, such an idea. Nevertheless, we argue that neo-liberal education policy has capitalized on a historical concern to care for the self, or the Greek *epimeleia heautou*.

Given our agreement with the idea that "[e]verything is political, but every politics is simultaneously a macropolitics and a micropolitics" (Deleuze & Guattari, 1987: 213), we discuss how neo-liberal education policy (aka, the 'macro') intra-acts with the subject/object (aka, the 'micro'). Again, we believe greater attention to how space or spacing operates in education policy studies is required. We discuss *epimeleia heautou* in relation to education policies that emphasize greater choice in educational offerings, and in relation to school choice policies more generally. Thus, a premise of our argument is that *neo-liberal policies produce and, therefore, accommodate a much greater range of selves to be cared for.* The analysis examines the neo-liberal subject, *homo œconomicus*, in relation to education policy that produce choices of the self and choices for its care. We conclude by discussing conceptions of the self in relation to two aporias of neo-liberal educational equality produced through ethno-culturally specific schools.

Foucault (2005: 5) noted that caring for the self, or the Greek *epimeleia heautou*, was a generalized precept that Hellenistic people used when applying the general rules of: "you must attend to yourself, you must not forget yourself, you must take care of yourself." Know yourself, or *gnōthi seauton*, was a phrase inscribed at the entrance to the Temple at Delphi and articulated an ethos about how to live one's life. Foucault (2005) discussed the idea of *gnōthi seauton* in relation to the more pervasive credo of *epimeleia heautou* during this period, noting how ideas of care

CHAPTER 6

shaped ideas about self-knowledge. Always 'knowledge' and rarely material. Oh well.

In this chapter, we argue that the neo-liberal subject, *homo œconomicus*, uses education policy to increase curricular choices for its respective care. We continue to examine how subjects/objects intra-act with a range of prolepses, intensions, and folds. We use social theory in relation to a set of policy concepts operating throughout the globe: deregulation, marketization, choice, innovation, human capital and, too often neglected or obscured, conceptions of the self. Our method is best described as presenting an argument that neo-liberal education policy promotes conceptions of the self that enunciate aporias of neo-liberal educational equality.

The term 'aporia' has been chosen deliberately to convey our sincere puzzlement about notions of neo-liberal educational equality. Furthermore, our use of the term 'aporia' signals an attempt to not resolve such conundrums, but rather, to examine and better understand how such a puzzle has been constructed and to discuss possible effects that such a puzzle produces – an example of what we term policy problematization (see Chapter Three).

The chapter begins by reviewing neo-liberalism and education policy. Next, we link this discussion to Foucault's (2008) conception of the self as expressed in the phrase *homo œconomicus*. We argue that the consumption practices of *homo œconomicus* constitute two ways to understand contemporary methods of caring for the self. Finally, our conclusion examines three biopolitical themes that emerge from our discussion of the education policies of *epimeleia heautou*:

- that practices of care are predicated on *a priori* notions of the self;
- that the care of the self is practised in relation to unequal and provisionally finite educational markets; and
- that the education policies of *epimeleia heautou* enunciate aporias of neo-liberal equality when deregulated schools care for a self (or plural, selves) that has been historically marginalized, threatened, or excluded.

The latter speaks to the possibility that the logical outcome of neo-liberal education may be that the juridical, legislative, and policy worlds continue to fail historically marginalized groups, leaving only economics as a site of redress. Nevertheless, if economics is the only site left for historically marginalized groups to pursue education, it places them in yet another very precarious and inherently unfair politics.

Our approach utilizes Michel Foucault's (2008: 232) lectures from 1978–82 where he discussed the concept of *education policy* and neo-liberalism explicitly. The posthumous lectures have been published relatively recently, and as such some of the points that follow may seem somewhat rehashed for scholars of neo-liberal education policy. We offer apologies in advance, but note that we make the unique argument that neo-liberal education policy is intimately connected to notions of the self and its care.

We also note that the themes of *epimeleia heautou* are increasingly enunciated in education policy as values of self-respect, self-freedom, self-equality, self-worth, self-determination, and, as we will examine shortly, self-separation. These registers of subject expression, then, are the very folds that emanate from our four folds of policy: material, knowledge, power, and existence that we discussed in the previous chapter. The significance of this analysis rests on identifying how different practices of self-care are developed through neo-liberal policy. Foucault (2008: 227) foresaw that 'designer babies' only signalled a beginning of an educational desire concerned with producing particular subject positions. Neo-liberal education policy complements and extends the production of desired selves through schooling practices chartered to produce particular subjects, such as the middle class (white) ideal student (Gewirtz, 2001).

NEO-LIBERALISM AND GOVERNMENTALITY

Neo-liberalism is a political-economic theory that utilizes the efficiencies of market economics to develop and legitimate government priorities and practices. Neo-liberalism also promotes a form of social organization where strong emphasis is placed on individual's freedom of choice (Friedman, 1962, 1980). No matter the location considered or the form adopted, neo-liberalism calls for 'freedom', mostly understood in relation to the rights of the individual to market participation and of markets themselves to operate without any intromission from the state (Clarke, 2004). From this viewpoint, then, social well-being rests on individual choice and can only take place within an unrestricted market-driven model of development.

Foucault (2008) understood neo-liberalism as government practices that operated through the techniques by which states and individuals govern and are governed. This form of governmentality differs from earlier forms of liberalism in that it conceives the market as something that government constructed by setting institutional, legal and political conditions deemed necessary for its effective operation. Moreover, the state needed to face the predicament of having to foster the development of 'autonomous' and 'free' individuals that neo-liberal styles of government depend upon (Johnson, 2000). In this sense,

> the problem of neo-liberalism is how the overall exercise of political power can be modeled on the principles of a market economy [and] of taking the formal principles of a market economy and referring and relating them to, of projecting them on to a general art of government. (Foucault, 2008: 131)

As a set of government practices, neo-liberalism seeks to reduce the social, political, and economic risks assumed by liberal (i.e., democratic) governments; and instead, transfer these risks onto individuals through their relationships with each other, and importantly, themselves (Olssen & Peters, 2005). That is, neo-liberalism provides self-regulated mechanisms through the devolution of risk onto the individuals who become responsible for their own care (i.e., they are 'empowered' to discipline themselves; e.g., Rose, 1999b). Through neo-liberalism, government practices are autonomized (Barry, Osborne, & Rose, 1996) and adjusted to an entrepreneurial model via the fabrication of techniques that emphasize "the greater individualization of society and the 'responsibilization' of individuals and families" (Peters, 2001: 85). As we will argue, 'responsible individualization' is intimately connected to developing specific practices to care for oneself.

Neo-liberalism, then, refers to the tactics, mechanisms, and other technologies used to persuade populations to discipline themselves economically and/or enterprisingly. Neo-liberalism birthed *homo œconomicus* which refers to a shift from overt forms of control or 'oppression' and toward more covert forms of control imbued with individuals' own desires and active participation in the development of an entrepreneurial self. As Edwards (2002: 357) put it,

> [g]overning, therefore, has less to do with a rational process of social reform [that is, policy scientificities *1.0* and *2.0*] and more to do with fashioning conduct based on certain cultural norms and values, wherein individuals are taken to be active subjects and not passive objects. In particular, these norms and values take the forms associated with responsible consuming and enterprise. Thus, subjectivities are themselves re-fashioned in eliciting a particular image of human beings as enterprising.

Neo-liberal Education Policy

Neo-liberal education policy enunciates values that emphasize deregulation, consumer choice, and competition (Basu, 2004). Consequently, neo-liberal education policy often involve shifts from central administration to managerial decentralization coupled with new forms of public provision (e.g., magnet and charter schools) and financing (e.g., voucher programs).

School choice alternatives are basically grounded on three arguments:

- with wider school choices the ability to exit under-performing public schools is distributed more fairly and socioeconomically disadvantaged students can gain access to better schools;
- a decentralized school system is likely to be more responsive to the different needs of students than schools dependent on a central district administration are (Chubb & Moe, 1988), and
- school choice initiatives create a competitive market environment which forces all schools to improve their academic standards to respond to the quality demands of their 'consumers' (Chubb & Moe, 1990).

The neo-liberal discourse of choice, which positions the rational, self-entrepreneurial subject, assumes that all subjects are equally positioned to recognize, mobilize and consolidate productive or successful choices. There is no space in this discourse for any consideration of the different and inequitable locations of subjects in terms of familial, cultural or socioeconomic privilege or disadvantage, or of age, education, gender, class and ethnicity. (Bansel, 2007: 298)

As Bansel suggested, this discourse of choice assumes that all subjects are able to choose in equal conditions from identical alternatives (see also, Ball, 2003).

Under neo-liberalism, educational institutions are not only expected to behave like actors in a market, but are also transformed by consumers' needs that respond to and shape the choice alternatives within an education system. School choice policy alternatives are coupled with management technologies that include increased exposure to competition, increased accountability measures, and the implementation of performance goals and quality assurance measures (Davies & Bansel, 2007). Education policies that promote self-responsibility and freedom of choice operate through a performativist culture that subjects different conceptions of the self "to what might be regarded as a regime that involves observation, surveillance, and examination in the form of monitoring of learning, intervention, 'programmes', and assessments" (Foucault, 1982a: 50). The neo-liberal self is an entrepreneurial one – *homo œconomicus* – that is 'freed' from the welfare state and responsible for its own care (Foucault, 2008).

Neo-Liberal Homo Œconomicus

Foucault (2008) used the figure of *homo œconomicus* to discuss the idea of an entrepreneurial and performing self. He situated *homo œconomicus* within conceptions of liberal governmentality (discussed above) and in relation to post-war economics of the United States and Europe, particularly Germany. At the risk of oversimplifying, the First and Second World Wars replaced an exchange-based *homo œconomicus* with an enterprising *homo œconomicus*. Now, *homo œconomicus* "is not at all a partner of exchange" but rather "an entrepreneur, an entrepreneur of himself [and herself]'" (Foucault, 2008: 226). Foucault (2008: 225) described the neo-liberal shift as a critique of classical economics that characterized *homo œconomicus* as a 'partner of exchange' that required,

> an analysis in terms of utility of what he [sic] is himself, a breakdown of his behavior and ways of doing things, which refer, of course, to a problematic of needs, since on the basis of these needs it will be possible to describe or define, or anyway found, a utility which leads to the process of exchange.

Foucault (2008: 221–2) argued that neo-liberalism capitalized on the ambiguity and 'abstractions' of *needs* which, in his view, ignored the "qualitative modulations" of labour. Instead, Foucault argued, neo-liberalism sought to capitalize on the qualitative

CHAPTER 6

modulations of labour, and specifically, to use them in relation to education policy in order to implement neo-liberal government practices at the level of the body.

Foucault (2008) claimed that the qualitative modulations of labour were evidenced through the choices labour made. Neo-liberalism, then, sought to capitalize on these choices. Importantly, neo-liberalism deregulated governmental systems in order to increase choice, which as Foucault (2008) wryly observed, were intimately linked to emerging post-war discourses on equality and freedom. Here, as Foucault (2008) noted, markets declared that they would free the state and free the self from government control.

While the concept of scarcity remained an integral feature to both pre- and post-war economics, neo-liberals capitalized on the equivocations of 'needs' to produce conceptions of *homo œconomicus*. Foucault (2008: 222) ventriloquized the neo-liberal logic of choice when he stated,

> [w]e have scarce means, [but] we do not have a single end or cumulative ends for which it is possible to use these means, but ends between which we must choose, and the starting point and general frame of reference for economic analysis should be the way in which individuals allocate these scarce means to alternative ends.

Foucault (2008) argued that neo-liberalism placed discussions of ends and means into the hands of *homo œconomicus* and away from the state. This shift was partly the result of replacing 'economy' – and shared ends – with 'catallaxy' – and different ends. *Homo œconomicus* now determined what was needed and what was not. This so-called democratization of needs "ensure[d] that the worker is not present in the economic analysis as an object – the object of supply and demand ... but as an active economic subject" (Foucault, 2008: 223). The shift from passive object to active subject characterized the neo-liberal shift on conceptions of the self. In education, this shift was evidenced in the emergence of educational markets in which families were responsible for selecting particular educational opportunities, or what we will discuss below as 'educational investments'.

HUMAN CAPITAL AS VOLUNTARY FORMATIONS OF THE SELF

> With what folds can I surround myself or how can I produce myself as subject?
> —Deleuze, 1988: 114

Historic conceptions of education policy that focused on producing 'human capital' were transformed into more contemporary technologies that economized the self, placing neo-liberal *homo œconomicus* into systems of entrepreneurial production (Foucault, 2008: 227). For our purposes, the shift from object to subject characterized how different conceptions of the self became different markets for different educational investments. Foucault (2008: 229) explained,

> The neo-liberals pose their problems and set out their new type of analysis. from the angle of. more or less voluntary formation of human capital in the course of individuals' lives. What does it mean to form human capital ... ? It means, of course, making what are called educational investments.

Foucault (2008: 231) noted that 'educational investments' were apparent through an economization of education policy that seeks innovations in the development of human capital, "that is to say, of the set of investments we have made at the level of man himself." Foucault's observation is a slightly different conception of education policy, whereas the prevalent 'human capital' discourse invariably enunciates conceptions of the self within incomplete and impoverished registers of the 'herd', or the more polite 'human capital stock' (OECD, 2011). Instead, Foucault's conception of education policy signals an emerging focus on discrete selves which develop innovations with/in themselves. Neo-liberal education policy, then, increases choices for a variety of necessarily innovative selves but still within particular markets and economies that enunciate available opportunities for self-creation.

Neo-liberal education policy sought markets for educational investments and thus altered prior notions of education policy that produced a workforce in relation to assessments of required human capital stock for the future. In 1979, Foucault presciently noted the wave of education policy reform about to occur throughout the 1980s and intensify into the 1990s.

> On the basis of this theoretical and historical analysis we can thus pick out the principles of a policy of growth which will no longer be simply indexed to the problem of the material investment of physical capital, on the one hand, and of the number of workers, [on the other], but a policy of growth focused precisely on one of the things that the West can modify most easily, and that is the form of investment in human capital. And in fact we are seeing the economic policies of all the developed countries, but also their social policies, as well as their cultural and *educational policies*, being orientated in these terms. (Foucault, 2008: 232, our emphasis)

While there is much more to be said about the neo-liberal shift of need, we pick up on the thematic that educational policy has been re-oriented away from a discourse of a nation-state conception of 'human capital' and towards discourses that sought specific entrepreneurial conceptions of the self. We note, however, that conceptions of the self and of specific human capital are entirely dependent on one another and articulated through education policy as contemporary values of choice, entrepreneurism, and, interestingly, equality and/or freedom (for example, the UK's so-called 'free school' movement; Miller, 2011). Resulting from this re-orientation, education policy is no longer interested in a liberal or public exchange of ideas, and certainly no longer interested, if ever, in developing democratic citizens (Brown,

2003). In a re-articulation of equality of opportunity, education policy now develops markets of care for entrepreneurial, innovative, and particular selves.

The Neo-Liberal Education Policies of Epimeleia Heautou

In contrast to an economic object, the neo-liberal subject is an "entrepreneur of himself, being for himself his own capital, being for himself his own producer, being for himself the source of [his] earnings" (Foucault, 2008: 226). Neo-liberal *homo œconomicus* is no longer a passive object of goods and services; instead, neo-liberal *homo œconomicus* is an active producer of capital. What does neo-liberal *homo œconomicus* produce? Foucault (2008: 226) answered,

> [w]ell, quite simply, he produces his own satisfaction. And we should think of consumption as an enterprise activity by which the individual, precisely on the basis of the capital he has at his disposal, will produce something that will be his own satisfaction.

We think 'she' and 'her' are implicated in this too. The key link in our argument is the relationship between the production of self-satisfaction and the practices of *epimeleia heautou*. The significance between self-satisfaction and care is illustrated by the activities of self-identification. In other words, *homo œconomicus* is faced with the challenge of identifying itself amidst a variety of (unequal and circumscribed) choices now available to it. Moreover, *homo œconomicus* is faced with identifying the requisite practices of care, which, as we have noted, are choices often equated with notions of freedom and equality. Dilts (2011: 143) argued likewise,

> [w]hat Foucault seems to be expressly attending to in the account of a subject formed through practices is the way in which freedom is only achieved through practices of the self that proceed from the 'rules, styles, and conventions' of a particular culture. To identify what practices constitute free practices requires an account of how some practices can be understood as ones that allow access to a self that is not sovereign, but which 'takes care of oneself' as a way of 'knowing oneself'. That is, the truth of a practice as a 'free' practice requires precisely an account of the specific rules and practices of a specific milieu, of the truth games or regimes of veridiction that are in play ...

We suggest that there are (at least) two ways to understand how self-satisfaction is related to self-care. The first is concerned with engaging in practices of care in relation to developing a particular self. The second understanding is concerned with developing the conditions, environments, or milieus to support particular educational investments.

Educational Investments: Caring for the Self

In the first sense, we posit that self-satisfaction is *an assessment regarding the uses of care techniques*. In relation to the explicit neo-liberal shift in governance, we measure ourselves and measure how well we have *produced-through-consumption self-satisfaction*. Indeed, as Foucault (1988a: 68) noted,

> the task of testing oneself, examining oneself, monitoring oneself in a series of clearly defined exercises, makes the question of truth – the truth concerning what one is, what one does, and what one is capable of doing – central to the formation of the ethical subject.

Underneath the constant examination of oneself lies an awareness – perhaps developing and certainly learned – of the care practices that produce satisfaction. As we noted earlier, practices of self-examination were designed through neo-liberal education policy when it promotes self-responsibility and freedom of choice within different performativist cultures in which the self is "subject to what might be regarded as a regime that involves observation, surveillance, and examination in the form of monitoring of learning, intervention, 'programmes', and assessments" (Foucault, 1982a: 50). Thus, as Foucault (1991: 5) noted, practices of *epimeleia heautou* appear invariably as educational investments into particular knowledges. He stated,

> [o]ne cannot care for the self without knowledge. The care for the self is of course knowledge of self but it is also the knowledge of a certain number of rules of conduct or of principles which are at the same time truths and regulations. To care for self is to fit one's self out with these truths.

Educational investments into these 'truths' denote the second sense in which self-satisfaction is related to care. In this second sense, self-satisfaction is designed as enterprising educational investments into knowledge of care practices. Significantly, however, *homo œconomicus* has the ability to develop specific milieus (i.e., schools) to support the requisite knowledges of the self. In other words, school choice policy provides *homo œconomicus* means to produce the milieus with which *epimeleia heautou* can be practised.

For instance, charter and magnet schools in the United States and Alberta, Canada have specialized curricula that are marketed to produce mathematicians, engineers, health science workers, athletes, and so forth. Human capital is differentiated along specific economic sectors (i.e., knowledge workers, symbolic analysts, Olssen & Peters, 2005) and creates unequal subject positions across strategic forms of self-knowledge and requisite practices of care.

However, school choice policies now further provide a sanctuary for selves that have been historically marginalized, threatened, or excluded (Rofes & Stulberg, 2004).

Marginalized ethno-cultural groups can utilize school choice policies to develop schools and curricula on specific conceptions of the self and its care (Rofes & Stulberg, 2004). Scholars have argued that school choice could provide opportunities to develop ethno-culturally – specific curricula for Native Hawai'ians (M. Buchanan & Fox, 2004), Native Americans (Belgarde, 2004), African Americans (Shujaa, 1988, 1992; Yancey, 2004), Black Canadians (Dei, 2005), and Aboriginal Canadians (Archibald, Rayner, & Big Head, 2011).

The production of self-satisfaction and the way this production relates to practices of *epimeleia heautou* are intimately related to a *politics of self-choice*, which is articulated through ideas of self-worth, self-determination, and self-respect. In a sociological sense, this politics may be one of belonging; a kind of politics that seeks practices of *epimeleia heautou* that are 'more like me' (inclusion), and entirely linked to avoiding practices of *epimeleia heautou* that are 'practised by them' (exclusion).

Because the self has been racialized, a *politics of self-choice* certainly produces a *politics of self-separation* (Dei, 2005) that pivots on determining who has the authority, perhaps copyright (Gilroy, 2000), to place parents and their children within particular milieus to practise discrete forms of care (Webb & Gulson, 2011). This has led some scholars to argue that education and economic policies that promote ethnic identity schools are a new force in educational politics that is simultaneously 'progressive' and 'conservative' in promoting educational choice and school competition (Pedroni, 2006).

In the end, neo-liberal education policy can be understood as a politics of *no longer waiting*. *Homo œconomicus* is the active subject in the creation of the self and no longer the passive – and waiting – object in juridical, legislative, and ideological debates about equal education. Finally, if 'education levels' continue to be an indicator for human capital, and eventually economic mobility, then the production of self-satisfaction and its relation to practices of *epimeleia heautou* are particular self-investments into uncertain and unequal futures.

THE APORIAS OF NEO-LIBERAL EQUALITY IN EDUCATION

We have argued that practices of care are intimately connected to neo-liberal entrepreneurialism and, curiously, neo-liberal equality. In its simplest form, our argument noted how practices of care coalesce into forms of consumption produced by, and for, discrete and innovative selves. We argued that these practices are a uniquely educational phenomenon once policy is used to increase choices of the self and its care through the development of choice schools.

We conclude by discussing three themes, noted in the introduction above, that emerge from the neo-liberal education policies of *epimeleia heautou*:

- that the care of the self is predicated on *a priori* notions of the self (in other words, who or what contain these truths of the self? Are schools the contemporary oracles of the self?);

THE NEO-LIBERAL POLICIES OF EPIMELEIA HEAUTOU

- that the care of the self is practised in relation to unequal and provisionally finite educational markets; and
- that the education policies of *epimeleia heautou* enunciate aporias of neo-liberal equality when choice schools practise care for a self that has been historically marginalized.

We draw upon an example of Afrocentric schooling in Toronto, Canada to illustrate this final point.

Our conclusion is framed as two 'aporias' of neo-liberal education equality in which these three themes operate together. Importantly, our conclusion is not an answer or solution to these aporias – for instance, an attempt to resolve such conundrums – and, instead, our conclusion is a concerted problematization of these conditions, as we argued for in Chapter Three.

We believe the aporias of neo-liberal equality cannot be resolved with a nostalgic return to democratic schooling because we contend that choice policies and the resulting catallaxy are the default mechanism in most discussions about curriculum, schools, ideas of the self and its care (Brown, 2003; Vázquez-Arroyoa, 2008). Equally vexing, if not more so, is the aporia concerning the role capitalism has in equal schooling for historically marginalized subjects (see also, Gerrard, 2013; Mirza & Reay, 2000). Our goal is to better understand these problems through a discussion of how neo-liberalism refigures ideas of equality, the self, and education policy.

The Aporia of a Freer Self

As credo, *epimeleia heautou* predicates an object – a self – to care for. What is this object, this self? The aporia of a freer self is, ironically, evidenced in the choices that regulate the self. The self may be 'freer' to choose its own care but the extent to which it is 'free' or 'completely emancipated' is questionable given the unequal distribution of political, social, economic, and educational choices. Instead, the regulating practices of *epimeleia heautou* produce a 'relation of oneself to oneself' (Foucault, 1988a). Foucault (1988a: 64–65) explained,

> [t]he common goal of these practices of the self, allowing for the differences they present, can be characterized by the entirely general principle of conversion of the self. in the activities that one ought to engage in, one had best keep in mind that the chief objective one should set for oneself is to be sought within oneself, in the relation of oneself to oneself.

The aporia of a freer self maintains a relation of oneself to oneself. *Homo œconomicus* may select more of its own care, but in other words, *homo œconomicus* selects more of its own folds, its own discipline.

The aporia of a freer self is largely determined *a priori* and regulated within appropriate identifications, metrics, and performances (Butler, 1990; Gilroy, 2000).

A priori conceptions of the self are identified prior to practices of *epimeleia heautou*, or perhaps, simultaneously identified, whereas practices of care are designed to produce a specific self. Nevertheless, *a priori* conceptions of the self are a significant factor in the development of choice schools and illustrate subtle differences between conceptions of the self that are not given, or already known. In contrast, for example, Foucault (1982b: 237) argued that "from the idea that the self is not given to us, I think that there is only one practical consequence: we have to create ourselves as a work of art."

A priori conceptions of the self signal many different micropolitical choices of, and for, self-development. Indeed, choices of the self, or 'qualitative modulations', are expressed through the consumption of particular educational experiences, educational investments, educational epistemologies, and educational 'truths'. If particular practices of care cannot be obtained within current educational economies, *homo œconomicus* is now freer, or perhaps more 'policy-enabled', to develop specialized schools and curricula for desired practices and expected 'truths'.

The aporia of a freer self is certainly not an exploration of possible or 'new' subjectivities. Nor is the aporia of a freer self utopian escapes or transcendental flights of the self. Instead, the aporia of a freer self maintains schooling as the disciplinary and reproductive machine that it always has been. But now, *neo-liberal schooling is the disciplinary and reproductive machine of self-selected investments.*

If returns to democratic education are troubled by neo-liberalism, we wonder what returns to self-identity will produce through school choice policies.

- Will 'culture' no longer be a process but simply a commodity used in school marketing campaigns?
- Who speaks for specific selves, and who does not?
- Can there be conceptions of the self outside of educational markets? This question identifies racialized catallaxies produced in neo-liberal education policy and the possibilities of educational eugenics.
- Will it even be conceivable to imagine a self outside of neo-liberal education investments?

In the end, the aporia of a freer self remains deeply indebted to *a priori* constructions of the self and indebted to the disciplining practices of schools. In this sense, the aporia of a freer self is a statement by *homo œconomicus* about how discipline is now applied equally.

The Aporia of Education Policy Equality

The aporia of neo-liberal equality is evidenced through school choice policies and self-selected investments in education. We agree with Foucault (2008) that educational policy seeks innovations of the self. However, and somewhat different from Foucault's conception of education policy, we note that choice policies provide the self with new forms of material from which to develop educational investments.

In other words, *homo œconomicus* is able to develop the milieus to support requisite forms of care.

Education policy is not just a technology that seeks innovations of the self; now, education policy provides *homo œconomicus* entrepreneurial opportunities to develop the very material to support those educational investments. Thus, neo-liberal education policies enunciate ideas of choice, freedom, and equality that invite *homo œconomicus* to develop milieus for specific subject positions. The use of neo-liberal education policies are ways of using one's entrepreneurial freedom, of making one's educational investment, of enacting one's self-responsibility, and of taking care of one's existence. Neo-liberal education policy tells us that this is a way to survive – *the fourth fold of policy geophilosophy* (see Chapter Five).

Importantly, the aporia of education policy equality is based on separation by choice. George Dei (2005), when discussing issues of segregation in relation to Afrocentric schooling, noted that "there is a meaningful difference, however, between forced segregation and separation by choice" (np). Dei's (2005) notion about separation by choice acknowledges the stark racialized separations that have operated covertly and disproportionately for particular groups. Thus, a politics of self-separation provides a register to articulate inequalities that have not been dealt with sufficiently. Within this politics of self-separation, *homo œconomicus* is freer to leave the lethal racisms of liberalism (Webb & Gulson, 2011).

More importantly, school choice policies provide mechanisms to address historic inequalities, at least in the sense of separating oneself from these histories. School choice policies certainly will not redress racisms; however, school choice policy does provide *homo œconomicus* with opportunities to speak for itself and to take responsibility for itself against persistent and historical educational inequalities. It does mean, however, keeping the racism of liberalism, by entering the new terrains of neoliberal racisms (Goldberg, 2009; Gulson, 2011). The price for equality, however, is the continuation of racialized separation – which is entirely related to the kinds of spatial politics we discussed in Chapters Four and Five.

Dei's (2005) ideas about self-separation raise questions about the authority, and perhaps the legitimacy, to develop particular milieus to practise discrete forms of care. For instance, who is able to lay claim to particular practices of *epimeleia heautou*? To some extent, we believe this question is a red herring. Educational markets ostensibly decide who is able to lay claim to particular practices of *epimeleia heautou*. Enrolments in choice schools, for instance, will determine who speaks for whom, and who is intelligible in the market. This is also to note that a liberal politics of representation "conserve or prolong an established historical order, or … establish a historical order which already calls forth in the world the forms of its representation" (Deleuze, 2004: 53). What seems more important to us when addressing the aporia of education policy equality is how one cares for and maintains the separations that provide entrepreneurial opportunities for the self in the first place. If liberal notions of equality are articulated through self-separations, then maintenance of these spaces must be cared for – the self depends on these separate spaces.

CHAPTER 6

In this sense, the aporia of education policy equality is admittedly a fine line – a line that must be constantly demarcated and cared for. A relatively straightforward way to care for the spatial separations is to essentialize *a priori* conceptions of the self. More importantly, and more insidiously, a straightforward way to maintain the spatial separations is to characterize 'other' conceptions of the self as inferior. For instance, in its most impoverished form – indeed, inhumane form – a politics of self-separation through school choice policies has produced characterizations of selves as a "feral underclass" (Miller, 2011). This utterance is produced when school choice policies ally themselves with principles of neo-liberalism that deliberately distort notions of freedom and equality – as in the case of UK's 'free school' policy initiatives (Miller, 2011).

Impoverished characterizations of a subject are produced as a way to maintain spatial separations and legitimate particular *a priori* conceptions of the self against other conceptions – 'them' and 'us'. Impoverished characterizations of a self are also produced when policy makers, economists, and politicians do not honestly discuss how the economy (really, catallaxy) is segmented: markets are not 'free' and 'self-regulating', but more importantly for our purposes, the consumption of self-satisfaction is not produced equally (Harcourt, 2011).

We imagine we could cite Alan Greenspan and his 'partial error' with regards to the failures of deregulation, but we don't want to give the impression that this confession signals anything close to an exoneration that places us on the 'road to educational recovery' (Andrews, 2008: B1). Again, the 'global cultural educational economy' and its privileging of the 'school' and the coercion of bodies are not the trajectories we believe we should be headed along (Chapter 1). The marketization of choice schools as 'free' is disingenuous and simply false. Again, there are costs to self-separation and these costs will be paid disproportionately depending on which practices of *epimeleia heautou* are selected. This is the clearest example of the fourth fold of education policy that we can think of, in which an affirmative biopolitics is mobilised (see Esposito, 2008). *How one thinks of death, existence, and survivability are central to understanding neo-liberal and biopolitical catallaxies in contemporary education policy.*

Further, the 'choices' of self-development that neo-liberal education policy promotes are made within local and global economic contingencies that provide unequal opportunities for self development. For instance, the politics of self-choice are practised within school districts with wildly unequal budgets and within communities with unequal resources to capitalize on self-choosing. Nevertheless, neo-liberal education policy is a problematic opportunity for some groups to equalize schooling for curricular interests that have been historically marginalized, threatened, or excluded. This statement might strike readers as an irony. Other readers might read such a statement as a kind of complicity in, or apology for, neo-liberal conservatism. Regardless, we note that for some diasporic groups this statement is an accurate description (even if they might not phrase it in such a way).

Thus, the aporia of education policy equality is no longer invested in debates around democratic ideologies. School choice policy invests in the production of different selves, by the self, for the self. Some groups are no longer waiting for the ideological debates of equality to be resolved so that educational investments can be made. In the end, such individualization and self-responsibilizations must confront the very forces that produce it. In its (re)creation, the self constantly positions itself within market principles and spatial separations that provide its very articulation. It must care for these separations because neo-liberal educational equality depends on market separations.

PART 3

CONNECTIONS

POLICY GEOPHILOSOPHY

How education policy positions and constitutes objects and subjects through emergent and adaptive arrangements that simultaneously influence how policy is sensed, embodied, and enacted.

This section works with:

- *Ambient fear*, noting how the affective registers of policy making are used, but in disproportionate ways depending on different representations of race and religion.
- *The city*, through a rethinking of representational conceptions of space and noting what new set of relations are produced when non-representational conceptions of space are used in relation to schooling and race and ethnicity.
- *Policy geophilosophy*, and what it can and cannot do.

CHAPTER 7

AMBIENT FEAR, ISLAMIC SCHOOLS AND THE AFFECTIVE GEOGRAPHIES OF RACE AND RELIGION

"We Had to Hide that We're Muslim All the Time."

This chapter is intended to be an example of what we have been talking about with regard to an education *policy geophilosophy* analysis. Perhaps, this chapter is even an enactment of such an analysis. This chapter, however, is not one of a 'model', 'precedent', or 'exemplar'. We do not employ the idea of an 'example' in order to provide a kind of paradigmatic tracing of some of the ideas that we have previously discussed. Our idiosyncrasies should not be the basis of anything, let alone a 'template' or 'recipe'. Moreover, the chapter might be quite weak depending on the evaluative criteria that you may or may not use to determine the strength of analysis.

The chapter does, however, use the concepts of *policy prolepsis* and *intension* deliberately as discussed in Chapters Four and Five, and in relation to an analysis characterized as a *policy problematization* that we discussed in Chapter Three. We pause throughout this chapter and indicate where these concepts are operating. We also note our construction of *policy apparitions* and the circulation of *policy phantasms* that emerge within the uncertainty produced in an *ambient fear* of neo-liberal education policy, or, in other words, the ambient fear enacted in neo-liberal raciologies and neo-liberal non-secularizations (school choice policies, in particular). Our policy problematization then – which is not designed to 'solve' anything, but rather understand the conditions the give rise to a particular problematic – takes up the ontological challenges related to ideas of race and religion. This last clause indicates both the fragility and difficulties of positing practices as part of an ontological assemblage (Mol, 2002).

The materialities of race and religion (objects, if you will) are not what constitutes a *policy geophilosophy* either; instead, these particular materialities are simply of our collective interests, and partly due to our contention that these materialities have been overlooked in relation to other preferred materialities that also produce education policy, like gender and social class. Paul Gilroy (2005: 7) argued that race has become an absent ontology in analyses due to a 'quiet period' of colonization, or in his words,

[i]nterest cooled as those [colonial] conflicts subsided, and at that point, would-be-practitioners of historical ontology became wary of both race and

CHAPTER 7

racism. Most opted to pursue their radical critiques of power and identity in calmer waters, usually where the creation of gender and sexual differences could be explored safely without trespassing on the political sensibilities of racial and ethnic minorities who did not appreciate their particularity being deconstructed and made to appear absurd. Critical reflections were easiest when the elaboration of cheap antihumanist positions was unlikely to be disrupted by any inconvenient clamour from the vulnerable groups whose rights had become entangled with demands for recognition as human beings in an unjust world that denied them even that protection.

While it is debatable which ontologies are 'safer' to examine, our problematization does provide analyses of *difference* and *representation* that we argued characterize a *policy geophilosophy*. And, our problematization also locates us in these kinds of analyses. It would be facile to simply state our racial and secular positions in attempts to locate ourselves within our analysis – the preferred practices of *policy scientificity 2.0,* including some of our previous work.

Instead, we treat ourselves as additional objects (White, agnostic/atheist, males) within registers of *difference* and *representation* that mark us in particular ways – and in ways that we work against. Again, alterity is a two-way street. Alterity is also delimited (conveniently) when defining it *a priori* within the humanist tropes that animate a liberal educational project within a rapidly encroaching (really, arrived) neo-liberal catallaxy of racial and religious differences and representations. Our focus on material, then, assists our problematization work within and against the entangled discourses of liberal and neo-liberal education policy.

Finally, even within the analytic contestations over policy objects (i.e., 'gender', 'class', 'race', etc.) – the 'ontological politics' we discussed earlier (Law, 2004) – very few education policy analyses examine the geographies of these materials as a concerted problematization. These materials are simply posited, avoided, or neatly (dis)counted in aggregate forms within registers of 'criticality' that continue to employ instrumental preferences in policy analyses as a form of quantifiable social justice. Again, it's just a matter of getting *your* epistemologies, evidence (i.e., 'data'), and commitments aligned.

Instead, this chapter provides readers an illustration of material, policy, and bodily enactments. As such, this chapter encourages others to problematize the conditions from which materialities emerge and operate within education policy. These enmeshed, multiple and non-representational materialities produce an array of policy enactments within the mutations of liberal and neo-liberal education projects. There is much work to do, and no more time in our opinion for techno-rational solutions that reify policy materials, and the associated practices, that are independent, singular and representational.

THE RELATIONAL GEOGRAPHIES OF RELIGION AND RACE

We argue, in this chapter, that urban politics around the establishment of Islamic schooling is understood through the geographies of race and religion, and specifically through affective geographies of threat and fear. This spatial analysis allows us to conceptualise the development of Islamic schools and the connected role that urban policy-making has with education policy and politics. While the chapter has an empirical focus on Sydney, Australia, we contend that we are identifying local, transversal, and heterarchical spatial-educational politics; again, "everything is political, but every politics is simultaneously a macropolitics and a micropolitics" (Deleuze & Guattari, 1987: 213). Furthermore, our identifications of the local, transversal, and heterarchical repudiate the supposed neutrality of market mechanisms in education that support the establishment of government-funded religious schools.

Over the past thirty years, there has been a virulent urban politics surrounding the provision of government-funded religious schooling in suburban south-western Sydney. We illustrate how race and religion constitute contestations of urban space around the establishment of government-funded Islamic schools. In the previous chapter, we argued that neo-liberal education policy depends on, and thus, creates, market separations for particular educational investments. In this chapter, we show how these separations are produced in education policy through fear of the racialized other. We argue these contestations are unique to specific groups, and fail to emerge when other types of government-funded religious schools, such as Christian schools, are proposed and established in Sydney. The politics surrounding Islamic schools reveals a coded urban politics, and geographies of fear and difference (England & Simon, 2010) pertaining to Islamophobia and racialisation. We argue that these codes can be understood by paying attention to the ambiance of racialised-religious fears produced, in part, through the apparently contradictory policies of government-funding of non-secular education.

To begin, we posit a relational geography of race and religion, with a focus on links between race and Islamophobia. Next, we provide detail on Muslim residents and Islamic schools in the local government area of Bankstown in south-western Sydney. We examine the role of religion in the management of urban space, illustrated through local government decisions concerning the rejection of Islamic schools. The penultimate section draws on the idea of "ambient fear", a concept developed by Papastergiadis (2012), to demonstrate how local urban and educational politics may be connected to various forms of Islamophobia, racialisation and everyday disorientations associated with encountering difference.

For our purposes, policy and its meanings are indeterminate, contingent, paradoxical, contradictory, and disorienting. Policy 'interpretations' are the enactments within attempts to control affective registers of meaning, if not, attempts to control affects themselves (see Chapter Four).

Discursive and Somatic Forms of Racial Representation

Our problematization focuses on the power relations that make both space and race a contingent accomplishment (Nayak, 2004, 2006). We are concerned with the performative constitution of race; in which designations of race and ethnicity, such as 'Black', 'White', 'Lebanese', are more than descriptions of *a priori* categories and identities. These designations "are part of on-going processes that create or *discursively constitute* these categories and the people allocated to them" (Gillborn & Youdell, 2009: 181). The performative aspect of race and ethnicity is made meaningful when these categorisations are mobilised and enacted through discourses that are intelligible in reference to "enduring relations of discursive, productive power" (Gillborn & Youdell, 2009: 181) and in relation to specific *policy materialities* or *policy somatics* that interact with these discursive categories. As we will show shortly, the particular policy materialities and somatics that we examine emerge within school choice policies, and in relation to the biopolitical catallaxies that we identified in previous chapters.

We are interested in how the phenomenon of Islamophobia interacts, rather than being conflated, with race and racism (Dunn, Klocker, & Salabay, 2007; Dwyer, 1993). This interaction occurs when religion moves between attachment to ethnicity – and thus to different cultural and geographical notions of belonging – to racialisation of the 'Other'. Islamophobia is based on assumptions and reductive characterisations, on stereotypes, about Islam and Muslim people; notably Islam is both Other as civilization and Other as religion.

Islamophobia, arguably, remains separate from racism as it is not devoid of a biological or somatic premise for pernicious action, being Muslim is not constituted as a genetic disposition (Miles & Brown, 2003). What is argued to make Islamophobia unique, however, is the combining of nationality, religion and politics, that is "frequently produced in Orientalist, Islamophobic and racist discourses. In contrast, most religions are not represented in an amalgam with terrorism, or even ethnic and national distinctiveness" (Miles & Brown, 2003: 164). The turn to race is made when a religion, and subsequently a religious group and/or individual is "seen as representing a racialised Other" (p. 165).

Here, then, a *policy prolepsis* – the representation of a thing as existing before it actually does or did so – emerges within the indeterminate, contingent, paradoxical, contradictory, and disorienting spaces of alterity. As we will show shortly, the specific spaces of alterity are produced through neo-liberal education policies (i.e., school choice) and the prolepses that emerge are circulated within these markets. We examine the collective affects that are produced in the constitution of both Islam as object and Muslim people as bodies. Anderson (2014: 4) gets at the heart of our analysis concerning how collective affects such as urban fear and Islamophobia are constituted, specifically, "how do collective affects take place so that they become part of the conditions for life?"

Racialising Islam: The Spatial and Somatic Unfolding of Biopolitics

The racialisation of Islam in Australia has rested on assumptions of Muslim homogeneity connected to geographical regions, such as the 'Middle East', and ethnicities, such as 'Arab' (Dunn et al., 2007). As Keith (2005: 9) suggests,

> race making sits between historically complex demographic trajectories and highly spurious systems of categorisation. Temporalities and spatialities are consequently not just the context of these processes, they are instead a constitutive feature of them.

In this we can see that race and space are contested, dynamic and temporal (Neely & Samura, 2011); *unfolding* in reference to contestation over religious space in particular areas of cities. This unfolding of religious space also enfolds or enacts particular bodies; bodies constituted through the four folds of policy that territorializes the self, politics, scientificities, and conceptualizations of existence and death/after-life. This unfolding of religious space, then, occurs within the intensions and localisations of transnational racisms that produces a racial-spatial biopolitics. This biopolitics entails the ways,

> [b]odily traits and 'ethnic' cultures are becoming the basis upon which peoples are allocated rights, identities, a place in the world…, at the expense of other modes of marking community and negotiating difference. (Amin, 2010: 10)

The somatic aspect is important as accessories and clothing become not merely material accoutrements but citational objects that ostensibly operate as both intensional markings and intensional threats. And, it is Muslim women wearing headscarves, Burqas, and Hijab, who bear the brunt of perceived threats, for "[t]he contemporary racialization of Muslims in Australia draws heavily upon observable elements of culture" (Dunn et al., 2007: 567).

While men's beards may be somatic markers-objects that conflate Lebanese Christian men with Lebanese Muslim men, both captured by the notion of the 'Arab' other, a woman's headscarf is simultaneously performative of Islam and interpreted as incontrovertible evidence of unassimilable difference. This performing materiality maintains disproportionate schooling, for many Islamic schools require female students to wear school uniforms with long sleeve pants and shirts, and Hijab. Bodies are the geographical and material markers of the distinctiveness of the Islamic school and bearers of a school's distinctiveness while coding gendered significations within and outside of schools.

CHAPTER 7

Muslim People and the South-Western Suburbs of Sydney

The south-western suburban areas of Sydney, approximately 25 kilometres from the Central Business District, has been the 'receiving' area for multiple generations of migrants (Collins & Poynting, 2000). This area has been characterised "as the 'other side' of a social boundary, one which contains several groups of society's 'others'" (Powell, 1993: xviii), and an area demonised in public discourses that conflate crime, poverty and ethnicity (Poynting, 2000).

The south-west, including the local government area of Bankstown, has historically high proportions of Muslim people – from a variety of geographical and ethnic backgrounds, with the largest proportion being Australian born residents – relative to national population and other local government areas (Saeed, 2003; Wise & Ali, 2008). In Bankstown in 1986, 10.3% (5,958 residents) of the population was Muslim. In 2001, 11.8% (19,499) was Muslim with a jump to 19.1% (34,796 residents) in 2011 (Bankstown City Council, 2012).

Key cultural institutions like mosques have been established in Bankstown, along with government-funded private Islamic elementary and secondary schools. In Australia parental choice of schools is the paramount policy framework in both federal and state government sectors, and Australia has one of the highest rates of government funding for private schools in the OECD (Musset, 2012). Of these choice schools, 94% are religious and over the past ten years, Islamic schools, along with small Christian schools – non-Anglican or Catholic – are among the fastest growing (Buckingham, 2010). Nonetheless, there are not many Islamic schools in Australia, 41 out of over 2000 government-funded private schools. Islamic schools educate approximately 20% of all Muslim students in Australia, with the majority of schools located in western and south western Sydney; twenty-three in all, with six in Bankstown.

Some of these proposed and established schools have been opposed at the local government level (Al-Natour, 2010). Government-funded private schools, in addition to being accredited by educational authorities, must gain development approval at a local government level. This is the only role for local government in the process of educational provision in Australia – aspects such as curriculum policy, overall accreditation, funding and so forth are the purview of other levels of government. All religious schools can receive government funding if they fulfil the requirements set down by state curriculum boards, and meet the requirements of local government through land-use approvals (Bugg & Gurran, 2011).

There is, however, no educational policy framework that advises local government on how to deal with development applications for private schools within the broader provision of education (Bugg & Gurran, 2011). In the absence of articulated frameworks for the establishment of schools in local government areas, urban policy becomes *de facto* and *ad hoc* education policy. The contestation over and decision making about urban space, thus, becomes significant for the provision of education and Islamic schools, for "culture is not simply contested within particular territories but is spatially as well as socially constituted" (Dwyer, 1993: 143).

THE MANAGEMENT OF RELIGIOUS, EDUCATIONAL (SUBURBAN) SPACE

The political configuration of the city allows certain kinds of individual and group identity to become visible. The technological arrangements through which patterns of identification emerge and transform ... (the planning of its urban form) become likewise implicated in the political constitution of urban cultures.
—Keith, 2005: 42

Planning decisions are not deterministic, but as Keith (2005: 40) contends, they may well be "inescapable": "There is no world untouched by the multiple regimes of power that structure the regulation of domesticity, labour, public and private life and the rights of the citizen". It is the very mundaneness of this power that leads to *"the banality of government"* (Keith, 2005: 40). Again, for our purposes, the 'multiple regimes of power' operate and enact difference and representation in ways that territorialize subjects/objects within the folds of the self, conflicting scientificities, and images of existence and death/after-life.

The regimes of power are also intensionalized in cities, and urban policy constitutes space as part of governing activities that manage space. As such, governmental intervention requires that "its spaces of intervention are not merely the sites of this governmental practice, but, first and foremost, its outcomes" (Dikeç, 2007: 280). Part of these outcomes concern the ordering and policing of racial spaces (Mitchell, 2000). In cases that reject Islamic school applications, the ordering and policing of race function as governmental interventions into the convergence of race and religion, and thereby, an ontological politics about the objects of reification vis-à-vis space.

Suburban Politics as a Proxy for Ontological Politics

Opposition to mosques and Islamic schools has intensified in Sydney's west over the past ten years or so (Dunn, 2001). This opposition, however, has a lineage back to the 1980s in Bankstown. The first Islamic school established in Sydney was *Al Noori Muslim Primary School*, founded by a small group of mothers, including a Muslim convert from a white, middle class Christian background. The school was opened in the backyard of a house, moving to a hall on a main road, and back into private homes. In the 1980s, like now, to be accredited and registered as a school required land use approval from a local government (council). As Adeeba (pseudonym), a Muslim female involved in founding the school, stated, the school's application to open was repeatedly rejected by councils in south-western Sydney,

CHAPTER 7

> Now the difficulty we had was we couldn't get any council to give us approval for any property ... Every council we would go to would say 'not here'... and we couldn't get funding, any sort of funding until we got council approval ... We just had to keep on moving and fighting to get approval, and we didn't have much [sic] funds. We were a group of mothers, a voluntary association ...

A local government level can only reject development applications on the grounds of amenity, such as land use, suitability of dwelling, traffic and parking concerns – the last especially significant for schools. In the case of Al Noori, the founders kept the school open without council approval, and thus, without registration. The school was moved nine times before finally being approved. Adeeba stated,

> To prepare an application was extensive ... we asked the council. They always rejected you on traffic grounds initially, that was usually the way they would knock you out [of the planning process].

In June 2007, twenty years after Al Noori was first proposed, an application proposed the establishment of the Al Amanah School, a 1200 student Islamic school, to be built next to an existing public secondary school. Bankstown council rejected this development application and an appeal was made to have this decision reviewed. Rejected planning applications can be appealed and are heard in the Land and Environment Court, a court of appeal for planning issues in New South Wales. In the hearing over the rejection of the Al Amanah School, a variety of reasons were given by Bankstown council including:

> Traffic and parking; Noise; Ecology; Character, scale and design; The site is too small; Social impact; Excessive impervious areas; Excessive cut and fill. (*Mohamad el Dana vs Bankstown City Council*, 2008: Point 10)

In the cases of both Al Noori and Al Amanah, twenty years apart, the outcome of rejecting development approval on similar grounds of urban amenity, elide other more complex processes around the contestation and negotiation of urban space and about what planning outcomes/objects are legitimate (Bugg & Gurran, 2011; Hackworth & Stein, 2012). At Bankstown, what perhaps is being managed through local government is multiculturalism; even issues of traffic in reference to the proposed schools are concerns tied up with cultural relations in suburbia.

While government-funded, private religious schools are common in Australia, controversy about the establishment of new religious schools has focused only on Islamic schools, despite many other religious schools such as Greek Orthodox and Anglican schools being proposed and established in western Sydney over the past thirty years. In the case of the rejection of Al Amanah School by Bankstown council, the magistrate in the Land and Environment Court noted:

> Throughout the hearing there was an unacknowledged presence in the courtroom: a topic of which, I suspect, everyone was aware, but which was not discussed because the discussion would have been too uncomfortable. That

topic was whether the council would have raised quite so many contentions as it did if the application had been for an Anglican school? Would, for example, a social impact statement have been required? (*Mohamad el Dana vs Bankstown City Council*, 2008: Point 46).

This issue of an absence of controversy concerning the opening of non-Islamic schools seems to be broader than merely the case of Al Amanah. In relation to a general question about how decisions are made on schools and planning decisions by council, and why it seems that there has not been similar attention paid to non-Islamic schools, Joe (pseudonym), a local politician, identified the possible role of religion in decision making.

Joe: Most of the other schools, that have been [approved] in the past everybody [on council], falls over backwards to make sure it happens ... anything they want approved it will just go through ... they sign off on it.
Interviewer: Why is that the case?
Joe: I think predominantly because ... [local politicians are] Christians, you know what I mean. When you've got an [Islamic] organisation that preaches to their people that we're all infidels and we've got to be got rid of ... that puts a bit of a blank in your mind.

Proposals over Islamic schools, while dealt with by councils as neutral – in process and as ostensive outcome – are planning issues imbued with residual and future encounters with difference (Bugg & Gurran, 2011). Joe noted that issues of race and religion were not discussed directly in local government meetings over planning decisions about Islamic schools. He stated,

[But] there's a ... perception that ... the Muslim's are, they're different, but there's a perception ... with some people that they're not good for our community. But I don't find that ... I mean ... they're no different to anyone else, you know. It's just the attitude – [Muslim people] get this attitude from their bloody clerics, and I think that's where a lot of the problems .... But you know, we've got a couple of, a few Muslims running for council, and they're some characters, even the women, they're really good, they're funny bastards, they don't take a backward step, they're on the attack right from the start. And that's what worries people, they're on ... they attack. But once you sit down and have a talk with them ... they're not bad people.

Joe both repudiates and reinforces the racialisation and racism (and gender) regarding the status of Muslim people in Australia. He exhibits precisely how lapses and contradictions challenge any claims to neutrality of planning. Islamic schools can, therefore, be opposed through council planning decisions on the basis of difference. Further, these decisions are occluded by claims that opposition is on neutral grounds of increased traffic flow or disputes over appropriate land use and zoning concerns.

The ostensibly neutral management of space risks both simplifying and misrepresenting the complexity of race and religion in the of oppositional practices to Islamic schools. At worst, the so-called neutral management of space perpetuates a colour-blind or naive diversity discourse in spatial-educational policy and politics. In this next section, we argue that this neutral management occludes prolepsis, in which possible objects (schools) are sensed as part of marketized education policy and planning processes.

ISLAMIC SCHOOLS AND THE GEOGRAPHIES OF AMBIENT FEAR

Urban geographers have examined "how fear shapes cities and those within them" (England & Simon, 2010: 202), with a focus on fear as activity or process rather than object. We are interested in tracing "how affects emerge from and express specific relational configurations, whilst also themselves becoming elements within those formations" (Anderson, 2014: 11). In this section we examine how the management of urban and, in turn, religious educational spaces can be re-articulated through reference to what Papastergiadis (2012) calls 'ambient fear', a fear generated in a post-9/11 world of new forms of terrorism and associated state violence. In the modern state, migrants are constituted as a 'problem' that has "always been cast in terms of the challenge to either convert them into national citizens, or keep them out" (Papastergiadis, 2012: 41).

This 'problem' is a psycho-geographic fear which permeates and pervades contemporary life post-9/11 in countries like the US, Australia, Canada, and England, and is a fear connected to the "the invisibility of the intimate enemy" (Papastergiadis, 2012: 24). This "[a]mbient fear is a kind of dread that has become so widespread that its sources appear to be both unlocatable and ubiquitous" (p. 24). This shifts the discussion of fear from the notion of an entity located in individual subjectivity to provide it with a social function, or we suggest in the case of managing space, with a socio-spatial-material function, and the circulation of *policy apparitions* and *policy phantasms* that emerge and fold subjects/objects within such an ambiance.

We discussed how fear can function as a *policy prolepsis* in Chapter Four, a circulation of ubiquitous affect that, in effect, becomes a technology to mobilize education policy-making and policy enactments in particular ways – the affective manipulation of manufactured crises. Here, we demarcate this particular genus with the affective species of a *policy apparition* and a *policy phantasm* that attempts to articulate both the fear and its invisibility that Papastergiadis (2012) discussed. Thus, *policy apparitions* arrange Islamic schools in Sydney in ways that are not afforded the status of crisis – as the Mayor of Bankstown noted in the epigraph above. Decisions to oppose Islamic schools were not about race but about planning, and these schools are not only objects of techno-rational policy making, but objects with 'agency' and to be encountered as such (see Chapter Eight).

Managing Difference, Managing the Ontological

The refusal to acknowledge the role of race and the racialisation of religion in planning decisions reinforces the mythology of the neutral decision, while fear continues to circulate about the Muslim other. Ambient fear does not simply happen; it is produced, even as it is simultaneously naturalized. Ambient fear, structures urban policy decisions and local politics that is concerned with movement, mobility, and direction, premised on a cohering of unstated and prior (White, Christian) boundaries. This managing of difference, like other bio-political spatial orderings such as apartheid and genocides (Mitchell, 2000), aims to contain and ideally purify any racial or cultural 'contagions' that may be inadvertently or by design brought to bear on an otherwise undefiled, imaginary space of homogeneity, in order for life to continue (e.g., see Esposito, 2008). Planning regulations point to an ontological politics of objects by managing the spaces of the city. Thus, we note that (a) neo-liberal education policy is not some errant variant of policy-making, but a consistent and symbiotic practice with other forms of policymaking that order and arrange city space, and (b) racial ontologies are produced in this policy amalgam.

The managing of space is the purview of governmental practices, and practised by disorienting others with *policy phantasms* like traffic regulations. It occurs, furthermore, in mundane and micro-geographic ways. In the Land and Environment case on the rejected Al Amanah School, the presiding magistrate referred to submissions by residents of Bankstown. These submissions included idea of violence, 'exclusive' and 'inclusive' spaces, and the need for 'buffers' between cultural groups – namely the Islamic school and the public high school; nominally between homogeneity and heterogeneity, as discussed below.

> [A female resident involved with the Bass Hill High School's Parents and Citizens Associated] … foresaw conflict between the two schools and believes there should be a buffer between them …. (*Mohamad el Dana vs Bankstown City Council*, 2008: Point 12).

> The social impact of building an '*exclusive*' school next to an '*inclusive*' one has not been assessed …. [A] retired teacher … said he is concerned about the safety of the Bass Hill pupils. Both sets of children are likely to congregate at Bass Hill Plaza, will fight each other making the shopping centre a battleground. (*Mohamad el Dana vs Bankstown City Council*, 2008: Point 13).

In describing opposition to things like mosques and temples in the UK, Westwood and Williams (1997: 10) suggested the politics of these sites is connected to the disruption of belonging, and the disorientations associated with becoming,

> [i]nvariably, extant, usually white residents complain about noise and traffic, about people and the 'alien' presence constituting a politics of space which has nothing to say about faith and religion but is organised around discourses of

the nation, culture and belonging. Those who complain run against time and to an imagined homogeneity of the neighbourhood.

This notion of homogeneity, and the threat and promise of heterogeneity in the idea of the public (inclusive) versus the Islamic (exclusive) Al Amanah school, relates to the framing of culture as attachment to place. This is a residentialist argument that frames mobility as a problem if there are competing claims to cultural authority in the same place (e.g., F. Freidman, 1999; for critique Papastergiadis, 2012), and that same places such as Islamic schools are objects out of place.

The Biopolitics of Residentialism

A key assumption in the residentialist position is that 'original' culture is connected to a place. This would mean most national identities would be disqualified for "loss of certain boundaries has not meant the disappearance of cultural differences, but rather the appearance of new forms of mixture and more complex patterns of differentiation" (Papastergiadis, 2012: 134). The residentialist position, nonetheless, perhaps suggests that place is fixed and bounded, a type of abstract space that bounds social relations and identity formation. In Chapter Four, we discussed this conception of space as one that is non-relational, or a kind of container for events, actions, and the clear demarcation of subjects/objects. One result of this type of thinking is to invoke a nostalgic notion of place in the sense of boundaries (re)inscribing identities; a territorializing politics that reterritorializes against the perceived threats of deterritorializing efforts (Deleuze & Guattari, 1987).

Residentialism is, further, connected to ambivalence and fear of migrants, what Papastergiadis (2012) calls 'kinetophobia' – or fear of mobility. This takes a variety of forms, from racist scapegoating to the notion that there is a political and social body that will be defiled by newcomers, unless they are adequately integrated or ideally assimilated. Adeeba notes how in Australia in the 1980s,

> there was this whole feeling amongst a lot of educated White Australians that Muslims were not deserving of recognition and support in any area, and they represented a foreign race that needed to be assimilated into Australian .... So there was just this attitude, 'you have to be like us, you have to do things the way we do it here. Your way of doing things is not what we want here'. So ... it was a ... conglomeration of foreign culture, foreign look, and foreign religion that [was to be rejected].

Assimilation as the necessary bio-power technology of the 'White Australia' immigration policy has been revived, in the early 2000s, by commentators and politicians, who have made reference to Muslim people who have not assimilated into 'Australian ways', and who are just one step away from being racialised into terrorists (Dunn et al., 2007; Humphrey, 2005). In talking about Australia and Sydney in the 1980s, Adeeba explained that,

All the time Muslims have been seen as being not Australian, and a threat because of the religion, because of the culture, because of the dress and the whole concept of having schools that are not 'like us' was un-Australian. So, for example with [one school site] ... the lady who's now passed away and who had the house directly adjoining it and who was most affected because it ... went around the back of her property. She went on media saying ... that 'they're like cockroaches, sweep them off our back step and go back to the bush where they came from'.... It was very, very hard, very irrational, always. Very, very emotional and ... there were allegations that, that you know if our school went ahead you know Australia, that we were going to convert the whole of Australia, we're going to try and make all of Australia Muslim and, and why couldn't we learn how to be Australian in Australian schools ... that was, that's been ... the, the current all the way through.

Dehumanising references to Muslim people as 'cockroaches' exemplifies the link between race and Islamophobia and the complex connections between nation, religion and politics, along with the assumptions of cultural inferiority that parallel that of biological racism (Dunn et al., 2007; Miles & Brown, 2003). It is also a clear indication of how easily subjects/objects are produced and the performative work of representations. And as Berlant (2011: 19) posits, "affective responses may be said significantly to exemplify shared historical time". As Dwyer (1993) argued, following Said (1978), this further resonates with a construction of Islam as the 'other' of the white Christian nation. This is to apportion these schools with the marker of fundamentalism, which is mobilised as explanation and description. The construction of fundamentalism builds upon "a long legacy of Orientalist discourse which relies upon the oppositions of West and East, rationality versus irrationality, modernity and liberal tolerance versus fundamentalism" (Dwyer, 1993: 155).

HISTORIES OF FEAR AND CITY SEDIMENTATIONS

The ambient fear produced through Islamic schools, we suggest, reflects not only post-9/11 but also are remnants of pre-9/11 fears about Islam, often located in reference to Iran and Ayatollahs, the Palestinian Liberation Organisation, and general unease about Muslim people. There is historical continuity embedded in shifting yet resilient geographies of xenophobia, racism and Islamophobia that are global and transnational in scope. As Papastergiadis (2012: 25) noted,

[t]his process of connecting disparate entities in the imagination gives rise to a much more intimate sense of threat. Each new formulation of fear proves to be highly unstable and quickly overlaps with the residual sediments of archaic fears, as well as inserting itself into the as yet undefined fears of the future.

CHAPTER 7

In reference to contestation over establishing the Al Noori Islamic School, Adeeba reflected on how fears of difference were tied to flippant yet pathologising ideas linking the school to the terrorist organisation of the day.

> There were allegations by ... locals, [who] would say, 'oh they're probably manufacturing bombs for the PLO [Palestinian Liberation Organisation] in their backyards, kind of thing. So there was a lot of hysteria, we're always in the news .... And then we managed to stay [in one place] ... for one year in relative peace but then they wouldn't renew the lease. So then we approached a Syrian church, we didn't tell them who we were, we have to hide that we're Muslim all the time.

Eventually, after moving nine times in five years, the school received approval as an Earth Integrated school, it was landscaped so it could not be seen. Not only was it necessary to pass as non-Muslim, as Adeeba noted, "eventually with this Earth Integrated School ... they couldn't see us and they couldn't hear us." The school gained recognition, finally, but only by becoming invisible, this was recognition through obscurity.

Islamic Schools as the 'Enemy Within'

Ambient fear takes shape, or is embodied, provisionally, in the form of 'sleepers' who lie amongst 'us', awaiting activation from a controller who is always overseas as a spectre of the other. "Sleepers' evoke fears that migrants and 'foreign cultures' will transgress borders and 'destroy all forms of social control'" (Papastergiadis, 2012: 71).

> It was very, very apparent that ... the biggest opposition [was from] ... people who thought we were bringing in something which was going to be unstoppable ... and was going to change their way of life. (Adeeba)

Opponents of Islamic schools mobilise a politics that simultaneously refuses and reifies ambient fear. Islamic schools are locatable and definable objects, if essentialised – Islamic schools as the 'face' of the other. Ambient fear, concomitantly, pervades this politics as these schools become the mark of the 'enemy within' – the unassimilable 'other' taking over suburbs and cities, one school at a time (Al-Natour, 2010; Al-Natour & Morgan, 2012).

> It's a factor ... and when they get funded to build these schools, they get funded by the Sunnis and stuff like that ... you think 'oh shit what the?' they're not funding it with they're own community, they're being funded by outside. So that gives ... some people ... a bit of a blank ... you know they think what the hell, this is not growing out of their own people that are here, its growing from something that's an external .... I think they're a bit worried .... And then you've got the enemy from within, you know, they get that sort of picture that

> 'can we trust them' ... because they're being funded by other organisations, where do their [loyalties] really lie? (Joe)

The reactions to Islamic schools posits that these schools will ostensibly operate as insertion points for Muslim people to proselytise and convert non-Muslims, to take over suburbs and undermine social stability (Al-Natour, 2010). This is despite the very small numbers of Islamic schools compared to other forms of schooling. As noted, there are only 41 schools in Australia with the majority in south-western Sydney.

We suggest the reaction to Islamic schools is redolent of what Appadurai (2006) calls "fear of small numbers" in which there is a disproportionate reaction of majority populations towards minority populations, that are reminders and remainders of the "anxiety of incompleteness". "'Minorities', in a word, are metaphors and reminders of the betrayal of the classical national project" in a globalised world (Appadurai, 2006: 43). This has been evident in other instances of Islamic schools in parts of Sydney that are characterised as 'non-Muslim' areas – a maintenance of the residentialist myth of homogeneity that is invoked to counter the possibility of encountering difference. In this way difference is inscribed as irreducible and separate, even in places like Bankstown where the majority of Muslim residents are Australian born.

> It's a fear, its an unknown, basically ... But it's not entrenched .... It's not something people openly bloody go on about ... they don't have debates about it or anything ... it's just something in the back ... of their minds. (Joe)

When discussing Islamic schools, ambient fear requires a materiality to be encountered – ambient fear is unknown and unlocatable but becomes manifest through proximity, in the possibility of being made concrete through mosques and schools. As Amin (2010: 10) noted, the result is that "[u]nder such a biopolitics, the taming of the errant body – in this case the Muslim body [and school] – is urged as a necessity, a matter of everyday vigilance from the responsible citizen, wronged for thinking and doing otherwise." The marking out and then blurring of migrant and assumed migrant – the Muslim other – distinction, is part of what Papastergiadis (2012: 31) proposes is perhaps prominent in these psycho-social geographies of fear; the monstrousness of all of this which comes from realising that despite elaborate denial, "the enemy is more similar than we could bear to consider."

The controversy over Islamic schools – and the lack of controversy over non-Islamic schools such as Christian schools – highlights the way that focusing on the racialisation and geographies of religion provides insight into what would otherwise be seen as a set of both techno-rational urban policy problems and a set of neutral educational policy initiatives around the provision of religious schools within choice frameworks – the quintessential labouring and reifying of *policy scientificity 1.0,* and refusing to acknowledge the concomitant scientificities of *3.0.*

CHAPTER 7

MARKETIZING SPACE AND COMMODIFYING EDUCATIONAL DIFFERENCE

We suggest these contestations of urban and religious educational space have been heightened through a confluence of market policies in education leading to the increased establishment of ethno-cultural schools like Islamic schools, and global shifts that are mediated in local instances and places. Thus, market mechanisms like choice schools provide impetus for commodifying difference – a quasi market of neo-pantheonism – while surreptitiously eroding a secular educational discourse. We argued that to understand these geographies of Islamic schools, and the contestation over urban space, it is necessary to identify the way that these schools are part of the management of space and the future of urban multiculture. As Murdoch (2006: 23) posits, "spaces are made of complex sets of relations so that any spatial 'solidity' must be seen as an accomplishment, something to be achieved in the face of flux and instability."

The (provisional) accomplishments of space through urban planning are part of the managing of race and religion that are emptied of complexity. The management of urban space is necessarily crude, and claims amenity as its primary foci, but is inexorably caught in the negotiations and accommodations over space in reference to the racialisation of Islam, and the mobilising of the ensemble of nation, religion and politics to constitute the racialised religious Other. This mobilisation is imbued with what we have, following Papastergiadis (2012), identified as ambient fear, in which Islamic schools are the material manifestation of ubiquitous and unlocatable fears about others connected to difference.

There are new geographies of suburbia, connected to race and global Islamophobia, in which local planning is playing a role in constituting a racialised religious politics in education. This is to note how *policy scientificity 1.0* perpetuates particular forms of difference, representation, and alterity under the techno-rational schemes of traffic management and other sundry 'rational' policies as 'solutions' to our 'problems'. And this is where schooling is significant in what we might see as new edges of race and fear that have shifted the emphasis of concentrated fear of the other to the suburbs. This is a shift from the visceral notions of close contact in the inner city and the idea of proximity as a proxy for dealing, or not dealing, with difference. In the next chapter we take this role further through exploring contact as encounters.

CHAPTER 8

POLICY E(A)FFECTS

Spatial and Racial Encounters in the City

Cities are, of course, demarcated, through planning and architectural rules and through transport and communications networks within and beyond the city. But the spatial and temporal porosity of the city also opens it to footprints from the past and contemporary links elsewhere ... the present is crossed by influences from the past.
—Amin & Thrift, 2002: 22

In this chapter we examine how the ideas of *policy effects* and *policy affects* disrupt the notion of separation. Specifically, the chapter examines policy e(a)ffects in relation to their production and enactments that come from the introduction of *ethno-culturally focused schools* as emergent objects within the city. This chapter builds upon some of the concepts we have developed so far in the book, and specifically extends our problematization regarding space and the relationships among the *aporias of neo-liberal education policy* that we discussed in Chapters Six and Seven.

Our focus is in relation to the spaces and separations of the city. We problematize the concept of 'separation' as an integral modality in education policy – for instance 'segregation' – and evidenced in the practices of care that 'separate the self' (or self-separation). Our analysis notes how these ideas of separation are related to the spatial demarcations that characterize educational markets or education catallaxies. In what follows, our analytic focus is in relation to the more overt spatial separations of choice schools and the requisite market catallaxy that provide choice schools the ability to articulate difference and representation within cities. This chapter, then, continues our discussion of Chapter Six to problematize the conditions of choice policies that provide the self opportunities to develop 'new' educational investments – i.e., materials and milieus – in cities.

The purposes for disrupting ideas of separation are part of extending our previous analysis on *homo œconomicus* and the ways this figure collapses previous conceptions of educational space. Rather than treating space as a nebulous concept, this chapter thinks through the idea of space as encounter. We posit that *homo œconomicus* is now able to develop the milieus – such as ethno-cultural schools – to support requisite forms of care, that are encountered as part of the footprints of a city's past and future. Education policy is not just a technology that seeks innovations of the self; now, education policy provides *homo œconomicus* entrepreneurial opportunities to develop the very material, that is the bricks and mortar of school buildings,

CHAPTER 8

curriculum choices and capacity to self-identify along ethno-cultural categories (e.g., Afrocentric, Islamic), to support specific educational investments. Moreover, our purposes for disrupting ideas of separation are part of a post-positivist move in spatial theory that focus on the affective dimension of policy in the city. We extend this to look at connections between *policy effects* and *policy affects*, including the geographies of racial encounters in cities.

This chapter extends a policy problematization of educational separation in three ways:

- to identify the connections between policy e/affects, marketized education and culturally focused schools;
- to conceptualize ethno-culturally focused schools in the city as events utilising relational forms of place, circulation and encounter; and,
- to posit that race and raciologies require analysis in relation to events, encounter and alterity as part of the assemblage of education policy and the city.

This chapter argues that ethno-culturally focussed schools have become non-human bodies encountered as racialised objects. We show how education policy e/affects can be understood through connecting the materiality and performativity of race to the idea of the encounter, and particularly to encountering attempts of education equality. These attempts are linked to the educational markets of cities that simultaneously complicate and position equity attempts within a city's catallaxies. Equity attempts are not necessarily in opposition to articulations of educational equality through juridical and/or legislative means, but *are part of* the contemporary neo-liberal logic in education that utilizes the legislative arena to legitimate attempts at 'racial equality' with market logics – i.e., choice. This chapter, thus, notes how the risks of racial equality are passed down to very groups that have been racialized as non-White; and through this *entrepreneurial move*, the risks and remainders of race continue to be levied in disproportionate ways. Markets are, we reiterate, not equal nor self-regulating.

We conclude by noting how *policy e/affects* function as unintended as well as intended spatial (dis)orderings that allow for a rethinking of the relationships between the city and education policy. Moreover, such a rethinking provides conceptual and material disruptions to settled notions of segregation, separation and educational equality. At least this is our goal.

OH, THE SPACES YOU WILL GO[1]: MARKETIZED EDUCATION AND CULTURALLY FOCUSED SCHOOLS

The tropes of 'separation' and 'segregation' are powerful in urban education, for instance, 'residualised schooling', 'ghetto schooling', and so forth, and are indicative of dichotomies such as working class, middle class; comprehensive/single sex; private/public, and so forth. Separation, at at times categorization, are enduring ways of characterising the processes of education. Alongside these dichotomies are the material separations of schools from the 'outside world' through barb-wire fences and new technologies of surveillance in schools (e.g., metal detectors), and the marking out of some schools as different and dangerous (Gallagher & Fusco, 2006; Mills & Keddie, 2010).

These ideas about schooling have a parallel, and affinity, with historical imaginaries of the city as segregated and separated – the geographies and wilderness of the city such as 'south central,' 'east side,' and the 'wrong side of the tracks'. These imaginaries are premised on understanding cities through notions of connections, separations, and the equivalence of social distance with spatial distance. This equivalence was central to the *policy scientificities of 1.0* that included British social, positivist geography in the 1970s and 80s, and social psychology's investigations of social interaction (Keith, 2008). The notion of a segregated and separated city by class and race is an entrenched and normalising component of *policy scientificities 1.0* and within some of the 'critical' literatures emanating from *policy scientificities 2.0* on the city and on urban education. This is most evident in the idea of a lack of social mix and social mixing, where populations are grouped according to demographic markers (for critique, see Cochrane, 2007).

These scientificities mobilise worries and fears about social mixing or lack thereof, and about the constitution and transgressing of racial and ethnic categories. For instance, the American 'public' became experts in school bussing debates directed towards desegregation during this period. In any event, demarcating parts of the city and schools as dangerous, the financial centre, tourist quarters, ethnic specialities ("Chinatown"), etc. – creates city cartographies and school geographies (just ask any real estate agent) that can conflate identities with bodies, both human and non-human. These cartographies have been crucial to the constituting of urban spaces and schooling as, for example, ghettos or as enclaves (Anyon, 1997; Leonardo, 2009; D. Massey & Denton, 1993; Wilson, 2007). 'Where are the "good" schools?' is a question that is often asked by prospective home owners when trying to navigate these cartographies.

Separation has become synonymous with governance of the city and education. As we argued in the previous chapter, policy is a key mechanism in the proliferation of economic and cultural zones in cities, or area-based initiatives in the UK and Australia, and the surveillance and management of those sites as 'dangerous' and 'outliers', the so-called enclaves, ghettos, and so forth (Cochrane, 2007; Dikeç, 2007). We note, then, that cities are *living up to* their *1.0 and 2.0 policy scientificities* despite significant re-readings in geography and social theory, notably those focused on multiplicity, relational spaces and hybridity (Keith, 2005, 2008; Phillips, 2008). Our attention is focussed on the ways education policy positions, transmutes, and enacts objects/subjects in cities through emergent and adaptive policy arrangements that simultaneously influence how policy is sensed and embodied – the *policy e(a)ffects* of educational raciologies.

CHAPTER 8

POLICY EFFECTS: REPRESENTATIONAL AND MATERIAL MANIFESTATIONS OF EDUCATION POLICY

The idea of *policy effects*, while extensive in political science, was explicitly outlined in critical education policy studies by Stephen J. Ball in a 1993 chapter titled 'What is policy?'. Ball (2006: 47) posited "that practice and the 'effects' of policy cannot be simply read-off from texts and are the outcome of conflict and struggle between 'interests' in contexts". Additionally, Ball (2006: 51) identified a distinction between what he terms first order and second order policy effects. He stated,

> [f]irst order effects are changes in practice or structure (which are evident in particular sites and across the system as a whole). And second order effects are the impact of these changes on patterns of social access and opportunity and social justice.

In this chapter we work with, and across, first and second order effects, whereas first order effects of marketized education policy includes:

- choice mechanisms such as changing enrolment procedures, opening up catchment or provider areas; and
- the changing nature of funding and provision to allow parents and community groups to establish schools.

Second order effects are the market policies that support school choice for social justice claims, by generating opportunities for students that have previously been denied through stringent admission and enrolment policies (Chubb & Moe, 1990). This 'opening up' of space is most commonly represented as the dissolution of catchment or admission boundaries for a public school where students within these boundaries were required to attend schools locally coded and mapped within the city (aka, the proverbial and idyllic 'neighbourhood school').

However, as we noted in Chapter Six, *homo œconomicus* is now able to develop the milieus to support requisite practices of care. Contemporary education policy provides *homo œconomicus* entrepreneurial opportunities to develop the very material to support specific educational investments, and, hence, to redraw the previous catchments, boundaries, and neighbourhoods. Marketized policies have led to the partial blurring of previous territories – or city demarcations – with students able to cross boundaries to other schools and districts, depending on whether there are places available and to what extent subject/objects possess the requisite mobility requirements.

Yet, as we noted in Chapter Six, marketized education policy confronts enduring notions of racial politics in cities. We want to explore the banal and everyday aspects of this confrontation and interactions through ideas of encountering schools as objects in the city. We use our *policy intensions* as another kind of second order *effect* and *affect* that can identify a variety of *policy prolepses* regarding racialized subjects/objects that we discussed in Chapter Seven. Neo-liberal education policy has become a forceful and predominant factor in the redesign of cities, and in particular, a powerful cartographer in the reshaping of neo-liberal racial bodies within the production of culturally focussed schools.

Ethno-Culturally Focussed Schools and Choice

School choice has long been a feature of the Global North with the provision of public and private schools in many nation-states. The difference in the 21st century is the solidification – almost beyond repudiation – of public funding for private schooling entrenched as part of education policy (Musset, 2012). Another key part of the increasing marketization of education relates to funding for different types of schools within public systems such as charter schools in the United States, and government funding for private religious schooling in Canada, especially British Columbia, and Australia, something we discussed in Chapter Seven.

These different types of schools include ethno-culturally focused schools – such as the Africentric elementary school in Toronto noted in Chapter Six, and Islamic elementary and secondary schools in Sydney – that identify with and are identified by particular ethno-cultural and ethno-racial premises, either in name or ethos. These schools are posited as providing crucial choice for parents and groups that have previously been unable to establish schools and have often been significantly disadvantaged by public schooling. These groups are now establishing some of these schools. While the lineage of these schools precedes the marketisation of education, the consolidation and expansion of markets into education has increased the funding to, and numbers of, these schools (Levin, 1979) and raise important questions about the role of education equity within cities that have been assembled, arranged, and separated in particular ways.

We use the examples of *ethno-culturally focused school* as a way to problematize the representational and material manifestations of education policy, in that these schools enter material and affective registers that transmit representations of difference in the education markets of cities. These registers are redolent of the notion of the symbolic and material realms of policy. As Rizvi and Lingard (2010: 9) distinguish,

> [s]ymbolic policies are often political responses to pressures for policy. They usually carry little or no commitment to actual implementation and usually do not have substantial funding attached …. A material policy, in stark contrast, is strongly committed to implementation. It is accompanied by funding, and sometimes effective evaluation mechanisms to ensure achievement of its goals.

Of course, the policy pre-condition of choice – that different schools operate as symbolic choices – functions within marketized policies that manifest these schools as material outcomes. Education policy intervenes in the world outside of school in

CHAPTER 8

ways that has unintended consequences. In this, we can see that education policy "offers an imagined future state of affairs, but in articulating desired change always offers an account somewhat more simplified than the actual realities of practice" (Rizvi & Lingard, 2010: 5).

This is all to say that market policies have e(a)ffects that are beyond that which are articulated in policy texts. As we noted in Chapter Three, one of goals with a *policy problematization* is to move beyond forms of textual and discourse analyses that characterize much of contemporary educational policy analyses. Further, our insistence on the materiality of policy obliges us to focus on the conditions of simultaneity and multiplicity that emerge from the symbolic and materiality of culturally focused choice.

All schools generate effects (and enactments) not measured by educational outcomes. Moreover, policy enactments or 'other' policy effects emerge relating to the way ethno-culturally focussed schools circulate in the creation of difference, representation and provisional accomplishments – or geographies – of race and space in the city. We have limited interest in this chapter, therefore, in what people might do with market policies – which we discussed in much more detail Chapter Six and Seven – although we have a strong sense that what people might do with neo-liberal education policy will be related to 'investing in' practices of care of some kind (e.g., racialized care, etc.).

Nevertheless, market policies enable the creation of certain schools to *become* objects in the urban education market. This is not about relations and processes within schools, which of course count in the kinds of practices of care that are imagined and enacted as part of these schools, but of education policy and schools in, and as, the urban world of the city. Schools are the non-human bodies that are circulated and encountered in the city – that is in the spatio-temporality of policy effects, including the commodification of these subject/objects inherent in neo-liberal education policy. We discuss these concepts next.

SPACE, PLACE AND ENCOUNTERS: A CONCEPTUAL TERRAIN FOR RETHINKING POLICY EFFECTS

That world no longer exists.
Yet from the architecture of longing
you continue to construct a bountiful edifice.
This is not exile.
You can return any day to the place that you came from
though the place you left has shifted a heartbeat
(Senior, 2005, *Blue Foot Traveller*)

In this chapter we work with a conception of space as emergent and exigent to social relations (see Chapter Two). This encapsulates the performative functions of space and time. As Gregory (2004: 18–19) argued, following Edward Said's work within the imaginative geographies of Orientalism, these (relational, colonial) geographies "are not only accumulations of time, sedimentations of successive histories; they are also *performances of space*". In this sense, space is not only "an effect of practices of representation, valorization, and articulation; it is fabricated through and in these practices and is thus not only a domain but also a "doing"' (p. 19). The relationships between educational policy effects and the city can be problematized through seeing that simultaneity and synchronicity are part of the imaginaries and materialities of space, the 'real' of space (cf., Soja, 1996).

Our four folds of policy – bodies, power, knowledge (i.e., scientificities), and thoughts on existence/death – are constitutive of the practices of space – "a topological theory of space, place and politics as encountered, performed, and fluid" (Jones, 2009: 492). The four folds of policy provide a way to understand the relationality of place as an event and its relationship to encounters – *to take place* as in territorialization attempts that we discussed earlier in relation to our four folds of education policy.

Education policy creates culturally focussed schools as new creations, as new policy effects, in the landscape of the city, and as places that are both the results of encounter and as objects to be encountered. This requires, we suggest, a relational notion of place and its connection to the encounter, for we are interested in "[p]laces not as points or areas on maps, but as integrations of space and time, as spatiotemporal events" (Lorimer, 2008: 130).

Events as breaks from extant conditions are important parts of thought-in-action, predicated on "the desire … to find a means of attending to the difference, divergence and differentiation that events open up, or may open up" (Anderson & Harrison, 2010: 22). This notion of the political requires "a world which demands the ethics of facing up to the event; where the situation is unprecedented and the future is open" (Anderson & Harrison, 2010: 22). This is space as the possibility of the unexpected occurring, but it seems, always awaiting the inevitable scientificities to solve the problems that emerge from difference, divergence, and differentiation.

This dealing with flux provides an uncertainty regarding place – and an opportunity. For as Massey (2005: 139) asks: "If there are no fixed points then where is here?" The encounter enters if place is not about a point, or that in the sense it is not a stable point, for it seems crucial to note the co-extensive nature of time and space which characterizes our *policy prolepsis*. That is, to repeat the point, "'here' is no more (and no less) than our encounter, and what is made of it. It is, irretrievably, here and now" (Massey, 2005: 141). We don't mean that uncertainty is a form of spatial 'presentism', and place is thus anachronistic. For, "if 'here' is the aggregation of multiple meetings and encounters that create a history, then what has come before is implicated in and constitutive of the multiple spatio-temporalities of now – that is now then and there" (Massey, 2005: 139).

CHAPTER 8

Performing, Enacting, and Encountering Educational Events: Prolepses, Intensions, and Prehensions

In this section we are interested in the notions of meetings and encounters in relation to *policy prolepses* and *intensions*. We work with the idea that place has no fidelity, for it is premised on 'throwntogetherness' – the heterogeneities of the assemblage – the dispositif – that is a "negotiation between both human and non-human" that makes place (Massey, 2005: 140). Amin and Thrift (2002: 30) noted that the,

> encounter, and the reaction to it, is a formative element in the urban world. So places, for example, are best thought of not so much as enduring sites but as moments of encounter, not so much as 'presents', fixed in space and time, but as variable events; twists and fluxes of interrelation.

'The reaction to it' – like the sensing through *policy intensions* – is a type of paradoxically, process-oriented, relational materiality in which place is open and multiple, and generates all kinds of encounters as predicated in some sense on interpretations, that are in themselves forms of historicising events and thus become 'places'. Interpretations worry us, in that they are a form of violence as Lim (2008: 228), following Foucault, noted,

> [i]n some sense, all interpretations involve violence (Foucault, 1991), appropriating systems of relation and subjecting them to secondary rules, and appropriating bodes and ideas and making them stand in for other ideal meanings, collectivities and histories. Interpretations asks that bodies and their relations obey a system of proper, explainable relations.

'Making sense' of the uncertainty in events is not necessarily what worries us. It is the assumptions within forms of interpretations that seek to order and regulate the uncertainty. We also worry that the prolepses of event are assumed to be independent of the *intensions* that represent the *prolepsis* in the first place. Representational accounts of events ignore or minimize the relational/materiality of space and further assume to precede, or be anterior, to the subject/object of its enactment. This anterior notion of space only reifies additional assumptions of material as something definite, as in constant, singular, and perhaps universal – what John Law (2004) discussed as 'primitive' and 'originary' Euro-American conceptions of representative ontology.

The policy effects of ethno-culturally focused schools enter realms, however, of interpretations concerned with (non-human) bodies in the city, and encountered in marketized systems that we never had to previously consider. In other words, the event of ethno-culturally focussed schools is quickly being coded into the *policy scientificities* of *1.0* and possibly *2.0* which assume a certain representative ontology. Instead of using *1.0* and *2.0*, we might consider how policy creates new schools as interventions into places already in process – as part of place-as-event – that create emergent, and uncertain materialities. Nevertheless, some of these educational materialities are not always necessarily open. Admissions procedures, curricula foci and daily religious observances can close place. And, marketized policy creates schools as commodities that are part of both financial exchanges, education for money, and encounters, perhaps even confusing and complex neo-liberal encounters of educational equality.

Ethno-culturally focused schools as commodities are made objects devoid of the complex processes and practices that go into the everyday life of a school, and the fluid and contested nature of the identities that become marked by and create the marking of the school. Folks just don't buy homes *there – there* can be *near* a school, or in a market where proximity to a school is not necessary then travel and movement become part of school life. The car, for example, becomes the replacement to walking to and home from school – the car as the quintessential and contemporary object that traverses the 'dangerous' city. The complexity of life is seen to happen outside rather than inside the school. Education policy has now constituted the complexity of everyday life of a school as a simplified, reduced and exchangeable entity – a 'thing'. As Amin and Thrift (2002: 35) noted (quoting Weiss),

> Things are central to human life, but more than this, they are actively consumed in all kinds of networks of use: "certain objects have social lives that are quantitatively different from others as well as correspondingly distinct potentials for constructing the lives of persons who control (or are controlled by) them". (Weiss 1996: 15)

When places are ethno-culturally focused schools, such as Islamic schools, these places are paradoxically provisional that circulate both as reifications and repudiations of the neo-liberalising of difference (i.e. all difference as equal) (Goldberg, 2009; Gulson, 2011). These schools are objects of difference that are encountered. We should note that difference, whiteness and the 'other' constitute the encounter (that is, Christian schools are rarely if ever identified as ethno-cultural). As Gregory (2004: 18) suggested, "distance – like difference – is not an absolute, fixed and given, but is set in motion and made meaningful through cultural practices."

Encountering the Count

Ethno-culturally focused schools are new representations of knowledge – new folds – about schooling in the city. Online websites provide access to information about standardised test results, demographics and finances, such as the Australian example, *My School* but that have become ubiquitous in the hegemonic foreclosures of educational spaces. These schools, these non-human bodies, are now commodified as part of new technologies that circulate knowledge and scientificities throughout the city and that simultaneously locate schools in reference to an already coded, stratified, city. The conflation of place and knowledge alongside 'demographics' and 'educational outcomes' of these schools, portend educational destinies within the already defined stratifications of the city.

These new technologies of circulation work along with re-articulating knowledge about the city, from the cartographies of demographics to the calculative cartographies of education policies. There is now the capability of undertaking enormous amount of calculation that this is creating 'a new calculative sense' (Thrift, 2008) that Thrift (2008, following Callon & Law, 2004) terms, 'qualcalculation'. This calculative sense is changing how we encounter objects such as schools, where constant calculations and updating are being done about education and school, and we now take note of the 'data' that exists about these schools in ways that were never previously available and rarely questioned. As Thrift (2008: 98) noted we have such faith in numbers despite their application.

> We might say that ... [an] obsessive faith in number ... has become generalized .... Almost anything is thought susceptible to counting, ranking and the like, as evidenced by the current mania for ranking just about anything, often in what might seem completely inappropriate ways.

These calculative representations of schools, posited as solutions to problems, are constituting education policy problems, and are creating new ways of understanding space. Yet, we are not quite sure what type of life is being created by these ways of calculating the work, for as Thrift posited, there have been few accounts that "have tended to work out in any detail what the space-time signatures of a lifeworld that was heavily calculated (or, as I would have it, qualcalculated) would look like ..." (Thrift, 2008: 103).

This could mean new notions of what it means to be 'human' or a policy actor or subject, and in relation to education policy. It means that ethno-culturally focused schools as objects are encountered through this qualcalculative world, that can be reductive but just might be generative. Encounters can be governed (of course, space, etc.), and particularly structured prior (e.g., memory). We might, therefore, also consider how encounters can be 'represented' prior to actually occurring, i.e., in anticipation – as *policy prolepsis* or becoming-policy (see Chapter Four). We might link the preconditions of 'encounter' to prolepsis, a representation before it actually does or did.

EDUCATION POLICY AND THE CONSTITUTING OF GEO-MEMORIES

Thrift (2003: 2022, cited by Nayak, 2010: 2378) suggested that "[s]paces can be stabilised in such a way that they act like political utterances, guiding subjects to particular conclusions". Following this, we suggest policy organizes and arranges space – attempts to stabilise the uncertainty and unpredictability of space – but, also the converse: that representational and material space stabilises policy. We might, for instance, propose there are no such thing as boundaries (e.g., Thrift, 2006) – everything is porous (though, we should note, performative materialities make some seem/are less so than others, such as the building of walls to separate people from land and the assertion of national boundaries (see Gregory, 2004).

Cities are demarcated in a variety of ways through planning and architecture, including the various cartographies of education policy such as school admission boundaries, and school districts that overlay multiple notions of spatiotemporal knowledge (e.g., maps of Indigenous lands, local government). Education policy that establish quasi-markets in education have reordered space to encourage an understanding of educational spaces as open, while removing any chance of managing difference in the city; this is policy constituting space as anachronistic. If we take the idea of relationality seriously, and relations as 'open, provisional achievements', then we need to examine how this relationality comes to be constituted. As Anderson and Harrison (2010: 16) maintain, "it becomes necessary to think through the specificity and performative efficacy of different relations and different relational configurations."

Each ethno-culturally focused school – as object, as commodity, as dispositif, as assemblage – is, for example, encountered in an ostensibly neutral policy market, yet as we have noted above, encountered always with particular spatio-temporalities that make up and constitute relations between (human and non-human) entities. These relations are significant in that they indicate how place as event is tied up with the struggles over memory and histories of place, objects and encounters. This is clear when schools are proposed and opened that carry with them an assemblage of geo-histories.

For example, an Afrocentric school in Toronto is a trans-scalar place; an assemblage of Black education in Toronto, slavery and segregation in Canada, contestations over belonging in multicultural cities and nations, and so forth. Furthermore, when an Afrocentric school is proposed and established it is encountered through readings of difference and negotiation in the city of Toronto (see Gulson & Webb, 2013a). If we constitute this within an understanding of the complex racialisations of education policy, we can understand that an Afrocentric school is encountered through what Amin calls the 'remainders of race'. For Amin (2010: 3–4) the remainders of race involve,

> the interplay between vernacular habits with long historical roots of reading racial and social worth from surface bodily differences and racial biopolitics that makes the critical difference to the real experience of race, arbitrating the choice between accommodation and discipline of the racialized other.

The remainder of race points to an emphasis on encounter, difference, negotiation and history. In thinking about the role of education policy in the city, we might consider what Soja (1996: 182–3) posited as "a de-centering of the historical imagination, and ... [the work] to un-learn its privilege and behave as it if is part of the margin, in a space-time or geohistory of radical openness." Histories matter – to prevent openness and multiplicity from being hollowed out, and to move from spatial fetishism and the hint of being anachronistic. Keith's (2005) idea of place might be useful in conceptualising places as temporary achievements but nonetheless located geo-historically that are no more and no less than moments of arbitrary closure.

Materially produced and multiply signified, "a 'place' in precise terms can have only a meaning of a particular moment" (Keith, 2005: 75). This is a moment of unequal encounter.

We remember parts of cities and the struggles for parts of cities through schooling. School buildings can be part of "the corporeal traces of buildings and landscapes that provide a kind of half-remembered poetics" (Thrift, 2006: 139). For example, in the inner city suburb of Redfern, an area long associated with urban Aboriginality in Sydney, the local primary school was to be closed as part of a policy initiative within a marketized inner city education market (Gulson, 2011; Gulson & Parkes, 2009). This closure could be understood as the on-going constitution of urban Aboriginality, for this school was symbolically significant for Indigenous urban politics, connected to national concerns for land rights in the 1970s and now seen as part of what Gregory (2004) calls 'the colonial present'. Memories of place are connected to other forms of the performativity of representation that are located in the very materiality of life, schools marked with and as racial encounters, marked by 'the scent of memory' (Nayak, 2010), and the triggers of activity.

Mobility is important as is the struggle over the meaning of movement (Cresswell, 2006). Schools, for example, have long been a key part of neighbourhoods and suburbs, with public schools playing a community hub role, while private schools have been associated with movement, as destinations in areas of cities – not so much as schools located in place as is the case in the public school, but rather of place, with travel to these schools seen as a way in which the city is made, rather than the school itself (Symes, 2007). Schools can be encounters with memories not yet made that are struggled over, repudiated, and connect schools to other forms of spatial politics. This resonates with how ethno-culturally focused schools are sensed and encountered in the city, and how these schools bring with them the 'scent of memory' that is connected to particular imaginings of the nation; for example, Islamic schools are connected to present and past notions of the racialised 'other' and contemporary terrorism.

We might similarly consider how a small Afrocentric school in Toronto, Canada, as an ethno-cultural school, was seen as a challenge to the fidelity of (white) Canadian multiculturalism (Gulson & Webb, 2012, 2013a). As Nayak (2010: 2384) noted in reference to 'Asian' shops on housing estates in England, "They come to symbolise larger transformations in the nation-state that are lived out and experienced in the micropolitics of the local." These micro-politics of the nation are similarly located in particular spatio-temporalities of race and whiteness, that are played out in reference to culturally focused schools in multicultural cities and nations like Australia and Canada. This requires us to reconsider the tendency to understand and reify, and thus the necessity if we are to think of the schools as more than mere repositories of raced bodies, as place as located "through history, through the past, through time-embeddedness" (Massey, 2006: 15).

Policy Effects/Race Redux

The ordering of the city has much to do with the governing of the city (Rose & Miller, 2008) and the practice of biopolitics of the city – "the practice of engineering the body and the senses – and life more generally – so as to produce governable subjects" (Amin & Thrift, 2002: 83) – and education's role in this, the being together of multiple existences. If policy contains triggers for activity, then policy can be constructed – symbolically or otherwise – to manage or govern these triggers, and, in the example of marketized education policy, all the while providing the illusion of choice. There are expected and unexpected consequences – effects – of the spatial ordering that is created through education policy. Effects in flux, but also always provisionally permanent, are generated, for example, through education policy delineating school boundaries, inside-outside areas, and curricula boundaries as spatial metaphors of knowledge, of the subject, of place. While place might be open it simultaneously has form through a provisional, and perhaps paradoxically, dynamic order. Education policy can therefore, be part of:

> the dynamic ordering processes which have produced our chief senses of urban space and time .... [T]hese have mainly been produced through the design of mundane instruments of encounter which themselves became the proof of the existence of particular spaces and times. (Massey, 2006: 46)

We suggest that the combination of policy and race constitute such 'mundane instruments'. This is not to suggest race is mundane in its consequence and necessary coupling with and as racism, but rather the need to be attendant to moments of articulation of race and racialization, that are constituted through different mechanisms such market based policies that reconfigure how schools are sensed in the city. We need to attempt to deal with notions of new (or are they old?) ways of talking with and working with (ideas of) race. It is the dividing force of race, what Goldberg (2009) called the 'threat of race' in that every encounter has the possibility of both something new and old, and under marketized conditions it is homogeneity through differentiation that is a possible paradox; that is, the precondition for a school in marketized conditions is differentiation while other parts of neoliberalisation require that every school is standardised through other realms of policy (such as accountability policies around curricula and testing).

As Nayak (2011: 554) asserted, "we must ask under what conditions is [race] summoned-to-life and allowed to materialise within time and place. In this respect race is not simply a fiction but an ultimate dividing practice in late-modern societies." Race and space are intertwined (Neely & Samura, 2011), and Saldanha (2006: 18) posited a notion of race and space, building on Massey, in which: "[w]hat is needed is a concept of space in which fixity can emerge from flux under certain conditions." Saldhana suggested the idea of viscosity to elucidate the ways in which there is a "continuous, but constrained dynamism of space" (p. 18). Difference sticks to particular bodies through contingent circumstances – which is not to eradicate history here in favour of geography.

Education policies supporting school choice allow for the creation of new schools, such as culturally focused schools, and provide new interventions in the ways difference circulates and is encountered in the city. A school that is identifiable as an 'other' identity, is sensed as an 'other' object – by a Mosque, or by a mission statement on a sign outside, or by its name – Islamic, Africentric, Baptist – is marked out materially and representationally – in ways that enter and create new forms difference and intensities. This is to work with the performative aspect of representations, that is "representation not as a code to be broken or as a illusion to be dispelled rather representations are apprehended as performative in themselves; as doings" (Dewsbury, Harrison, Rose, & Wylie, 2002: 438 cited in Anderson & Harrison, 2010: 14–5).

THE RACIALIZATIONS OF SUBJECTS/OBJECTS: MATERIAL ENCOUNTERS IN THE CITY

If we think of schools as bodies in the city, then the encounter is with the school as an object of difference, rather than the students, and we might, further, note how policy effects are creating the accomplishment of space and race. These relational spaces now structure our senses through the logics of commodified schools in education markets. This is to think of a non-deterministic regime of classification and differentiation, in which some things stick to human and non-human bodies, and why this occurs (Swanton, 2008). This is part of what we might identify as "a materialist engagement of race that recognises ... the 'force of things' and how raced memories and affects congeal around particular bodies, things and spaces and how these things then exert a kind of agency in the event of an encounter" (Anderson & Harrison, 2010: 18).

A focus on the encounter with human and non-human bodies (or perhaps we should just think of these as objects) requires us to examine not the interpretations of race (i.e., how do we know race?), important as this question is, but what Swanton suggested following Deleuze and Guattari (1987) that we might see as 'experimentation'. For Swanton (2010: 2338), this meant asking: "what does race do? How does race function?" Can it exist without recognition (Grosz, 2002)? How is it produced differently by marketized education policy? Race does not look the same in all times and spaces – that it looks different depending on the connections between policy and the city; and depending on the types of encounter, and co-constitutively what emerges from the encounter.

We posit that ethno-culturally focused schools have become part of the 'rubric' and 'grammar' of race, and that school choice makes this possible as policy effects; these are the generative, yet certainly not innocent, aspects of policy affects and policy effects. Ethno-culturally focused schools circulate as reputations, as threats, where racialised memories and affects surround and constitute some bodies and objects – in this case schools.

In this chapter, we were interested in material relationality, on the connections between the human and the non-human, that are constitutive and constituted by relations of race; and that that these relationships have changed both through urban change and educational change, particularly policy. We wanted to emphasize encounters and multiplicity, but this is not about equivalence. It is about how some orders are made durable, which in this instance we are taking as the orders of race.

That is, we can continue to see the materiality of the representations and the work that goes into making these provisional, pernicious racialisations of non-human bodies. We are talking about the management and ordering of bodies (human and non-human) in times and spaces – about legitimate and illegitimate bodies in microgeographies of schooling and the city. This ordering tells us something about how the education market is creating new, yet durable and pernicious, and at times complexly (dis)empowering notions of race that never quite emerge from the 'weight of race' (Goldberg, 2009). For if education policies and markets are meant to be neutral then the encounter tells something about how *policy prolepses* work, and why some schools are marked out more than others, and how schooling articulates new, not just reflects, urban forms.

NOTE

[1] A concerted play on Geisel, T. S. (1960). *Oh, the places you'll go!* New York, NY: Random House.

CHAPTER 9

3.0: LINES

The Vectors of a Policy Geophilosophy

I tend to think of things as sets of lines to be unraveled but also to be made to intersect. I don't like points; I think it's stupid summing things up. Lines aren't things running between two points; points are where several lines intersect.
—Deleuze, 1995: 160–161

I can't help but dream of the kind of criticism that would try not to judge but to bring an oeuvre, a book, a sentence, an idea to life; it would light fires, watch grass grow, listen to the wind, and catch the sea foam in the breeze and scatter it. It would multiply not judgements but signs of existence; it would summon them, drag them from their sleep. Perhaps it would invent them sometimes – all the better. All the better. Criticism that sends down sentences sends me to sleep; I'd like a criticism of scintillating leaps of imagination. It would not be sovereign or dressed in red. It would bear the lightening of possible storms.
—Foucault, 1997: 323

We are wondering – albeit cautiously in light of Deleuze's distaste for summing things up, but then a book always needs to finish, at least materially – whether this chapter is an epitaph for the impossibility of recuperating policy analysis, or the beginning of another form of policy analysis; to see if *policy geophilosophy* is part of what we have constituted as *policy scientificity 3.0*?

The difficulty for poststructural policy research, a field in which we reluctantly but likely inevitably will be positioned as part of what Murdoch (2006) called a 'material poststructuralism', has been to critique and change political structures and practices (Peters & Humes, 2003). As St. Pierre (2011: 613) suggested,

The difficulty for the poststructural researcher lies in trying to function in the ruins of the structure after the theoretical move that authorizes its foundations has been interrogated and its limits breached so profoundly that its center no longer holds .... Of course, *the structure had always already been ruptured, ruined.*

In this book we have used *3.0* to ask ontological questions about the ossified worlds of policy scientificities *1.0* and *2.0*. Moreover, we have asked about the possibilities of other representations, non-representations, the possibilities contained with developing new translation registers perhaps born from earlier forms of difference and representation, but which are also not necessarily tied to those either.

We might characterize, but not equate, *policy scientificity 3.0* in the same way that Anderson and Harrison (2010: 3) described the emergence of non-representational theory as a set of ideas that as an 'event', "arrives somewhat unexpectedly, whose outcome is never guaranteed in advance, and which is composed across but irreducible to a multiplicity of sites, desires, fears, contingencies and tendencies". Education policy attempts to reduce these multiplicities into 'controllable' singularities. Like an event, in this chapter we outline three precarious vectors of policy geophilosophy. Please bear with us (and, for this final chapter, we recommend a Shiraz or Malbec).

We think about these lines or vectors as provocations, ruminations and abutments – unfinished thoughts and struggles about what constitutes the theories and methodologies for an emerging set of analyses. *Policy scientificity 3.0* may include any or all of the following, or, in fact, be something completely different. We continue to think that the notion of a transversal politics carries some purchase, as Raunig (2007: n.p.) contended, where "transversal lines tend to transsectorally cross through several fields, they link together social struggles and artistic interventions and theory production." We hope the following thoughts are leaps, but remain acutely aware that they are just as likely to be intellectual stumbles.

LINE ONE: THE SPATIAL AND AFFECTIVE

The first line in *policy geophilosophy* is to articulate a policy dispositif that produces sensings of all kinds that are subsequently used in analysis of education, broadly conceived, while simultaneously recognizing that material subjugations occur within those very spaces. This relates to what we see as the necessity to understand policy and policy analysis as spatial and affective. As Berlant (2011: 53) claimed, "affect theory is another phase in the history of ideology theory; the moment of the affective turn brings us back to the encounter of what is sensed with what is known and what has impact in a new but also recognizable way". Here, we would acknowledge both the capacity to generate new encounters, and the caution provided by Rose regarding the renewed focus on, or borrowing from, biology in the 'human' sciences. Rose (2013: 12) points out that the link between biology and human sciences, especially affect theories and the non-cognitive, has meant:

> Biology is translated into ontology, ontology is transmuted into politics. We have seen a similar move in recent history, appealing to a different biology, with political consequences that, to say the least, should give us pause.

Working against this background, in this book, we have been thinking in educational modalities, and the material subjectifications involved in policy becomings. This is why we like mapping so much. Simons, Olssen, and Peters (2009b: 68) concisely state what we think is at stake in the first line of *policy geophilosophy*,

The aim is to draw precise attention to what is familiar today and to what is often invisible due to this familiarity (Foucault, 1978a, pp. 540–541). What is needed to achieve this aim is a kind of "cartography" (Deleuze, 1986) that "maps" (Flynn, 1994) the present or, as Rose (1999, p. 57) puts it, an "empiricism of the surface" focusing on what is said and what allows it to be said. Thus what is at stake, according to Rose (1999, p. 20) is "introducing a critical attitude towards those things that are given to our present experience as if they were timeless, natural, unquestionable" and "to enhance the contestability of regimes" that seek to govern us.

Perhaps in a city. Perhaps in a school in a city. Perhaps in a classroom in a school in a city. We suspect that much of what we have written is part of what is amorphously referred to as 'urban education' for the city is a significant part of what we are exploring. Particularly the ordinariness of education policy in the city, and the sense of the everyday life that pervades much thinking about education (e.g., the rhythms of the day, the segmentation and normalisation of differences in space-times, that both replicate and are disjunctures of what is always problematically separated as education policy domains, such as schools, and always defined in opposition to the outside world). But this is precisely what we are attempting to grapple with the technologies of spatial – material – affective analysis.

What we suspect – indeed as we noted in the chapters on prolepsis and apparitions as action in the world – is that policy implementation is closer to *intuition*, with "'intuition' as the process of dynamic sensual data-gathering through which affect takes shape in forms whose job it is to make reliable sense of life" (Berlant, 2011: 52). This is intuition as possibility, where: "People follow their intuitions about what they don't know and so change the shape of the present, which is not fleeting at all, but a zone of action in a space marked by its experiments in transitioning" (Berlant, 2011: 77).

This is evident in the affective politics of choice. Thrift (2008: 182–3) posits that what is occurring, or has occurred,

> consists of the general changes in the *form* of such politics that are taking place in the current era, changes which make affect a more and more visible element of the political. In particular, I want to point towards so-called 'agencies of choice' and 'mixed-action repertoires' in line with a general move to more and more areas of life the subject of a new set of responsibilities called 'choice.'

These 'responsibilities of choice' alter notions of educational change and action. We examined how in education markets, for example, people practice and encounter 'choice' schools as a variety of affects – through fear, opportunity, investments. Thrift (2008: 182) noted that, "affect has always been a key element of politics and the subject of numerous powerful political technologies which have knotted thinking, technique and affect together in various potent combinations".

CHAPTER 9

Sellar (2014), along with Staunes (2011), has mapped how the notion of affect can help to rethink notions of policy at a distance, the spatial-affective aspects of organizations and programs like Organisation for Economic Co-operation and Development (OECD) and Programme for International Student Assessment (PISA). This includes the transforming of multiple qualities of, for example, education into a common metric, as what is termed 'commensuration', which "has become a central practice with the rise of data and its usage to manage capitalist society" (Sellar, 2014: 131). Performance data is generated by an intergovernmental organization like OECD through PISA, to change perceptions precisely as its purpose, not as a secondary, unintended consequence.

Commensuration is a new form of affective governing, for as Thrift (2008: 182) notes, there is "a tendency towards the greater and greater engineering of affect …". Nonetheless, there is a need to understand the dimensions of affect as a way to evoke new creativities concerning educational data. Sellar (2014) proposes that an engagement with new forms of data is "to open up possibilities for imagining approaches to education policy research that embrace the creative effects that can be produced by performance data in its relation to affective-sense making, but which do not mobilise the authority that is gained by simultaneously disavowing the creativity of commensuration" (Sellar, 2014: 143). Education policy, thus, constitutes objects and subjects through emergent formations that simultaneously influence how policy is sensed, embodied, and enacted in complex and often paradoxical ways.

LINE TWO: PROBLEMATIZATION FOR EMERGENT ONTOLOGIES

The second line in *policy geophilosophy* is specifically designed to problematize, or what Ball (1995) discussed as 'defamiliarize', education policy. Bacchi (2012b: 7) suggested,

> A study of problematizations … offers researchers the possibility of getting inside thinking – including one's own thinking – observing how 'things' come to be. It gives access to the spaces within which 'objects' emerge as 'real' and 'true', making it possible to study the strategic relations, the politics, involved in their appearance. Examining thought in this way puts into question the presumed fixity of the thing 'thought' and, by so doing, makes it possible to think other-wise.

Problematization is a key aspect to our geophilosophizing, as we have examined some of the normative practices in education that are attuned to improving educational conditions through the historical registers of instrumentalism.

Our goal has been to deliberately problematize the 'unquestionable' and the 'familiar' but in ways that provide a certain amount of latitude in analysis to attempt to avoid a reterritorialization of this work into the positivistic rationalities always ready to digest 'research recommendations' (Lather, 2009). We think that problematization is more than just a 'troubling' method; it is a practice of sorts, perhaps even a commitment to not knowing. With regard to not knowing, Deleuze (2004: 130) helps:

> ... here and there isolated and passionate cries are raised. How could they not be isolated when they deny what 'everybody knows...?' And passionate, since they deny that which, it is said, nobody can deny? Such protest does not take place in the name of aristocratic prejudices: it is not a question of saying what few think and knowing what it means to think. On the contrary, it is a question of someone – if only one – with the necessary modesty not managing to know what everybody knows, and modestly denying what everybody is supposed to recognise.

As modestly (or should that be as obviously) as we can, we certainly do not claim that we are the only ones not knowing. Such a claim would smack of an aristocratic arrogance; and really, such a claim would be completely disingenuous given that so many kindergarteners deliberately 'not know' everyday. However, such a stance is a difficult one within academia and the schoolhouse and their increasingly instrumental foci. We just hope that kindergarteners might let us stand with them and not know together.

Problematization is an attempt to enhance the contestability of regimes and involves creative attempts to think through the possibilities of analysis involved in uncertain modalities, chaotic virtualities, and emergent time-spaces, and unsettled "hinterlands" (Law, 2004). It is also helps, if we may pay some credence to those that have come before us, "to recognize the non-innocence of how 'problems' get framed within policy proposals, how the frames will affect what can be thought about and how this affects possibilities for action" (Bacchi, 2000: 50). Our problematization is oriented to when choices have been made and modalities have been closed (for a time), even if certain possibilities palpate sensings of otherworlds (Adkins-Cartee, 2014). It is not all fun and games when possible ontologies are closed.

We can see this notion, for example, in the critiques made by Barnett, who identified what he sees as the limits of ontological politics, namely reifications of normative politics. Barnett has argued that there is a recurrent feature of what he terms "political ontologies of affect". Barnett (2008: 195) contended that,

> political ontologies of affect lay themselves open to the charge of *cryptonormativism*: in order to elaborate on the political relevance of their claims, they implicitly invoke the persuasive force of norms that theorists of affect are unwilling to openly avow, and which their own theories seem to undermine.

We try to remain cognisant of 'cryptonormativism' in our second line with *policy geophilosophy* as we posit it is markedly different than the predictions that lie in positivists account of intervention, or in 'implementation'. We have been interested in the ontological politics of policy, comprising: (a) not independent of those who make, or independent of other policies; (b) not 'out there', firmly conceived, made, practiced somewhere (i.e., time/space, and in different time/spaces); (c) not anterior (i.e, not statements from God, truth, or science – even if statements are couched in these arenas); (d) multiple; and, (e) non representational. This approach is cognate with what Mol (2002: 155) posited as the practice of research methods, where "methods are not a way of opening a window on the world, but a way of interfering with it. They act, they *mediate* between an object and its representation". As Bacchi (2012a: 150) suggested, this type of politics of research challenges, indeed repudiates, the scientificities of *1.0* that endure today, where evidence based policy posits that "[d]ifferent policy options … can be tested much in the way of a scientific experiment to see which one works." We are not suggesting that problematization and the closing of any particular modalities are entirely our choice.

LINE THREE: PROBLEMATIC ATTACHMENTS AND NEW CONCEPTS

The third line on our *policy geophilosophy* is the deliberate design of new educational policy concepts, with most being spatial-affective types. We do this as part of what Bacchi (2012: 151) identified as "theoretical interventions as *themselves political practice*". The importance of creating concepts is to develop a language to create other ways of thinking, acting and sensing, as a possibly beneficial way to move educational subjugation along new paths rather than (only) the path of capitalist labor and other sundry practices of self care that have their (neo-liberal) educational registers always already defined (e.g., gender, race, class, dis/ability, etc.). We recognize that concept creation is also the domain of policy entrepreneurs who market solutions to schools and systems[1] (e.g., 'brain-based learning' – as if there were any other learning type?). We are hopeful that our commitment to not knowing as part of problematizations will maintain our criticality.

We are, nonetheless, attempting to propose *policy geophilosophy* as a viable form of analysis with an enduring sense of futility. We find some solace, if that is the term, in what Berlant (2011) called 'cruel optimism'. Berlant (2011: 24) stated that, "Cruel optimism is the condition of maintaining an attachment to a significantly problematic object." As would be clear, we hope, we have some serious qualms about both policy and policy analysis. Yet, we continue to expend energy, labour, affect, in thinking about both these things, despite our continued identification of the failure of policy to 'solve' any of the enduring 'problems' of education.

While we have been interested with concepts in this book, we place these ideas as part of the despairingly optimistic endeavour of education. It is this 'matter' that matters, for, as Stengers (2005), following Deleuze notes, "we should be interested in tools for thinking, not in an exegesis of ideas. An idea is always engaged in what [Deleuze] called a matter, always a specific one". If we consider policy, and its futurist orientation, we can see why we might need new tools for understanding policy and to be attuned to its becoming and uncertainties. Becoming-policy provides moments for thinking differently.

Concept creation as part of *policy geophilosophy* provides us with the possibility of sustaining policy and analysis but with new tools. We are attempting to make connections to new forms of policy analysis for people struggling through, as part of a "turn toward thinking about the ordinary as an impasse shaped by crisis in which people find themselves developing skills for adjusting to newly proliferating pressure to scramble for modes of living on" (Berlant, 2011: 8).

The idea of 'turning toward the ordinary' might seem strange in a field of governance like policy, but it fits precisely with the ideas of having tools for thinking about and with the mundane representational and material aspects of policy and policy analysis. We think this is what Brinkmann (2014) is getting at, when he advocates an abductive approach to research,

> Abduction is … a never-ending process, something that goes on as long as humans are alive. There is, according to this model, no hard and fast line between life, research, theory and methods. One "learns about methods by thinking about how one makes sense of one's own life" (Denzin, 2005, p. 449). Or, as Tim Ingold (2011) has put it in his exposition of C. Wright Mills, "There is no division in practice, between work and life. [An intellectual craft] is a practice that involves the whole person, continually drawing on past experience as it is projected into the future" (p. 240). According to the abductive model, we do research, inquiry, analysis, for purposes of living, and theories and methods are some of the tools used in the process.

We see again the tempting refrains, the 'muddling through' of Lindblom, and the requirement to persevere in a failed endeavour; this is the precariousness and capture of education and education policy, to make better, to intervene in the world through heroic impositions.

We are, if anything, then seemingly attached to the idea, as Bacchi (2012a: 142) proposed, that *"research is an active component in the shaping of different realities* and therefore is, at its core, *a political practice"*. This is a move away from 'epistemology' as a terrain of irreconcilability and a move toward an ontological politics that examines the "effects of the real" (to follow Foucault), or what Bacchi proposed as the "effects as the real" that identifies the ways that research produces realities. Bacchi (2012a: 151) noted that, "The point here is that references to effects 'in the real' continue to assume a reality within which interferences take place." This is the role of the creation of concepts, where in this book we have been fascinated with policy materials, encounters, with *policy prolepses* and *policy phantasms, policy intensions* and the encounters with non-human bodies of difference, the multiplicity of racialised thinking, of the representational, socially constructed notions of race and the ontological aspects of bodies in the world.

Are we, we must ask, as policy analysts, compelled, driven, to be attached to that which will never provide solace? As Sellar (2013: 247) characterised Berlant's thesis: 'cruel optimism' is what "arises when objects of desire that sustain people's life projects simultaneously undermine them" (and for us, it is how this is done – the scientificities that sustain us – for example, the comfort of certainty in *1.0*).

In this sense, our philosophical perspective is very much related to, but very distinct in the roles it plays, to 'complexity theory'. Bonta and Protevi (2004: 29) are helpful here:

> Philosophy gives consistency to the virtual, mapping the forces composing a system as pure potentials, what ... [a] system is capable of. Meanwhile, science gives it reference, determining the conditions by which systems behave the way they actually do. Philosophy [abstracts] an event or change of pattern from bodies and states of affairs and thereby laying out the transformative potentials inherent in things, the 'roads not taken' that coexist as compossibles or as include disjunctions, while science tracks the actualization of the virtual, explaining why the one road was 'chosen' in a a divergent series of exclusive disjunction.

What roads, we might ask, are you *not* travelling? Traveling these roads would add the lines +1 of a *policy geophilosophy*.

MOVING WITH A GEOPHILOSOPHY

We are well aware that education policy is obsessed with a *tyranny of the immediate* – the practical, the day-to-day, the so-called 'real'. Taking a moment to think about and question 'the real' is often an affront to policy makers in the busy, busy world of education. "Dreamers, academics, *theorists*" – these are the pejoratives slung from the mighty vantages of those who *know* education realities. "What education needs is answers", the realists demand, "not more theory!"

How sad it is when education disparages imagination – when we might posit that imagination precedes politics (Papastergiadis, 2012)? How nuts is it that people claim to know the real? *That* is crazy. Or as Whitehead (2010/1978: xiv) stated,

> [t]here remains the final reflection, how shallow, puny, and imperfect are efforts to sound the depths of the nature in things. In philosophical discussion, the merest hint of dogmatic certainty as to finality of statement is an exhibition of folly.

More importantly, how dangerous is it when people claim to know reality? Of course, they have (always) already had the answers, because they have (always) already defined what the real is. And this is just what all the little despots did for the past thousand years when they governed us in other ways, with other forms of 'education'. They told us what to think and know because they knew what the real was, or more precisely what real was to be necessary.

Not anymore. The 'real' just got real chaotic. It is with this chaos that there are innumerable[2] opportunities to re-create education for emergent futures – just like kindergarteners do – and this is the project to which *policy geophilosophy* aims to contribute.

NOTES

[1] Thanks to Sam Sellar for raising this point with us.
[2] Actually, "more than one and less than many" (Law, 2004: 62).

REFERENCES

Achinstein, B., & Ogawa, R. T. (2006). (In)Fidelity: What the resistance of new teachers reveals about professional principles and prescriptive educational policies. *Harvard Educational Review, 76*(1), 30–63.
Adkins Cartee, M. R. (2014). *Otherworlds: Teachers' experiences of power vis à vis accountability policies in South Carolina* (MA Thesis). University of British Columbia.
Ahluwalia, P. (2005). Out of Africa: Post-structuralism's colonial roots. *Postcolonial Studies, 8*(2), 137–154.
Al-Natour, R. J. (2010). Folk devils and the proposed Islamic school in Camden. *Continuum, 24*(4), 573–585.
Al-Natour, R. J., & Morgan, G. (2012). Local Islamophobia: The Islamic school controversy in Camden, New South Wales. In G. Morgan & S. Poynting (Eds.), *Global Islamophobia: Muslims and moral panic in the West* (pp. 101–118). Farnham, England: Ashgate.
Altieri, C. (2012). II Affect, intentionality, and cognition: A response to Ruth Leys. *Critical Inquiry, 38*(4), 878–881.
Amin, A. (2010). The remainders of race. *Theory, Culture & Society, 27*(1), 1–23.
Amin, A., & Thrift, N. (2002). *Cities: Reimagining the urban*. Cambridge, UK: Polity Press.
Anderson, B. (2008). Non-representational theory. In R. Johnston & G. Pratt (Eds.), *Dictionary of human geography*. London, UK: Arnold.
Anderson, B. (2014). *Encountering affect: Capacities, apparatuses, conditions*. Farnham, UK: Ashgate.
Anderson, B., & Harrison, P. (2010). The promise of non-representational theories. In B. Anderson & P. Harrison (Eds.), *Taking-place: Non-representational theories and geography* (pp. 1–36). Farnham, England: Ashgate.
Andrews, E. L. (2008, October 24). Greenspan concedes error on regulation. *New York Times*, p. B1.
Anyon, J. (1997). *Ghetto schooling: A political economy of urban educational reform*. New York, NY: Teachers College Press.
Appadurai, A. (1990). Disjuncture and difference in the global cultural economy. *Theory, Culture & Society, 7*(2), 295–310.
Appadurai, A. (1996). *Modernity at large: Cultural dimensions of globalization*. Minneapolis, MN: University of Minnesota Press.
Appadurai, A. (2006). *Fear of small numbers: An essay on the geography of anger*. Durham, NC: Duke University Press.
Archibald, J. A., Rayner, A., & Big Head, R. (2011). *Community responses to creating a school with an Aboriginal focus*. Vancouver, Canada: Vancouver School Board.
Armstrong, F. (2003). *Spaced out: Policy, difference and the challenge for inclusive education*. Dordrecht, The Netherlands: Kluwer Academic Publishers.
Ash, J., & Simpson, P. (2014). Geography and post-phenomenology. *Progress in Human Geography*. doi: 10.1177/0309132514544806
Bacchi, C. (2000). Policy as discourse: What does it mean? Where does it get us? *Discourse: Studies in the Cultural Politics of Education, 21*(1), 45–57.
Bacchi, C. (2012a). Strategic interventions and ontological politics: Research as political practice. In A. Bletsas & C. Beasley (Eds.), *Engaging with Carol Bacchi: Strategic interventions and exchange* (pp. 141–156). Adelaide, South Australia: University of Adelaide Press.
Bacchi, C. (2012b). Why study problematizations? Making politics visible. *Open Journal of Political Science, 2*, 1–8.
Bailey, P. L. J. (2013). The policy dispositif: Historical formation and method. *Journal of Education Policy, 28*(6), 807–827.
Ball, D. (1990). Reflections and deflections of policy: The case of Carol Turner. *Educational Evaluation and Policy Analysis, 12*(3), 247–259.

REFERENCES

Ball, S. J. (1990). *Politics and policy making in education: Explorations in policy sociology.* London, UK: Routledge.
Ball, S. J. (1994). *Education reform: A critical and post-structural approach.* Philadelphia, PA: Open University Press.
Ball, S. J. (1995). Intellectuals or technicians? The urgent role of theory in education studies. *British Journal of Educational Studies, 43,* 255–271.
Ball, S. J. (2003). *Class strategies and the education market: The middle classes and social advantage.* London, UK: Routledge.
Ball, S. J. (2006). *Education policy and social class: The selected works of Stephen J. Ball.* London, UK: Routledge.
Ball, S. J. (2007). *Education Plc: Understanding private sector participation in public sector education.* London, UK: Routledge.
Ball, S. J. (2009). Beyond networks? A brief response to 'which networks matter in education governance?' *Political Studies, 57*(3), 688–691.
Ball, S. J. (2012). *Global education Inc.: New policy networks and the neoliberal imaginary.* London, UK: Routledge.
Ball, S. J. (2013). *Foucault, power and education.* London, UK: Routledge.
Ball, S. J., & Junemann, C. (2012). *Networks, new governance and education.* Bristol, UK: The Policy Press.
Ball, S. J., Hoskins, K., Maguire, M., & Braun, A. (2011a). Disciplinary texts: A policy analysis of national and local behaviour policies. *Critical Studies in Education, 52*(1), 1–14.
Ball, S. J., Maguire, M., Braun, A., & Hoskins, K. (2011b). Policy subjects and policy actors in schools: Some necessary but insufficient analyses. *Discourse: Studies in the Cultural Politics of Education, 32*(4), 611–624.
Ball, S. J., Maguire, M., & Braun, A. (2012). *How schools do policy: Policy enactments in secondary schools.* London, UK: Routledge.
Bankstown City Council. (2012). Community Profile. Retrieved January 10, 2012, from http://profile.id.com.au/Default.aspx?id=101
Bansel, P. (2007). Subjects of choice and lifelong learning. *International Journal of Qualitative Studies in Education, 20*(3), 283–300.
Barad, K. (2003). Posthumanist performativity: Toward an understanding of how matter comes to matter. *Signs, 28*(3), 801–831.
Barad, K. (2007). *Meeting the universe halfway: Quantum physics and the entanglement of matter and meaning.* Durham, NC: Duke University Press.
Barnett, C. (2008). Political affects in public space: Normative blind-spots in non-representational ontologies. *Transactions of the Institute of British Geographers, 33*(2), 186–200.
Barry, A., Osborne, T., & Rose, N. (Eds.). (1996). *Foucault and political reason: Liberalism, neoliberalism, and rationalities of government.* Chicago, IL: University of Chicago Press.
Basu, R. (2004). The rationalization of neoliberalism in Ontario's public education system. *Geoforum, 35*(5), 621–634.
Bauman, Z. (2001). The great war of recognition. *Theory, Culture & Society, 18*(2–3), 137–150.
Belgarde, M. J. (2004). Native American charter schools: Culture, language, and selfdetermination. In E. Rofes & L. Stulberg (Eds.), *The emancipatory promise of charter schools: Towards a progressive politics of school choice* (pp. 107–124). Albany, NY: State University of New York Press.
Bennett, J. (2009). *Vibrant matter: A political ecology of things.* Durham, NC: Duke University Press.
Bensimon, E. M., & Marshall, C. (1997). Policy analysis for postsecondary education: Feminist and critical perspectives. In C. Marshall (Ed.), *Feminist critical policy analysis: A perspective from post-secondary education* (pp. 1–20). London, UK: Falmer Press.
Berlant, L. G. (2011). *Cruel optimism.* Durham, NC: Duke University Press.
Berliner, D. C., & Biddle, B. J. (1996). *The manufactured crisis: Myths, fraud, and the attack on America's public schools.* New York, NY: Basic Books.
Biesta, G. (2010). Five theses on complexity reduction and its politics. In G. Biesta & D. Osberg (Eds.), *Complexity theory and the politics of education* (pp. 5–14). Rotterdam, The Netherlands: Sense Publishers.

REFERENCES

Bifo. (2008). Alterity and desire. In S. O'Sullivan & S. Zepke (Eds.), *Deleuze, Guattari and the production of the new* (pp. 22–32). London, UK: Continuum

Bignall, S., & Patton, P. (2010). Introduction: Deleuze and the postcolonial: Conversations, negotiations, mediations. In S. Bignall & P. Patton (Eds.), *Deleuze and the postcolonial* (pp. 1–19). Edinburgh, Scotland: Edinburgh University Press.

Blackburn, S. (1990). Filling in space. *Analysis, 50*(2), 62–65.

Bonta, M., & Proveti, J. (2004). *Deleuze and geophilosophy: A guide and glossary*. Edinburgh, Scotland: Edinburgh University Press.

Bosteels, B. (1998). From text to territory: Felix Guattari's cartographies of the unconscious. In E. Kaufman & K. J. Heller (Eds.), *Deleuze and Guattari: New mapping in politics, philosophy, and culture* (pp. 145–174). Minneapolis, MN: University of Minnesota Press.

Bourdieu, P. (1990). *In other words: Essays towards a reflexive sociology*. Stanford, CA: Stanford University Press.

Bourriaud, N. (1998). *Relational aesthetics*. Dijon, France: Les Presses Du Reel.

Bowe, R., Ball, S. J., & Gold, A. (1992). *Reforming education and changing schools: Case studies in policy sociology*. London, UK: Routledge.

Braun, A., Ball, S. J., Maguire, M., & Hoskins, K. (2011). Taking context seriously: Towards explaining policy enactments in the secondary school. *Discourse: Studies in the Cultural Politics of Education, 32*(4), 585–596.

Brinkmann, S. (2014). Doing without data. *Qualitative Inquiry, 20*(6), 720–725.

Brown, W. (2003). Neo-liberalism and the end of liberal democracy. *Theory and Event, 7*. http://muse.jhu.edu/journals/theory_and_event/v007/7.1brown.html>

Brown, W. (2010). Political theory is not a luxury: A response to Timothy Kaufman-Osborn's 'Political theory as a profession'. *Political Research Quarterly, 63*(3), 680–685.

Buchanan, I. (2005). Space in the age of non-place. In I. Buchanan & G. Lambert (Eds.), *Deleuze and space* (pp. 16–35). Edinburgh, Scotland: Edinburgh University Press.

Buchanan, I., & Lambert, G. (2005). Introduction. In I. Buchanan & G. Lambert (Eds.), *Deleuze and space* (pp. 1–15). Toronto, Ontario, CA: University of Toronto Press.

Buchanan, N. K., & Fox, R. A. (2004). Back to the future: Ethnocentric charter schools in Hawai'i. In E. Rofes & L. Stulberg (Eds.), *The emancipatory promise of charter schools: Towards a progressive politics of school choice* (pp. 77–106). Albany, NY: State University of New York Press.

Buckingham, J. (2010). *The rise of religious schools*. Sydney, Australia: Centre for Independent Studies.

Bugg, L., & Gurran, N. (2011). Urban planning process and discourses in the refusal of Islamic Schools in Sydney, Australia. *Australian Planner, 48*(4), 281–291.

Bukowski, C. (1984). *War all the time*. New York, NY: HarperCollins.

Bullen, E., Fahey, J., & Kenway, J. (2006). The knowledge economy and innovation: Certain uncertainty and the risk economy. *Discourse: Studies in the Cultural Politics of Education, 27*(1), 53–68.

Burke, K. (1966). *Language as symbolic action: Essays on life, literature, and method*. Berkeley, CA: University of California Press.

Burns, L., & Kaiser, B. M. (2012). *Postcolonial literatures and Deleuze: Colonial pasts, differential futures*. New York, NY: Palgrave Macmillan.

Butler, J. (1990). *Gender trouble: Feminism and the subversion of identity*. New York, NY: Routledge.

Butler, J. (1993). *Bodies that matter: On the discursive limits of 'sex'*. New York, NY and London, UK: Routledge.

Butler, J. (2001). What is critique? An essay on Foucault's virtue. Retrieved from http://eipcp.net/transversal/0806/butler/en

Butler, J. (2004). *Undoing gender*. London, UK: Routledge.

Calvino, I. (1986). *The uses of literature*. London, UK: Harcourt Brace & Company.

Chubb, J. E., & Moe, T. M. (1988). Politics, markets and the organization of schools. *American Political Science Review, 82*(4), 1065–1089.

Chubb, J. E., & Moe, T. M. (1990). *Politics, markets and America's schools*. Washington, DC: Brookings Institution.

Clarke, J. (2004). *Changing welfare, changing states: New directions in social policy*. London, UK: SAGE.

REFERENCES

Cochrane, A. (2007). *Understanding urban policy: A critical approach*. Oxford, UK: Blackwell.
Cohen, D. (1990). A revolution in one classroom: The case of Mrs. Oublier. *Evaluation and Policy Analysis, 12*(3), 311–329.
Coleman, G. (2013). Anonymous and the politics of leaking. In B. Brevini, A. Hintz, & P. McCurdy (Eds.), *Beyond Wikileaks: Implications for the future of communications, journalism and society* (pp. 209–228). Basingstoke, UK: Palgrave Macmillan.
Collins, J., & Poynting, S. (2000). Introduction: Communities, identities and inequalities in Western Sydney. In J. Collins & S. Poynting (Eds.), *The other Sydney, Australia: Communities, identities and inequalities in Western Sydney* (pp. 19–33). Melbourne, Australia: Common Ground Publishing.
Conley, T. (2005). Folds and folding. In C. J. Stivale (Ed.), *Gilles Deleuze: Key concepts* (pp. 170–181). Montreal, Canada: McGill-Queen's University Press.
Connolly, W. E. (2011). I The complexity of intention. *Critical Inquiry, 37*(4), 791–798.
Coole, D., & Frost, S. (2010). Introducing the new materialisms. In D. Coole & S. Frost (Eds.), *New materialisms: Ontology, agency, and politics* (pp. 1–46). Durham, NC: Duke University Press.
Crang, M., & Thrift, N. (2000). Introduction. In M. Crang & N. Thrift (Eds.), *Thinking space* (pp. 1–30). London, UK: Routledge.
Cresswell, T. (2006). *On the move: Mobility in the modern western world*. New York, NY: Routledge.
Cresswell, J. W. (2013). *Research design: Qualitative, quantitative, and mixed methods approaches*. Thousand Oaks, CA: Sage.
Datnow, A., Lasky, S., Stringfield, S., & Teddlie, C. (2006). *Integrating educational systems for successful reform in diverse contexts*. Cambridge, MA: Cambridge University Press.
Datnow, A., & Park, V. (2009). Conceptualising policy implementation: Large-scale reform in an era of complexity. In G. Sykes, B. Schneider, & D. Plank (Eds.), *Handbook of education policy research* (pp. 348–361). New York, NY: Routledge.
Davies, B. D., & Bansel, P. (2007). Neoliberalism and education. *International Journal of Qualitative Studies in Education, 20*(3), 247–259.
Davis, B., & Sumara, D. (2008). Complexity as a theory of education. *Transnational Curriculum Inquiry, 5*(2), 33–44.
Dei, G. J. S. (2005). The case for black schools. *The Toronto Star*. Retrieved from http://www.diversitywatch.ryerson.ca/media/cache/blackschoolsdei_star_feb4.htm
deLeon, P. (2005). Social construction for public policy. *Public Administration Review, 65*(5), 635–637.
Deleuze, G. (1983). *Nietzsche and philosophy*. New York, NY: Columbia University Press.
Deleuze, G. (1988). *Foucault*. Minneapolis, MN: University of Minnesota Press.
Deleuze, G. (1990). *The logic of sense*. New York, NY: Columbia University Press.
Deleuze, G. (1992). Postscript on the societies of control. *October, 59*, 3–7.
Deleuze, G. (1993). *The fold: Leibniz and the Baroque* (T. Conley, Trans.). London, UK: The Athlone Press.
Deleuze, G. (1995). *Negotiations: 1972–1990* (M. Joughin, Trans.). New York, NY: Columbia University Press.
Deleuze, G. (2004). *Difference and repetition*. New York, NY: Continuum International Publishing Group.
Deleuze, G., & Foucault, M. (1972). Intellectuals and power: A conversation between Michel Foucault and Gilles Deleuze. *L'Arc, 49*, 3–10.
Deleuze, G., & Guattari, F. (1983). *Anti-Oedipus*. Minneapolis, MN: University of Minnesotta Press.
Deleuze, G., & Guattari, F. (1986a). *Kafka: Toward a minor literature*. Minneapolis, MN: University of Minnesota Press.
Deleuze, G., & Guattari, F. (1986b). *Nomadology: The war machine*. New York, NY: Semiotext(e).
Deleuze, G., & Guattari, F. (1987). *A thousand plateaus: Capitalism and schizophrenia*. Minneapolis, MN: University of Minnesota Press.
Deleuze, G., & Guattari, F. (1994). *What is philosophy?* London, UK: Verso.
Derrida, J. (1994). *Spectres of Marx: The state of debt, the work of mourning, and the new international*. New York, NY: Routledge.
Dewsbury, J. D., & Thrift, N. (2005). 'Genesis eternal': After Paul Klee. In I. Buchanan & G. Lambert (Eds.), *Deleuze and space* (pp. 89–108). Toronto, Canada, ON: University of Toronto Press.

REFERENCES

Dikeç, M. (2007). Space, governmentality, and the geographies of French urban policy. *European Urban and Regional Studies, 14*, 277–289.
Dilts, A. (2011). From 'entrepreneur of the self' to 'care of the self': Neo-liberal governmentality and Foucault's ethics. *Foucault Studies, 12*(2), 130–146.
Doel, M. A. (2000). Un-glunking geography: Spatial science after Dr. Seuss and Gilles Deleuze. In M. Crang & N. Thrift (Eds.), *Thinking space* (pp. 117–135). London, UK: Routledge.
Doel, M. A., & Clarke, D. B. (2011). Gilles Deleuze. In P. Hubbard & R. Hitchin (Eds.), *Key thinkers on space and place* (2nd ed., pp. 141–147). London, UK: Sage.
Dreyfus, H. L., & Rabinow, P. (1982). *Michel Foucault: Beyond structuralism and hermeneutics.* Chicago, IL: University of Chicago Press.
Dunn, K. M. (2001). Representations of Islam in the politics of mosque development in Sydney. *Tijdschrift voor economische en sociale geografie, 92*(3), 291–308.
Dunn, K. M., Klocker, N., & Salabay, T. (2007). Contemporary racism and Islamaphobia in Australia. *Ethnicities, 7*(4), 564–589.
Dwyer, C. (1993). Constructions of Muslim identity and the contesting of power: The debate over Muslim schools in the United Kingdom. In P. Jackson & J. Penrose (Eds.), *Constructions of race, place and nation* (pp. 143–159). London, UK: UCL Press.
Easton, D. (1953). *The political system.* New York, NY: Knopf.
Edwards, R. (2002). Mobilizing lifelong learning: Governmentality in educational practices. *Journal of Education Policy, 17*(3), 353–365.
Edwards, R. (2012). Theory matters: Representation and experimentation in education. *Educational Philosophy and Theory, 44*(5), 522–534.
Eisenhart, M., & Towne, L. (2003). Contestation and change in national policy on 'scientifically based' education research. *Educational Researcher, 32*(7), 31–38.
Eisner, E. W. (1992). The federal reform of schools: Looking for the silver bullet. *Phi Delta Kappan, 73*, 722–723.
Ellsworth, E. (1989). Why doesn't this feel empowering? Working through the repressive myths of critical pedagogy. *Harvard Educational Review, 59*(3), 297–325.
Elmore, R. F. (1979–1980). Backward mapping: Implementation research and policy decisions. *Political Science Quarterly, 94*(4), 601–616.
England, M. R., & Simon, S. (2010). Scary cities: Urban geographies of fear, difference and belonging. *Social & Cultural Geography, 11*(3), 201–207.
Esposito, R. (2008). *Bios: Biopolitics and philosophy.* Minneapolis, MN: University of Minnesota Press.
Fay, B. (1975). *Social theory and political practice.* London, UK: Allen and Unwin.
Fenwick, T., & Edwards, R. (2010). *Actor network theory in education.* London, UK: Routledge.
Fenwick, T., & Edwards, R. (2011). Considering materiality in educational policy: Messy objects and multiple reals. *Educational Theory, 61*(6), 709–726.
Feuer, M. J., Towne, L., & Shavelson, R. J. (2002). Scientific culture and educational research. *Educational Researcher, 31*(8), 4–14.
Foucault, M. (1970). *The order of things: An archaeology of the human sciences.* London, UK: Tavistock.
Foucault, M. (1974). *The archaeology of knowledge.* London, UK: Tavistock Publishers.
Foucault, M. (1982a). *The archaeology of knowledge.* New York, NY: Pantheon.
Foucault, M. (1982b). On the genealogy of ethics: An overview of work in progress. In H. Dreyfus & P. Rabinow (Eds.), *Michel Foucault: Beyond structuralism and hermeneutics* (pp. 229–252). Chicago, IL: Chicago University Press.
Foucault, M. (1985). *The use of pleasure: The history of sexuality* (*Vol. 2*). New York, NY: Random House.
Foucault, M. (1986). Of other spaces. *Diacretics, 16*, 22–27.
Foucault, M. (1987). Questions of method. In K. Baynes, J. Bonman, & T. McCarthy (Eds.), *After philosophy, end or transformation* (pp. 100–118). Cambridge, Mass.: MIT Press.
Foucault, M. (1988a). *The history of sexuality, Volume 3: The care of the self.* New York, NY: Vintage.
Foucault, M. (1988b). *Politics, philosophy, culture: Interviews and other writings, 1977–1984.* New York, NY: Routledge.

REFERENCES

Foucault, M. (1988c). Practicing criticism. In L. D. Kritzman (Ed.), *Politics, philosophy, culture: Interviews and other writings, 1977–1984* (pp. 152–156). New York, NY: Routledge.
Foucault, M. (1990). *The history of sexuality: An introduction (Vol. 1)*. New York, NY: Vintage Books.
Foucault, M. (1991). The ethic of care for the self as a practice of freedom. In J. Bernauer & D. Rasmussen (Eds.), *The final Foucault* (pp. 1–20). Cambridge, MA: MIT Press.
Foucault, M. (1994a). Polemics, politics, and problematizations. In P. Rabinow (Ed.), *Ethics, subjectivity and truth* (pp. 111–119). New York, NY: The New Press.
Foucault, M. (1994b). The subject and power. In J. Faubion (Ed.), *Power: Essential works of Foucault 1954–1984* (Vol. 3, pp. 326–348). London, UK: Penguin.
Foucault, M. (1997). The masked philosopher. In P. Rabinow (Ed.), *Michel Foucault - Ethics: Subjectivity and truth* (pp. 321–328). London, UK: Penguin.
Foucault, M. (2003). *Society must be defended: Lectures at the Collège de France 1975–1976* (D. Macey, Trans.). New York, NY: Picador.
Foucault, M. (2004). *Society must be defended*. London, UK: Penguin.
Foucault, M. (2005). *The hermeneutics of the subject: Lectures at the College de France 1981–1982*. New York, NY: Picador.
Foucault, M. (2007). What is critique? In S. Lotringer (Ed.), *The politics of truth* (pp. 41–81). Los Angeles: Semiotext(e).
Foucault, M. (2008). *The birth of biopolitics: Lectures at the Collège de France 1978–1979*. New York, NY: Palgrave MacMillan.
Fowler, F. C. (2003). School choice: Silver bullet, social threat, or sound policy? *Educational Researcher, 32*, 34–39.
Fraser, N. (2000). Rethinking recognition. *New Left Review*(3), 107–120.
Freidman, J. (1999). The hybridization of roots and the absence of the bush. In M. Featherstone & S. Lash (Eds.), *Spaces of culture: City-nation-world*. London, UK: Sage.
Friedman, M. (1962). *Capitalism and freedom*. Chicago, IL: University of Chicago.
Friedman, M. (1980). *Free to choose*. New York, NY: Harcourt Brace Jovanovich.
Gage, N. L. (1989). The paradigm wars and their aftermath: A 'historical' sketch of research on teaching since 1989. *Educational Researcher, 18*(7), 4–10.
Gale, T. (2001). Critical policy sociology: Historiography, archaeology and genealogy as methods of policy analysis. *Journal of Education Policy, 16*(15), 379–393.
Gallagher, K., & Fusco, C. (2006). I.D.ology and the technologies of public (school) space: An ethnographic inquiry into the neo-liberal tactics of social (re)production. *Ethnography and Education, 1*(3), 301–318.
Gerrard, J. (2013). Self help and protest: The emergence of black supplementary schooling in England. *Race, Ethnicity and Education, 16*(1), 32–58.
Gewirtz, S. (2001). Cloning the Blairs: New Labour's programme for the re-socialization of working-class parents. *Journal of Education Policy, 16*, 365–378.
Gillborn, D., & Youdell, D. (2009). Critical perspectives on race and schooling. In J. A. Banks (Ed.), *The Routledge international companion to multicultural education* (pp. 173–185). New York, NY: Routledge.
Gilroy, P. (2000). *Against race: Imagining political culture beyond the color line*. Camridge, MA: Harvard University Press.
Gilroy, P. (2005). *Postcolonial melancholia*. New York, NY: Columbia University Press.
Ginsberg, R., & Cooper, B. S. (2008). Introduction: What's fear got to do with it? *Educational Policy, 22*(1), 5–9.
Giroux, H. A. (2000). Postmodern education and disposable youth. In P. Trifonas (Ed.), *Revolutionary pedagogies: Cultural politics, instituting education, and the discourse of theory* (pp. 174–195). New York, NY: RoutledgeFalmer.
Goldberg, D. T. (2009). *The threat of race: Reflections on racial neoliberalism*. Oxford, UK: Wiley-Blackwell.
Greene, B. (2011). *The hidden reality: Parallel universes and the deep laws of the cosmos*. New York, NY: Knopf.

REFERENCES

Gregory, D. (2004). *The colonial present.* Oxford, UK: Blackwell.
Gribbins, J. (2010). *In search of the multiverse.* London, UK: Penguin.
Grosz, E. (2002). A politics of imperceptibility. *Philosophy and Social Criticism, 28*(4), 463–472.
Gulson, K. N. (2006). A white veneer: Educational policy, space and 'race' in the inner city. *Discourse: Studies in the Cultural Politics of Education, 27*(2), 251–266.
Gulson, K. N. (2011). *Education policy, space and the city: Markets and the (in)visibility of race.* New York, NY: Routledge.
Gulson, K. N., & Parkes, R. J. (2009). In the shadows of the mission: Education policy, urban space and the 'colonial present' in Sydney. *Race, Ethnicity and Education, 12*(3), 267–280.
Gulson, K. N., & Symes, C. (Eds.). (2007). *Spatial theories of education: Policy and geography matters.* New York, NY: Routledge.
Gulson, K. N., & Webb, P. T. (2012). Education policy racialisations: Afrocentric schools, Islamic schools and the new enunciations of equity. *Journal of Education Policy, 27*(6), 697–709.
Gulson, K. N., & Webb, P. T. (2013a). A raw, emotional thing: School choice, commodification and the racialised branding of Afrocentricity in Toronto, Canada. *Education Inquiry, 4*(1), 805–825.
Gulson, K. N., & Webb, P. T. (2013b). We had to hide we're Muslim: Ambient fear, Islamic schools and the geographies of race and religion. *Discourse: Studies in the Cultural Politics of Education, 34*(4), 628–641.
Hacking, I. (2004). *Historical ontology.* Cambridge, MA: Harvard University Press.
Hackworth, J., & Stein, K. (2012). The collision of faith and economic development in Toronto's inner suburban industrial districts. *Urban Affairs Review, 48*(1), 37–63.
Hale, C. R. (2005). Neoliberal multiculturalism: The remaking of cultural rights and racial dominance in Central America. *PoLAR: Political and Legal Anthropology Review, 28*(1), 10–28.
Hall, S. (1990). The emergence of cultural studies and the crisis of the humanities. *October, 53,* 11–23.
Hall, S. (1997). *Representation: Cultural representations and signifying practices.* Thousand Oaks, CA: Sage.
Hall, S., & Du Gay, P. (1996). *Questions of cultural identity.* London, UK: Sage
Harcourt, B. E. (2011). *The illusion of free markets: Punishment and the myth of natural order.* Cambridge, MA: Harvard University Press.
Harvey, D. (1989). *The condition of postmodernity.* Cambridge, MA: Blackwell.
Heimans, S. (2012). Coming to matter in practice: Enacting education policy. *Discourse: Studies in the Cultural Politics of Education, 33*(2), 313–326.
Honan, E. (2004). (Im)plausibilities: A rhizo-textual analysis of policy texts and teachers. *Educational Philosophy and Theory, 36*(3), 267–281.
Honig, M. I. (2006). *New directions in education policy implementation: Confronting complexity.* New York, NY: State University of New York.
Honneth, A. (1995). *The struggle for recognition: The moral grammar of social conflicts.* Cambridge, MA: Polity Press.
Howe, K. R. (2009). Positivist dogmas, rhetoric, and education sciences. *Educational Researcher, 38,* 428–440.
Humphrey, M. (2005). Australian Islam, the new global terrorism and the limits of citizenship. In S. Akbarzadeh & S. Yasmeen (Eds.), *Islam and the West: Reflections from Australia* (pp. 132–148). Sydney, Australia: UNSW Press.
Jackson, A. Y., & Mazzei, L. A. (2012). *Thinking with theory in qualitative research: Viewing data across multiple perspectives.* New York, NY: Routledge.
Jacob, E., & White, C. S. (2002). Theme issue on scientific research in education. *Educational Researcher, 31*(8), 3–29.
Johnson, C. (2000). *Governing change: From Keating to Howard.* St Lucia, QLD: University of Queensland Press and API Network.
Jones, P. (2009). Phase space: Geography, relational thinking, and beyond. *Progress in Human Geography, 33*(4), 487–506.
Keith, M. (2005). *After the cosmopolitan? Multicultural cities and the future of racism.* London, UK: Routledge.

REFERENCES

Keith, M. (2008). After the cosmopolitan? New geographies of race and racism. In C. Dwyer & C. Bressey (Eds.), *New geographies of race and racismNew geographies of race and racism* (pp. 193–206). Aldershot, UK: Ashgate.

Kurzweil, R. (2005). *The singularity is near: When humans transcend biology*. London, UK: Penguin.

Laplanche, J., & Pontalis, J. B. (1964/1968). Fantasy and the origins of sexuality. *The International Journal of Psychoanalysis, 49*(1), 1–18.

Lasswell, H. D. (1970). The emerging conception of the policy sciences. *Policy Sciences, 1*(1), 3–14.

Lather, P. (2004a). Foucauldian 'indiscipline' as a sort of application: Qu(e)er(y)ing research/ policy/ practice. In B. M. Baker & K. E. Heyning (Eds.), *Dangerous coagulations: The uses of Foucault in the study of education* (pp. 279–304). New York, NY: Peter Lang.

Lather, P. (2004b). Scientific research in education: A critical perspective. *British Educational Research Journal, 30*(6), 759–772.

Lather, P. (2006a). Foucauldian scientificity: Rethinking the nexus of qualitative research and educational policy analysis. *International Journal of Qualitative Studies in Education, 19*(6), 783–791.

Lather, P. (2006b). Paradigm proliferation as a good thing to think with: Teaching research in education as a wild profusion. *International Journal of Qualitative Studies in Education, 19*(1), 35–57.

Lather, P. (2009). 2007 Kneller Lecture, AESA getting lost: Social science and/as philosophy. *Educational Studies, 45*(4), 342–357.

Law, J. (2004). *After method: Mess in social science research*. London, UK: Routledge.

Lemke, T. (2014). New materialisms: Foucault and the 'government of things'. *Theory, Culture & Society.* doi:10.1177/0263276413519340

Leonardo, Z. (2009). *Race, whiteness and education*. New York, NY: Routledge.

Lerner, D., & Laswell, H. D. (1951). *The policy sciences: Recent developments in scope and method*. Stanford, CA: Stanford University Press.

Levin, M. (1979). Review of 'Understanding the alternative schools movement: The retransformation of the school' by Daniel L. Luke. *Curriculum Inquiry, 9*(4), 337–349.

Leys, R. (2011). The turn to affect: A critique. *Critical Inquiry, 37*(3), 434–472.

Leys, R. (2012). III Facts and moods: Reply to my critics. *Critical Inquiry, 38*(4), 882–891.

Lim, J. (2008). Encountering South Asian masculinity through the event. In C. Dwyer & C. Bressey (Eds.), *New geographies of race and racism* (pp. 223–238). Aldershot, UK: Ashgate.

Lindblom, C. E. (1959). The science of 'muddling through'. *Public Administration Review, 19*(2), 79–88.

Lingard, B. (2006). Globalisation, the research imagination and deparochialising the study of education. *Globalisation, Societies and Education, 4*(2), 287–302.

Lingard, B., & Rawolle, S. (2004). Mediatizing educational policy: The journalistic field, science policy, and cross–field effects. *Journal of Education Policy, 19*(3), 361–380.

Lipman, P. (2011). *The new political economy of urban education: Neoliberalism, race and the right to the city*. New York, NY: Routledge.

Lorimer, H. (2008). Cultural geography: Non-representational conditions and concerns. *Progress in Human Geography, 32*(4), 551–559.

Lubienski, C., Gulosino, C., & Weitzel, P. C. (2009). School choice and competitive incentives: Mapping the distribution of educational opportunities across local education markets. *American Journal of Education, 115*(4), 601–647.

Lubienski, C., Scott, J., & DeBray, E. (2011). The rise of intermediary organizations in knowledge production, advocacy, and educational policy. *Teachers College Record*, ID Number: 16487. Retrieved from http://www.tcrecord.org

Malins, P. (2004). Body-space assemblages and folds: Theorizing the relationship between injecting drug user bodies and urban space. *Continuum, 18*(4), 483–495.

Marcus, G. E. (2010). Contemporary fieldwork aesthetics in art and anthropology: Experiments in collaboration and intervention. *Visual Anthropology, 23*(4), 263–277.

Masny, D., & Cole, D. R. (2009). *Multiple literacies theory*. Rotterdam, The Netherlands: Sense Publishers.

Massey, D. (1992). Politics and space/time. *New Left Review, 196*, 65–84.

Massey, D. (2005). *For space*. London, UK: Sage Publications.

REFERENCES

Massey, D. (2006). Landscape as a provocation: Reflections on moving mountains. *Journal of Material Culture, 11*(1–2), 33–48.
Massey, D. S., & Denton, N. A. (1993). *American apartheid: Segregation and the making of the underclass*. Cambridge, MA: Harvard University Press.
Maxcy, S. J. (1991). *Educational leadership: A critical pragmatic perspective*. New York, NY: Bergin and Garvey.
May, T. (2005a). *Gilles Deleuze: An introduction*. Cambridge, UK: Cambridge University Press.
May, T. (2005b). *The political philosophy of poststructural anarchism*. Pennsylvania, PA: Pennsylvania State University.
May, T. (2006). *The philosophy of Foucault*. Montreal, Québec, Canada: McGill-Queen's University Press.
McCann, E., & Ward, K. (2012). Assembling urbanism: Following policies and 'studying through' the sites and situations of policy making. *Environment and Planning A, 44*(1), 42–51.
McCann, E., & Ward, K. (2013). A multi-disciplinary approach to policy transfer research: Geographies, assemblages, mobilities and mutations. *Policy Studies, 34*(1), 2–18.
McGann, J. G., & Sabatini, R. (2011). *Global think thanks: Policy networks and governance*. New York, NY: Routledge.
McGlynn, C., Bekerman, Z., Zembylas, M., & Gallagher, T. (2009). *Peace education in conflict and post-conflict societies*. London, UK: Palgrave Macmillan.
McLaughlin, M. W. (1987). Learning from experience: Lessons from policy implementation. *Educational Evaluation and Policy Analysis, 9*(2), 171–178.
Metcalfe, A. S. (2010). Examining the trilateral networks of the triple helix: Intermingling organizations and academy-industry-government relations. *Critical Sociology, 36*(4), 503–519.
Miles, R., & Brown, M. (2003). *Racism* (2nd ed.). New York, NY: Routledge.
Miller, J. (2011). School choice for the 'feral underclass'. Retrieved November 5, 2011, from http://www.inthesetimes.com/article/12121/school_choice_for_the_feral_underclass
Miller, P., & Rose, N. (2008). *Governing the present: Administering economic, social and personal life*. Cambridge, MA: Polity Press.
Mills, M., & Keddie, A. (2010). Cultural reductionism and the media: Polarising discourses around schools, violence and masculinity in an age of terror. *Oxford Review of Education, 36*(4), 427–444.
Mirza, H. S., & Reay, D. (2000). Spaces and places of black educational desire: Rethinking black supplementary schools as a new social movement. *Sociology, 34*(3), 521–544.
Mitchell, D. (2000). *Cultural geography: A critical introduction*. Oxford, UK: Blackwell Publishing.
Mohamad el Dana vs Bankstown City Council. (2008). NSW Land and Environment Court.
Mol, A. (2002). *The body multiple: Ontology in medical practice*. Durham, NC & London, UK: Duke University Press.
Morton, T. (2010). *The ecological thought*. Cambridge, MA: The Harvard University Press.
Murdoch, J. (2006). *Post-structuralist geography: A guide to relational space*. London, UK: SAGE Publications.
Musset, P. (2012). School choice and equity: Current policies in OECD countries and a literature review, *OECD education working papers, No. 66* (p. 52). Paris, France: OECD Publishing. doi: http://dx.doi.org/10.1787/5k9fq23507vc-en
Nayak, A. (2004). White lives. In K. Murji & J. Solomos (Eds.), *Racialization: Studies in theories and practice* (pp.141–162). Oxford, UK: Oxford University Press.
Nayak, A. (2006). After race: Ethnography, race and post-race theory. *Ethnic and Racial Studies, 29*, 411–430.
Nayak, A. (2010). Race, affect and emotion: Young people, racism, and graffiti in the postcolonial English suburbs. *Environment and Planning A, 42*, 2370–2392.
Nayak, A. (2011). Geography, race and emotions: Social and cultural intersections. *Social & Cultural Geography, 12*(6), 548–562.
Neely, B., & Samura, M. (2011). Social geographies of race: Connecting race and space. *Ethnic and Racial Studies, 34*(11), 1933–1952.
Nietzsche, F. (1996). *Nietzsche: Human, all too human: A book for free spirits*. Cambridge, MA: Cambridge University Press.

REFERENCES

O'Sullivan, S. (2006). *Art encounters Deleuze and Guattari*. Basingstoke, UK: Palgrave MacMilllan.
O'Sullivan, S. (2010). Fold. In A. Parr (Ed.), *The Deleuze dictionary* (2nd ed., pp. 107–109). Edinburgh, Scotland: Edinburgh University Press.
Olssen, M. (1999). *Michel Foucault: Materialism and education*. Westport, CT: Greenwood Publishing Group.
Olssen, M. (2008). Foucault as complexity theorist: Overcoming the problems of classical philosophical analysis. *Educational Philosophy and Theory, 40*(1), 96–117.
Olssen, M., & Peters, M. A. (2005). Neoliberalism, higher education, and the knowledge economy: From the free market to knowledge capitalism. *Journal of Education Policy, 20*(3), 313–347.
Olssen, M., Codd, J., & O'Neill, A. (2004). *Education policy: Globalization, citizenship and democracy*. London, UK: Sage publications.
Organisation for Economic Co-operation and Development. (2011). Education at a glance 2011: OECD indicators. Paris, France: OECD.
Osberg, D., Biesta, G., & Cilliers, P. (2008). From representation to emergence: Complexity's challenge to the epistemology of schooling. *Educational Philosophy and Theory, 40*(1), 213–227.
Ozga, J. (1987). Studying education through the lives of policy-makers: An attempt to close the micro-macro gap. In L. Barton & S. Walker (Eds.), *Changing policies, changing teachers*. Milton Keynes, England: Open University Press.
Ozga, J. (2000). *Policy research in educational settings: Contested terrain*. Buckingham, UK: Open University Press.
Ozga, J., & Jones, R. (2006). Travelling and embedded policy: The case of knowledge transfer. *Journal of Education Policy, 21*(1), 1–17.
Papastergiadis, N. (2012). *Cosmopolitanism and culture*. Cambridge, MA: Polity Press.
Parsons, W. (1995). *Public policy: An introduction to the theory and practice of policy analysis*. Cheltenham, England, UK: Edward Elgar.
Patterson, J. A., & Marshall, C. (2001). Making sense of policy paradoxes: A case study of teacher leadership. *Journal of School Leadership, 11*(5), 372–398.
Pedroni, T. (2006). Acting neoliberal: Is Black support for vouchers a rejection of progressive educational values? *Educational Studies, 40*(3), 265–278.
Peters, M. A. (2001). *Poststructuralism, Marxism and neoliberalism*. Oxford, UK: Rowman & Littlefield Publishers, Inc.
Peters, M. A. (2004). Geophilosophy, education and the pedagogy of the concept. *Educational Philosophy and Theory, 36*(3), 217–226.
Peters, M. A. (2008). Editorial: Complexity and knowledge systems. *Educational Philosophy and Theory, 40*(40), 1–3.
Peters, M. A., & Humes, W. (2003). Editorial: The reception of post-structuralism in educational research and policy. *Journal of Education Policy, 18*(2), 109–113.
Peters, M. A., & Kessl, F. (2009). Space, time, history: The reassertion of space in social theory. *Policy Futures in Education, 7*, 20–30.
Petersen, E. B. (2007). Negotiating academicity: Postgraduate research supervision as category boundary work. *Studies in Higher Education, 32*(4), 475–487.
Petersen, E. B., & Davies, B. (2010). In/Difference in the neoliberal university. *Learning and Teaching in the Social Sciences, 3*(2), 92–109.
Phillips, D. (2008). The problem with segregation: Exploring the racialisation of space in Northern Pennine towns. In C. Dwyer & C. Bressey (Eds.), *New geographies of race and racism* (pp. 179–192). Aldershot, UK: Ashgate.
Pickering, A. (1995). *The mangle of practice: Time, agency, and science*. Chicago, IL: University of Chicago Press.
Pickering, A. (2008). New ontologies. In A. Pickering & K. Guzik (Eds.), *The mangle in practice: Science, society, and becoming* (pp. 1–16). Durham, NC and London, UK: Duke University Press.
Pile, S., & Thrift, N. (Eds.). (1995). *Mapping the subject: Geographies of cultural transformation*. London, UK: Routledge.
Popkewitz, T. S. (1984). *Paradigm and ideology in educational research: The social functions of the intellectual*. Philadelphia, PA: The Falmer Press.

REFERENCES

Popkewitz, T. S. (1991). *A political sociology of educational reform: Power/knowledge in teaching, teacher education, and research.* New York, NY: Teachers College Press.
Powell, D. (1993). *Out west: Perceptions of Sydney's western suburbs.* Sydney, Australia: Allen & Unwin.
Poynting, S. (2000). Ethnicising criminality and criminalising ethnicity. In J. Collins & S. Poynting (Eds.), *The other Sydney, Australia: Communities, identities and inequalities in Western Sydney* (pp. 63–78). Melbourne, Victoria, Australia: Common Ground Publishers.
Protevi, J. (2004). *Manuel DeLanda, intensive science and virtual philosophy.* London, UK: Continuum. Retrieved from http://proteviblog.typepad.com/protevi/files/delanda_jbsp_review_long_version.pdf
Protevi, J. (2006). Deleuze, Guattari and emergence. *Paragraph, 29*(2), 19–39.
Protevi, J. (2009). *Political affect: Connecting the social and the somatic.* Minneapolis, MN and London, UK: University of Minnesota Press.
Prunty, J. J. (1985). Signposts for a critical educational policy analysis. *Australian Journal of Education, 29*(2), 133–140.
Rabinow, P. (2003). *Anthropos today: Reflections on modern equipment.* Princeton, NJ: Princeton University Press.
Rabinow, P., & Rose, N. (2003). Introduction. In *The essential Foucault: Selections from essential works of Foucault 1954–1984* (pp. vii–xxxv). New York, NY: The New Press.
Raunig, G. (2007). *Art and revolution: Transversal activism in the long twentieth century* (A. Dereig, Trans.). Los Angeles, CA: Semiotext(e).
Rawolle, S. (2005). Cross-field effects and temporary social fields: A case study of the mediatization of recent knowledge economy policies. *Journal of Education Policy, 20*(6), 705–724.
Rizvi, F., & Lingard, B. (2010). *Globalizing educational policy.* London, UK: Routledge.
Robbins, T. (2004). *Another roadside attraction.* Harpenden, UK: No Exit Press.
Roberston, S. L., & Dale, R. (2008). Researching education in a globalising era: Beyond methodological nationalism, methodological statism, methodological educationism and spatial fetishism. In J. Resnik (Ed.), *The production of educational knowledge in the global era* (pp.19–32). Rotterdam, The Netherlands: Sense Publishers.
Rofes, E., & Stulberg, L. (Eds.). (2004). *The emancipatory promise of charter schools: Towards a progressive politics of choice.* Albany, NY: State University of New York Press.
Rose, N. (1999a). *Governing the soul: The shaping of the private self* (2nd ed.). New York, NY: Free Association Books.
Rose, N. (1999b). *Powers of freedom: Reframing political thought.* Cambridge, MA: Cambridge University Press.
Rose, N. (2013). The human sciences in a biological age. *Theory, Culture & Society, 30*(1), 3–34.
Rose, N. & Miller, P. (2008). *Governing the present: Administering economic, social and personal life.* Malden, MA: Polity Press
Roy, K. (2003). *Teachers in nomadic spaces: Deleuze and curriculum.* New York, NY: Peter Lang.
Saeed, A. (2003). *Islam in Australia.* Sydney, Australia: Allen & Unwin.
Said, E. (1978). *Orientalism.* London, UK: Penguin Publishers.
Sahlberg, P. (2011). *Finnish lessons.* New York, NY: Teachers College Press.
Saldanha, A. (2006). Reontologising race: The machinic geography of phenotype. *Environment and Planning D: Society and Space, 24*, 9–24.
Sarason, S. B. (1990). *The predictable failure of educational reform: Can we change course before it's too late?* San Francisco, CA: Jossey-Bass.
Savage, M., & Burrows, R. (2007). The coming crisis of empirical sociology. *Sociology, 41*(5), 885–899.
Scheurich, J. (1994). Policy archaeology: A new policy studies methodology. *Journal of Education Policy, 9*(4), 297–316.
Schwille, J., Porter, A., Belli, G., Floden, R., Freeman, D., Knappen, L., & Kuhs, T. (1983). Teachers as policy brokers in the content of elementary school mathematics. In L. Shulman & G. Sykes (Eds.), *Handbook on teaching and policy* (pp. 370–391). New York, NY: Longman.
Sellar, S. (2013). Equity, markets and the politics of aspiration in Australian higher education. *Discourse: Studies in the Cultural Politics of Education, 34*(2), 245–258.
Sellar, S. (2015). A feel for numbers: Affect, data and education policy. *Critical Studies in Education, 56*(1), 131–146.

REFERENCES

Semetsky, I. (2006). *Deleuze, education and becoming*. Rotterdam, The Netherlands: Sense Publishers.

Shore, C., & Wright, S. (Eds.). (1997). *Anthropology of policy: Critical perspectives on governance and power*. London, UK: Routledge.

Shujaa, N. J. (1988). Parental choice of an Afrocentric independent school: Developing an explanatory theory. *Sankofa, 2*(1), 22–25.

Shujaa, N. J. (1992). Afrocentric transformation and parental choice in African American independent schools. *Journal of Negro Education, 61*(2), 148–159.

Simons, M., Olssen, M., & Peters, M. A. (2009a). Re-reading education policies: Part 1: The critical policy orientation. In M. Simons, M. Olssen, & M. A. Peters (Eds.), *Re-reading education policies: A handbook studying the policy agenda of the 21st century* (pp. 1–35). Rotterdam, The Netherlands: Sense Publishers.

Simons, M., Olssen, M., & Peters, M. A. (2009b). Re-reading education policies: Part 2: Challenges, horizons, approaches, tools, styles. In M. Simons, M. Olssen, & M. A. Peters (Eds.), *Re-reading education policies: A handbook studying the policy agenda of the 21st century* (pp. 36–95). Rotterdam, The Netherlands: Sense Publishers.

Simons, M., Olssen, M., & Peters, M. A. (2009c). Handbook on matters of public concern: Introduction and overview. In M. Simons, M. Olssen, & M. A. Peters (Eds.), *Re-reading education policies: A handbook studying the policy agenda of the 21st century* (pp. vi–xvi). Rotterdam, The Netherlands: Sense Publishers.

Singh, P., Heimans, S., & Glasswell, K. (2014). Policy enactment, context and performativity: Ontological politics and researching Australian National Partnership policies. *Journal of Education Policy, 29*(6), 826–844.

Soja, E. W. (1996). *Thirdspace: Journeys to Los Angeles and other real-and-imagined spaces*. Malden, MA: Blackwell.

Spillane, J. P., Gomez, L. M., & Mesler, L. (2009). Notes on reframing the role of organizations in policy implementation. In G. Sykes & B. Schneider (Eds.), *Handbook of education policy research* (pp. 409–425). New York, NY: Routledge.

Spivak, G. C. (1988). Can the subaltern speak? In C. Nelson & L. Grossberg (Eds.), *Marxism and the interpretation of culture*. Urbana, IL: University of Illinois Press.

St. Pierre, E. A. (1997). Methodology in the fold and the irruption of transgressive data. *International Journal of Qualitative Studies in Education, 10*(2), 175–189.

St. Pierre, E. A. (2008). Decentering voice in qualitative inquiry. *International Review of Qualitative Research, 1*(3), 319–336.

St. Pierre, E. A. (2011). Post qualitative research: The critique and the coming after. In N. K. Denzin & Y. S. Lincoln (Eds.), *The SAGE handbook of qualitative research* (4th ed., pp. 611–625). Thousand Oaks, CA: SAGE.

St. Pierre, E. A., & Jackson, A. Y. (2014). Qualitative data analysis after coding. *Qualitative Inquiry, 20*(6), 715–719.

St. Pierre, E. A., & Pillow, W. S. (2000). *Working the ruins: Feminist poststructural theory and methods in education*. New York, NY: Routledge.

Stagoll, C. (2010). Difference. In A. Parr (Ed.), *The Deleuze dictionary*. Edinburgh, Scotland: Edinburgh University Press.

Staunæs, D. (2011). Governing the potentials of life itself? Interrogating the promises in affective educational leadership. *Journal of Educational Administration and History, 43*(3), 227–247.

Stengers, I. (2005). Deleuze and Guattari's last enigmatic message. *Angelaki, 10*(2), 151–167.

Swanton, D. (2008). Everyday multiculture and the emergence of race. In C. Dwyer & C. Bressey (Eds.), *New geographies of race and racism* (pp. 239–254). Aldershot, UK: Ashgate.

Swanton, D. (2010). Sorting bodies: Race, affect, and everyday multiculture in a mill town in Northern England. *Environment and Planning A, 42*(10), 2332–2350.

Symes, C. (2007). On the right track: Railways and schools in late nineteenth century Sydney. In K. N. Gulson & C. Symes (Eds.), *Spatial theories of education: Policy and geography matters* (pp. 175–194). New York, NY: Routledge.

REFERENCES

Taylor, C. (1994). *Multiculturalism: Examining the politics of recognition*. Princeton, NJ: Princeton University Press.
Taylor, C. (2007). Geographical Information Systems (GIS) and school choice: The use of spatial research tools in studying educational policy. In K. N. Gulson & C. Symes (Eds.), *Spatial theories of education: Policy and geography matters* (pp. 77–94). New York, NY: Routledge.
Taylor, C. A., & Ivinson, G. (2013). Material feminisms: New directions for education. *Gender and Education, 25*(6), 665–670.
Thompson, G., & Cook, I. (2014). Education policy-making and time. *Journal of Education Policy*, 1–16. doi: 10.1080/02680939.2013.875225
Thrift, N. (2006). Space. *Theory, Culture & Society, 23*(2–3), 139–155.
Thrift, N. (2008). *Non-representational theory: Space, politics, affect*. New York, NY: Routledge.
Torres, C. A., & Van Heertum, R. (2009). Education and domination: Reforming policy and practice through critical theory. In G. Sykes, B. Schneider, & D. Plank (Eds.), *Handbook of education policy research* (pp. 221–239). New York, NY: Routledge.
Troyna, B. (1994). Critical social research and education policy. *British Journal of Educational Studies, 42*(1), 70–84.
van Reijen, W., & Veerman, D. (1988). An Interview with Jean-François Lyotard. *Theory, Culture & Society, 5*(2), 277–309.
Vázquez-Arroyoa, A. Y. (2008). Liberal democracy and neoliberalism: A critical juxtaposition. *New Political Science, 30*(2), 127–159.
Vidovich, L. (2007). Removing policy from its pedestal: Some theoretical framings and practical possibilities. *Educational Review, 59*(3), 285–298.
Virilio, P., & Lotringer, S. (1997/1983). *Pure war* (M. Polizzotti, Trans.). New York, NY: Semiotext(e).
Warf, B., & Arias, S. (2009). Introduction: The reinsertion of space in the humanities and the social sciences. In B. Warf & S. Arias (Eds.), *The spatial turn: Interdisciplinary perspectives* (pp. 1–10). Abingdon, UK: Routledge.
Weaver-Hightower, M. B. (2008). An ecology metaphor for educational policy analysis: A call to complexity. *Educational Researcher, 37*(3), 153–167.
Webb, P. T. (2001). Reflection and reflective teaching: Ways to improve pedagogy or ways to remain racist? *Race, Ethnicity and Education, 4*(3), 245–252.
Webb, P. T. (2008). Re-mapping power in educational micropolitics. *Critical Studies in Education, 49*(2), 127–142.
Webb, P. T. (2009). *Teacher assemblage*. Rotterdam, The Netherlands: Sense Publishers.
Webb, P. T. (2013). Nial-a-pend-de-quacy-in: Teacher-becomings and the micropolitics of self-semiotics. In D. Masny (Ed.), *Cartographies of becoming in education: A Deleuze-Guattari perspective* (pp. 163–177). Rotterdam, The Netherlands: SensePublishers.
Webb, P. T., & Gulson, K. N. (2011). Education policy as proto-fascism: The aesthetics of racial neo-liberalism. *Journal of Pedagogy, 2*(2), 173–194.
Wedel, J. R., Shore, C., Feldman, G., & Lathrop, S. (2005). Toward an anthropology of public policy. *The ANNALS of the American Academy of Political and Social Science, 600*(1), 30–51.
West, C. (1993). *Race matters*. New York, NY: Random House.
West-Pavlov, R. (2009). *Space in theory: Kristeva, Foucault, Deleuze*. Amsterdam, New York, NY: Rodopi B.V.
Westwood, S., & Williams, J. (1997). Imagining cities. In S. Westwood & J. Williams (Eds.), *Imagining cities: Scripts, signs, memory* (pp. 1–16). London, UK: Routledge.
Whatmore, S. (2006). Materialist returns: Practising cultural geography in and for a more-than-human world. *Cultural Geographies, 13*(4), 600–609.
Whitehead, A. N. (2010/1978). *Process and reality*. New York, NY: Simon and Schuster.
Willig, R. (2012). Grammatology of modern recognition orders: An interview with Axel Honneth. *Distinktion: Scandinavian Journal of Social Theory, 13*(1), 145–149.
Wilson, D. (2007). *Cities and race: America's new black ghetto*. New York, NY: Routledge.

REFERENCES

Wise, A., & Ali, J. (2008). *Muslim-Australians and local government: Grassroots strategies to improve relations between Muslim and non-Muslim-Australians.* Sydney, Australia: Centre for Research on Social Inclusion, Macquarie University.

Wiseman, A. W. (2010). The use of evidence for educational policymaking: Global contexts and international trends. *Review of Research in Education, 34*(1), 1–24.

Wittgenstein, L. (1953). *Philosophical investigations.* Oxford, UK: England.

Wittgenstein, L. (1965). *The blue and brown books: Preliminary studies for the 'Philosophical investigations'.* Rush Rhees, NY: Harper Torchbooks.

Wolcott, H. (2008). *Ethnography: A way of seeing* (2nd ed.). Walnut Creek, CA: AltaMira Press.

Yancey, P. (2004). Independent black schools and the charter movement. In E. Rofes & L. Stulberg (Eds.), *The emancipatory promise of charter schools: Towards a progressive politics of school choice* (pp. 125–158). Albany, NY: State University of New York Press.

Youdell, D. (2010). Pedagogies of becoming in an end-of-the-line 'special' school. *Critical Studies in Education, 51*(3), 313–324.

Youdell, D. (2011). *School trouble: Identity, power and politics in education.* London, UK and New York, NY: Routledge.